LEADING PROFESSIONALS

Further Praise for *Leading Professionals: Power, Politics, and Prima Donnas*

'Laura Empson tackles a hugely complex phenomenon: the nature of leadership in professional service firms, where no one wants to be a follower and leaders only survive through the consent of their colleagues. She has created a truly fascinating portrait of what it means to be a leader in such settings. The book is full of rich insights engagingly told, and often revealed in the words of the professional leaders themselves. This portrait will resonate strongly with practising and aspiring professional leaders who will find much to learn from the stories she tells and the insights she develops. Scholars of management will appreciate her work, not only for its significant contribution to academic knowledge, but also because it speaks to us directly—we are, after all, professionals and struggle with similar issues of leadership in our own working lives.'

Professor Ann Langley, HEC Montréal

'A richly detailed analysis of the complexities of modern professional organizations. The observations, based on more than twenty years of research, show a deep understanding of the tensions inherent in all successful firms. For those of us who lead or aspire to lead such firms, the lessons and conclusions are telling and valuable.'

Philip Davidson, Managing Partner, KPMG UK

'Professor Empson has made a major contribution to the literature on how professional services firms work and how they are best led. This is very well-researched and insightful analysis, based on a wealth of interviews, and written in a very readable style. All in all, a "must" on the reading list.'

Edward Braham, Global Senior Partner,
Freshfields Bruckhaus Deringer

'A modern global management consultancy practice contains a complex mix of people from differing backgrounds with different cultures and aspirations. Leading them is a daunting task but a task which is helped significantly by the insights within the book. I wish I could have read this book fifteen years ago.'

Mike Cullen, Former Global Managing Partner (Talent), EY

'Partnerships play a vital role in the modern economy. The spirit of partnership is a mystery to those who have not experienced it directly and also sometimes to partners themselves. This book is a highly readable explanation of what makes professional firms work and, importantly, how they are successfully led.'

Sir Gerry Grimstone, Chairman of Standard Life,
Deputy Chairman of Barclays

'This is an exciting and challenging book. It manoeuvres extremely well between what we know, academically, about professional leadership, and the concerns of thinking practitioners. The central ideas of plural leadership, leadership constellations, and ambiguity challenge all of us to re-evaluate our notions of leading professionals. Professor Empson has made an important contribution.'

Professor C. R. (Bob) Hinings, University of Alberta

'This is a must-read for anyone wondering why it is so challenging to lead in professional environments and how to do it more effectively. Empson masterfully brings together findings from research with the lived experiences of those she has studied to provide in-depth and detailed analysis of what it takes to survive and thrive in these politicized, but highly rewarding, work environments.'

Professor Mary Uhl-Bien, Neeley School of Business, TCU

'It's accepted wisdom that leading a professional services firm is different from other leadership roles, but very few have been able to explain why and in what ways. Laura Empson unravels this mystery, shining light deep into the underlying challenges leaders face and explaining ways to navigate them. An important book in a neglected and misunderstood area.'

Hugh Verrier, Chairman, White & Case

'Professor Empson has done an exceptional job making theory understandable and relevant to those actually involved in leading professional organizations whilst helping those more interested in the theory better understand how the real world works. Leading a professional organization can be lonely and Laura's research insights will help those grappling with the challenges of leadership to realize that they are not alone.'

Jeremy Newman, Former Global CEO, BDO

'Empson's latest book lifts the lid on the idiosyncrasies, paradoxes, and tensions of leadership in professional services firms. Featuring insights drawn from hundreds of interviews, *Leading Professionals* offers invaluable guidance to current/future leaders and management professionals alike.'

Wim Dejonghe, Global Senior Partner, Allen & Overy

LEADING PROFESSIONALS

POWER, POLITICS, AND PRIMA DONNAS

LAURA EMPSON

OXFORD
UNIVERSITY PRESS

OXFORD

UNIVERSITY PRESS

Great Clarendon Street, Oxford, OX2 6DP,
United Kingdom

Oxford University Press is a department of the University of Oxford.
It furthers the University's objective of excellence in research, scholarship,
and education by publishing worldwide. Oxford is a registered trade mark of
Oxford University Press in the UK and in certain other countries

First Edition published in 2017

Impression: 8

Published in the United States of America by Oxford University Press
198 Madison Avenue, New York, NY 10016, United States of America

British Library Cataloguing in Publication Data

Data available

Library of Congress Control Number: 2017931550

ISBN 978–0–19–874478–8

Printed and bound by
CPI Group (UK) Ltd, Croydon, CR0 4YY

For Michael and Daisy

Acknowledgements

First, thank you to the more than 500 professionals I have interviewed over the course of this research. I am grateful for the many hundreds of valuable hours they have given me, and for their thoughtfulness, eloquence, and honesty in responding to my questioning.

Second, I would like to thank the Economic and Social Council of Great Britain, who have funded three of the research studies on which this book is based.

Third, thank you to my colleagues with whom I have co-authored over the years: Johan Alvehus, Mats Alvesson, Louise Ashley, Joe Broschak, Chris Chapman, Imogen Cleaver, Royston Greenwood, Bob Hinings, Ann Langley, Ioana Lupu, Tim Morris, Daniel Muzio, and Crawford Spence.

Fourth, I would like to thank Caroline Scotter-Mainprize for the tremendous work she has done to help me translate my academic research into practitioner-friendly language. Writing a book is a long and lonely process and I have very much appreciated her encouragement and support throughout this time.

Fifth, thank you to my colleagues in the Cass Centre for Professional Service Firms who have provided such a constructive forum for discussion. In particular, I would like to thank Tony Angel and David Morley for their meticulous and thoughtful feedback on key chapters.

And finally, I would like to thank my husband, Michael, for the endless cups of Earl Grey which have appeared silently beside me while I have been writing, and more generally for being the remarkable man that he is.

Contents

PART IV. CONCLUSIONS

List of Figures

List of Tables

List of Boxes

I

Introduction and Overview

Introduction

Professional organizations—such as accounting, consulting, and law firms, investment banks, hospitals, and universities—embody some of the most complex and challenging interpersonal and leadership issues that organizations present.[1] All organizations exist as a means of encouraging individuals to cooperate with each other to achieve some kind of collective goal. In professional organizations this challenge, of reconciling the interests of the individual with the interests of the collective, is thrown into particularly sharp focus. Leaders of professional organizations must contend with ambiguous authority structures, complex interpersonal relations, and idiosyncratic professional colleagues: in other words, with the power, the politics, and the prima donnas. Or as one senior professional I have studied explains:

> I am responsible for a large group of partners, all of whom are very bright, at least as bright as I am, all of whom have big egos, all of whom are owners of the business with as much right to vote and draw profits as I have. The process of leading is about building consensus. It's not easy because most people are attracted to this business because they are independent, they like doing their own thing. Essentially, they want to be left alone until it's something that kind of connects with them and then it's: 'Why wasn't I consulted?' (Practice Head, Law Firm)

I have been conducting academic research into professional organizations for twenty-five years. My research as an academic was initially inspired by my experiences working as an investment banker and strategy consultant. Frustrated by, and curious about, the mismanagement and poor leadership

---

1. The research literature and empirical data which underpin this chapter are presented in detail throughout the subsequent chapters of this book.

I witnessed in these sectors, I returned to academia and began my research. I wanted to make sense of my own experiences and to understand better why supposedly 'smart' people do stupid things.

The complexities and peculiarities of professional organizations start with the complexities and peculiarities of the professionals who work within them. Professional organizations typically have relatively little in the way of tangible assets. Their value resides primarily in individual professionals, or rather in the technical knowledge, client relationships, and reputation which they possess. Senior professionals may choose to delegate authority to their elected leaders, but reserve the right to undermine or remove them. The same applies in professional organizations where individuals are appointed rather than elected to senior leadership roles, such as hospitals and universities. Without the cooperation of senior professionals, leaders of professional organizations will struggle to get anything done and may find themselves marginalized and removed. This is the distinctive nature of power in a professional organization.

Because power is possessed by many professionals and, therefore, widely diffused, it is often difficult to implement strategy within a professional organization. Leaders need to persuade numerous professionals to cooperate. They must devote considerable time to building consensus, making trade-offs, winning support, and doing deals. This is the distinctive nature of politics in professional organizations.

And what of the powerful professionals themselves? They are typically highly educated, highly trained, highly motivated, and highly opinionated individuals. To a colleague who attempts to lead them, they may appear like prima donnas. However, far from behaving unreasonably, these professionals may in fact be behaving highly rationally, protecting their own interests rather than compromising for the sake of 'the greater good'. After all, in a professional organization, the so-called greater good is simply the interests of the collective as defined by its leaders at a particular point in time.

For all these reasons, professional organizations are particularly difficult to lead. Yet professionals are often promoted or elected to leadership positions with very little preparation for these roles, and may have limited appetite or ability to perform them. Professionals may be obliged to give up their first love—their professional work—in return for the uncertain rewards and questionable status of a senior leadership role.

Newly appointed leaders of professional organizations may turn to the management literature for guidance (a logical response—professionals value expertise and are conscientious students). Yet they are likely to be disappointed when they realize that most leadership research is based on conventional hierarchical organizations and is, therefore, of limited relevance to professionals.

There is now an extensive body of sociological and organizational theory derived from the study of professional organizations (for a comprehensive compendium of state-of-the-art research in this area see *The Oxford Handbook of Professional Service Firms*,[2] which contains numerous chapters by leading scholars in this field). Yet, to date, there has been almost no systematic, rigorous academic research into leadership in professional organizations.

Who Should Read this Book: Practitioners and Academics

If you are a professional looking for a simple 'how to lead' book, you will be disappointed. This book is intended for more thoughtful and intellectually curious professionals who want to dig below the superficialities of conventional leadership books written for practitioners and to see their organization from a different perspective. You may be a fee-earning professional who has recently moved into a leadership role and who is trying to work out what is expected of you; or a long-established senior executive, frustrated by your ongoing difficulties in realizing your vision for the organization; or a manager in a business services function, new to the professional services sector and baffled by the peculiar dynamics you are encountering.

Each professional organization is complex and unique and it would be misleading to suggest that there is a set of generically applicable solutions to the challenges you face. So this book does not attempt to offer generic answers. Instead, it will enable you to ask better questions of your organization and the people you work with, and to understand why your previous attempts at leadership may have failed (or indeed succeeded). It will provide you with new perspectives on how to approach your ongoing leadership challenges.

2. L. Empson, D. Muzio, J. Broschak, and B. Hinings, eds. 2015. *The Oxford handbook of professional service firms*. Oxford: Oxford University Press.

If you are a scholar looking for esoteric theorizing, methodological exactitude, and narrowly defined, 'gap-filling' research, you will also be disappointed. This book wears its theory lightly. The theoretical and methodological foundations are explained but not dwelt upon. It highlights the key theories that provide the best insights into the phenomena under investigation and directs you to relevant further reading.

From an academic perspective, this book is most likely to appeal if you are a scholar of professional services who is new to the field of leadership research, or a leadership scholar new to the field of professional services research. It brings together data from several research studies I have conducted over the years and reinterprets them through a leadership lens. It is my hope that, inspired by this book, more academics will seek to engage in high-quality, empirically rigorous, theoretically informed research into leadership in professional organizations. This book is just the beginning.

Scale and Significance of the Professional Services Sector

The lack of research into leadership of professionals is potentially a serious problem because professional organizations are fundamental to the functioning of the global economy. When the definition of professional organizations is expanded beyond the traditional focus on accounting, consulting, and law firms to include organizations such as investment banks, hospitals, and universities, the impact of the professional services sector on society is clearly monumental.

In 2015, the accountancy, management consulting, and legal sectors alone generated revenue of US$1.6 trillion and employed sixteen million people (see Table 1.1). If sectors such as investment banking, engineering, architecture, advertising, and reinsurance are included, the figures rise to US$3.4 trillion and twenty-four million respectively. Moving beyond the more conventional definition of professional services to encompass professions such as academia and healthcare, it becomes impossible to accurately estimate the scale of the sector. A government report has identified more than 130 different professions.[3]

---

3. Panel on Fair Access to the Professions. 2009. *Unleashing aspiration: The final report of the Panel on Fair Access to the Professions*. London: Cabinet Office. <http://webarchive.nationalarchives.gov.uk/+/ http:/www.cabinetoffice.gov.uk/media/227102/fair-access.pdf>, accessed 15 February 2017.

Table 1.1 Scale of professional services sector (2015/16)

	Global revenue (US$ billion)	Employment ('000)
Accountancy[4]	$464	5,652
Advertising[5]	$206	1,191
Architecture[6]	$204	1,817
Engineering[7]	$773	4,081
Investment banking and brokerage[8]	$282	217
Law[9]	$593	6,081
Management consultancy[10]	$554	4,664
Reinsurance[11]	$295	333
Relative scale of comparable sectors		
Commercial banking[12]	$2,000	6,898
Pharmaceuticals[13]	$1,000	4,910

Professionals, and the services they offer, permeate and underpin the functioning of the global economy. Yet the significance of professional organizations (as defined in Box 1.1) extends far beyond their scale. They

4. As of December 2015. IBISWorld. Global accounting services: Market research report. <http://www.ibisworld.com/industry/global/global-accounting-services.html>, accessed 14 October 2016.

5. As of July 2016. IBISWorld. Global advertising agencies: Market research report. <http://www.ibisworld.com/industry/global/global-advertising-agencies.html>, accessed 14 October 2016.

6. As of December 2015. IBISWorld. Global architectural services: Market research report. <http://www.ibisworld.com/industry/global/global-architectural-services.html>, accessed 14 October 2016.

7. As of March 2016. IBISWorld. Global engineering services: Market research report. <http://www.ibisworld.com/industry/global/global-engineering-services.html>, accessed 14 October 2016.

8. As of April 2016. IBISWorld. Global investment banking & brokerage: Market research report. <http://www.ibisworld.com/industry/global/global-investment-banking-brokerage.html>, accessed 14 October 2016.

9. MarketLine. 2016. MarketLine Industry Profile: Global Legal Services. June 2016.

10. As of June 2016. IBISWorld. Global management consultants: Market research report. <http://www.ibisworld.com/industry/global/global-management-consultants.html>, accessed 14 October 2016.

11. As of March 2016. IBISWorld. Global reinsurance carriers: Market research report. <http://www.ibisworld.com/industry/global/global-reinsurance-carriers.html>, accessed 14 October 2016.

12. As of June 2016. IBISWorld. Global commercial banks: Market research report. <http://www.ibisworld.com/industry/global/global-commercial-banks.html>, accessed 14 October 2016.

13. As of June 2016. IBISWorld. Global pharmaceuticals & medicine manufacturing: Market research report. <http://www.ibisworld.com/industry/global/global-pharmaceuticals-medicine-manufacturing.html>, accessed 14 October 2016.

Box 1.1 What is a professional organization?

The term 'professional organization' merits some clarification, as its def-inition has long preoccupied scholars and policymakers alike.[14] In its narrowest sense, a professional service firm can simply be an organization where the majority of income-generating staff are members of an estab-lished, accredited, and regulated profession, such as accounting, law, engineering, architecture, or actuarial science. The definition is often expanded to include a wider range of knowledge-intensive activities and aspirant professions, such as management consulting, investment banking, executive search, and advertising. In its broadest sense, the term 'professional organization' can encompass a wide variety of organ-izations, such as hospitals, universities, and religious institutions, which employ a significant proportion of highly trained staff who view them-selves as professionals and who have the status (though not necessarily the income) that goes with that designation.

Any organization that possesses *all* the following characteristics can justifiably be considered a *professional service firm*:

Primary activity—application of specialist technical knowledge to creation of customized solutions to clients' problems.

Knowledge—core assets are professionals' specialist technical know-ledge and in-depth knowledge about clients.

Governance—extensive individual autonomy and contingent man-agerial authority, where core producers own or control core assets.

Identity—core producers recognize each other as professionals and are recognized as such by clients and competitors.

Professional organizations more broadly possess some but not necessarily all the above characteristics. They may use different terminology (e.g. doctors talk of patients rather than clients). They may have different resource endow-ments (e.g. the core assets of an investment bank will include financial capital as well as intellectual capital). They may have different governance structures (e.g. universities may be not-for-profit or public-sector organizations). All these organizations are entirely dependent on their professional workforce for the delivery of customized services. And with that comes a whole basket of complex leadership challenges.

---

14. For a detailed examination of this issue and a comprehensive derivation of a definition, see L. Empson, D. Muzio, J. Broschak, and B. Hinings. 2015. Researching professional service firms: An introduction and overview. In *The Oxford handbook of professional service firms*, ed. L. Empson, D. Muzio, J. Broschak, and B. Hinings. Oxford: Oxford University Press, 1–24.

play an important role in creating innovative business services, reshaping public services, ensuring access to capital, administering justice, setting financial reporting standards, protecting our health, discovering new knowledge, and educating our youth. They recruit many of the brightest and best graduates, attracted by the opportunities for rapid advancement and intellectual challenge on offer, as well as the high salaries and high status often associated with professional careers.

In recent years, the influence of professionals and professional organizations has been thrown into sharp focus by their involvement in a series of high-profile scandals, highlighting dishonesty and incompetence within professional organizations, and undermining the public's confidence in the professions.[15,16,17] In particular, the global banking crisis has raised serious concerns about the failings of leaders across a variety of professional organizations, and the wide-ranging and potentially catastrophic consequences that have ensued. Therefore, for the sake of the effective functioning of our society and economy, there is a desperate need for good leadership in professional organizations.

Empirical Foundations of the Book

The data in this book is based on a series of in-depth research studies I have conducted, funded by the Economic and Social Research Council of Great Britain. As part of these studies, in addition to detailed observational and archival analysis, I have formally interviewed more than 500 professionals in sixteen countries (comprising more than 750 hours of recorded and transcribed empirical material). The majority of interviews have been conducted in the US and UK, but I have also interviewed

15. R. Dinovitzer, H. Gunz, and S. Gunz. 2015. Professional ethics: Origins, applications and developments. In *The Oxford handbook of professional service firms*, ed. L. Empson, D. Muzio, J. Broschak, and B. Hinings. Oxford: Oxford University Press, 113–34.

16. C. Gabbioneta, R. Prakash, and R. Greenwood. 2014. Sustained corporate corruption and processes of institutional ascription within professional networks. *Journal of Professions and Organization* 1(1): 16–32.

17. D. Muzio, J. Faulconbridge, C. Gabbioneta, and R. Greenwood. 2016. Bad apples, bad barrels and bad cellars: A 'boundaries' perspective on professional misconduct. In *Organizational wrongdoing*, ed. D. Palmer, R. Greenwood, and K. Smith-Crowe. Cambridge: Cambridge University Press, 141–75.

professionals in China, Russia, India, Canada, Continental Europe, Scandinavia, and South America. The gender balance of the interviewees reflects the gender balance of most professional organizations; i.e. almost all of the senior leaders I have interviewed are male. These interviews have been supplemented by detailed observational and archival analysis, and a further 100 interviews which my co-researchers have conducted.

Detailed quotations from these interviews are presented throughout the book. I wanted the voices of professionals to come through strongly, to represent authentically the lived experiences of the leaders of professional organizations, and the professionals they seek to lead—their preoccupations and frustrations, their hopes and achievements.

The organizations in this book are drawn primarily from the accounting, legal, and consulting sectors. Fifteen have been analysed in considerable depth and additional interviews have been conducted in a further fifty organizations. Most of the accountants interviewed come from the very largest accounting firms, including all the Big Four; a small number of founder-led firms are also included. Most of the law firms are drawn from elite global firms headquartered in the City of London, including all the Magic Circle; firms headquartered in the US and other parts of Europe are also included. The consulting firms are drawn from a range of sectors, including mainstream management consulting sectors such as strategy, operations, change management, and human resource management, as well as other forms of consulting such as actuarial consulting and executive search.

The organizations include partnerships and privately held and publicly quoted corporations. The smallest earns US$4 million in fees and has fewer than thirty staff. The largest generates tens of billions of dollars and employs hundreds of thousands of staff. I have emphasized the generalizability of my findings, rather than focus on the vagaries of specific professions and professional organizations, to ensure my analysis is relevant to leaders and scholars across a range of professional sectors.

Throughout I have disguised the organizations in order to fulfil my commitment to interviewees that I would preserve confidentiality. This guarantee of anonymity ensures that the leaders of professional organizations have spoken extraordinarily honestly to me about their regrets, frustrations, and fears. From the basis of their sometimes brutal honesty they have also been able to express their most hard-won and heartfelt insights into leadership in professional organizations.

Overview of the Book

Part I: Foundations of Leadership

Chapter 2—Leadership Constellation: Power, Politics, and Professionals. This chapter presents the conceptual foundations of the book. It identifies key concepts developed from my research and explains how they relate to each other. The peculiar challenges of leading professionals arise from two interrelated organizational characteristics, which coexist in constant dynamic tension within professional organizations: (1) extensive autonomy and (2) contingent authority. To manage this tension, leaders need to develop a deep level of insight into the implicit power dynamics and covert political processes that permeate professional organizations, and strike an appropriate balance between challenging and propitiating powerful prima donna professionals.

Plural leadership[18] is a relatively new and rapidly developing leadership theory which is particularly relevant to professional organizations.[19] This approach examines leadership as a collective phenomenon that is distributed among multiple individuals. Building on research in this area, this chapter introduces the concept of the 'leadership constellation', developed to represent the informal power dynamics among leaders of professional organizations.

Chapter 3—Leadership Dynamics: Co-Constructing an Unstable Equilibrium. This chapter explains in detail how leadership actually happens in a professional organization—how people become part of the leadership constellation and what they actually do once they get there.

The plural leadership approach emphasizes that leadership is something that happens between people and is therefore co-constructed through interaction. This chapter develops a model of plural leadership dynamics in professional organizations, which identifies three microdynamics: 'legitimizing', 'negotiating', and 'manoeuvring'. The model demonstrates how leadership in professional organizations is the result of a complex and highly nuanced set of interactions among peers, rather than a simpler more

---

18. J.-L. Denis, A. Langley, and V. Sergi. 2012. Leadership in the plural. *Academy of Management Annals* 6: 211–83.

19. L. Empson and A. Langley. 2015. Leadership and professionals. In *The Oxford handbook of professional service firms*, ed. L. Empson, D. Muzio, J. Broschak, and B. Hinings. Oxford: Oxford University Press, 163–88.

transactional exchange between leaders and followers. In professional organizations, leadership represents an unstable equilibrium—it changes and adapts as relations between professionals change and adapt, and a small change in any one of the microdynamics may destabilize the leadership dynamics as a whole. The leaders who misjudge the subtleties of these microdynamics will quickly discover that nobody has to 'follow' them.

Chapter 4—Leadership and Governance: Reconciling the Individual with the Collective. The previous chapter focuses on leadership dynamics within the plural leadership group. This chapter expands the focus, to explore the dynamics which govern the interactions of professionals more generally, and to examine the implications for leaders of professional organizations.

There may be several hundred senior professionals working inside a large professional organization. At any moment, these individuals may stop thinking of themselves as part of the collective and start pursuing their individual interests. Despite its many limitations, partnership remains the optimal legal form of governance for reconciling these competing interests; this chapter explains why. It identifies the socialization processes, management systems, and governance structures which create and sustain the partnership ethos. By distinguishing partnership as a legal form from partnership as an ethos, this chapter identifies how valuable aspects of the partnership ethos can survive and thrive within a corporation. It explains how leaders with a sophisticated understanding of their organization's partnership ethos will find it easier to influence its partnership dynamics and avoid falling foul of them.

Part II: Leadership and Individuals

Chapter 5—Leadership Dyads: The Ideal Leader Is Two People. The dual leadership model, or 'leadership dyad', is common in professional organizations. While this arrangement is most typically found at the most senior level, leadership dyads can occur throughout a professional organization. This chapter asks whether leadership dyads can be effective and, if so, how they work in practice. It presents a framework which identifies and analyses four different leadership dyads that occur in professional organizations: 'intuitive collaboration', 'structured coordination', 'negotiated cohabitation', and 'careful cooperation'.

It explains why each of these dyads can be effective, in very different ways and for very different reasons. It argues that it is notionally possible for one individual to be in charge of a professional organization and to embody and reconcile the inherent tension between the individual and collective, but it is much easier when two are involved. It demonstrates how even the most discordant dyads can be effective if their members are able to embody, express, and repeatedly resolve the conflict which permeates the organization as a whole. This chapter examines the serious consequences when leadership dyads break down and explains what leaders can do if they become involved in a dysfunctional dyad.

Chapter 6—Leading Insecure Overachievers: The Comforts of Social Control. So far, the book has focused on leaders and leadership at a senior level within professional organizations. This chapter focuses on the rank-and-file fee earners, who represent the lifeblood of these firms. It examines the origins of insecurity among professionals and explains how their organizations amplify and exploit this insecurity. Elite professional organizations identify insecure overachieving individuals and provide them with the security of exceptional psychic as well as financial rewards through offers of employment. This chapter explains how and why professionals enjoy the comforts of being associated with an elite organization and how they are able to incorporate its elite status into their own identity.

The 'comforting' social control mechanisms embodied in strong cultures can translate into cult-like conformity among senior professionals in elite professional organizations. This chapter, therefore, also explores the dark side of social control and its most typical manifestation—overwork. It asks: why do senior professionals in many elite professional organizations 'choose' to exercise their autonomy by overworking to such an extent that they risk their personal relationships and physical and mental health? It concludes by examining the responsibilities of leaders in this context.

Chapter 7—Leading Discreetly: Management Professionals as Consummate Politicians. This chapter introduces a new group of individuals into the leadership constellation: senior management professionals. These individuals have overall responsibility for the business services functions, such as Finance, Human Resources, and Marketing. Just like the other members of the leadership constellation, management professionals need to be able to engage in the microdynamics of negotiating and manoeuvring outlined in Chapter 3. However, the dynamics they must contend with are even more complex.

As this chapter explains, management professionals need to develop a very close working relationship with the senior leadership dyad and engage in a complex range of political activities to bring about the change they have been tasked with achieving. To be effective, they must become consummate politicians, displaying a range of political skills from networking ability and interpersonal influence, to social astuteness and apparent sincerity. Through a complex set of political activities, management professionals work with the Managing and Senior Partners to help shift the balance of power, away from the senior fee-earning professionals and towards the leadership of the organization, without the fee-earning professionals necessarily recognizing or accepting that there is a need for such a change. In other words, this chapter shows how it is possible for outsiders to lead discreetly.

Part III: Leadership and Organizations

Chapter 8—Leadership Evolution: Growing Up and Growing Older. How does the locus of power shift around a professional organization as it grows, and what are the implications for leadership? How is ownership and power transferred from an organization's entrepreneurial founders to a wider group of professionals? And when the organization becomes too unwieldy to manage collectively, how does a large group of professionals delegate authority to an emerging group of leaders?

This chapter presents a multi-stage model of evolutionary and revolutionary growth in professional organizations. It shows how, as professional organizations increase in size and complexity over time, unresolved governance problems may precipitate organizational crises which can in turn lead to dramatic shifts in the locus of power. It explains the complex and messy reality of leadership in a professional organization, emphasizing the crises and reversals that can occur during aborted attempts at governance change. It emphasizes how leaders need to be sensitive to the consequences of these changes as the locus of power shifts around their organization, and explore how they can adapt their approach to leadership accordingly.

Chapter 9—Leading Mergers: The Ultimate Change Challenge. The previous chapter explains how organizational forms which are suitable for younger, smaller organizations may inhibit growth past a certain point. This can prompt leaders of professional organizations to pursue mergers. While potentially resolving one kind of crisis, mergers can provoke another.

Leaders may initiate a merger but have very limited power to ensure its success. Post-merger integration in professional organizations is largely dependent upon the cooperation of professionals who control access to key resources. However, sharing these resources potentially undermines the power base of these professionals. This chapter identifies two reasons why professionals may be reluctant to cooperate with merger objectives: fear of exploitation and fear of contamination. It presents the 'School Dance' model of post-merger integration, which outlines the gradual process by which professionals across the organization take responsibility for making the merger a success. Leaders of merging professional organizations require a subtle understanding of what drives professionals in a post-merger context, the willingness to hold back from direct action, and the perception to judge when to intervene.

Chapter 10—Leadership and Ambiguity: Acting Decisively without Authority.   This chapter examines in intricate detail the leadership dynamics of the plural leadership group: who they are, who has the power to decide who they are, how they work together under normal circumstances, and how their dynamics change in response to a crisis. In the previous chapter, the leaders have the luxury of time—they instigate change and control the timetable. In this chapter, leaders have change forced upon them—they must respond quickly but lack the authority to act decisively.

The conventional view is that organizational crises demand clear and decisive responses from 'strong' leaders. Yet this approach is hard to reconcile with the extensive autonomy and contingent authority which determine the distinctive power dynamics of professional organizations. At the heart of the analysis, therefore, is the question: how, when authority is ambiguous, are leaders able to respond effectively in a crisis? The answer is that, under the cloak of ambiguity, leaders may be able to exercise considerable informal power by mobilizing and exploiting an organization's hidden hierarchy. In the process, they move from an intuitive to a more deliberate form of mutual adjustment. This chapter explains exactly how it is done.

Part IV: Conclusions

Chapter 11—Paradoxes of Leading Professionals: From Unstable to Dynamic Equilibrium.   The theme of paradox runs throughout the book, albeit implicitly. This chapter makes paradox explicit, by drawing together multiple strands of argument contained in each of the preceding chapters. In recent years, paradox theory has developed into a particularly intriguing and highly influential body of management research. A paradox comprises two or more elements that are inherently contradictory, inter-related, simultaneous, and persistent.

Having presented some foundational concepts from paradox theory, this chapter goes on to identify ten paradoxes of professional organizations. These are: (1) autonomy and control, (2) reluctance and ambition, (3) political and apolitical leadership, (4) individual and collective interests, (5) harmony and conflict, (6) insecurity and confidence, (7) commercial and professional priorities, (8) centralized power and distributed leadership, (9) active and passive leadership, and (10) ambiguity and clarity. This chapter concludes with some final reflections for those seeking answers to the questions that remain.

PART
I

Foundations
of Leadership

2

Leadership Constellation

Power, Politics, and Professionals

I thought once I was elected Chairman I would finally have access to the levers of power. But when I moved into my new office I realized there was nothing there—just a desk.

(Chair, Accounting Firm)

Empson: Does anyone have power over you?
Partner: Not as far as I'm concerned, no.
Empson: Does anyone think they have power over you?
Partner: I don't think so.

(Client Relationship Partner, Law Firm)

Introduction

Leaders, by definition, must have followers. In most studies of leadership, this statement is axiomatic. Amongst professionals, however, it is too simplistic to talk in terms of leaders and followers. Many professionals have no ambition to become leaders, and they are equally reluctant to view themselves as followers (see Chapter 3).

In this context, conventional hierarchies are replaced by more ambiguous and negotiated relationships amongst professional peers, as highlighted in the quotes at the start of this chapter. Or, as the Senior Partner of a consulting firm explains:

Compared to a corporate, we need a softer style of leadership—you know, arm round the shoulder, gently nudging people in the right direction. (Senior Partner, Consulting Firm)

In such a context, where authority is contingent and power is contested, leadership is a matter of guiding, nudging, and persuading. So, what can the so-called leaders of professional organizations do with the highly driven, highly demanding, and sometimes highly insecure prima donnas for whom they are responsible?

This chapter presents the conceptual foundations of the book. It identifies the key concepts I have developed from my research and explains how they relate to each other. It begins with a general overview of the concept of leadership (see Box 2.1) before examining leadership in a professional context. The peculiar challenges of leading professionals arise from two interrelated organizational characteristics, which coexist in constant dynamic tension within professional organizations. These are extensive autonomy and contingent authority. To manage this tension, leaders need to develop a deep level of insight into the implicit power dynamics and covert political processes that permeate professional organizations, and to strike an appropriate balance between challenging and propitiating their powerful prima donna colleagues. Plural leadership is a relatively new and rapidly developing leadership theory which is particularly relevant to professional organizations. Building on plural leadership theory, I have developed the concept of the leadership constellation to represent the informal power dynamics among leaders of professional organizations.

Twin Leadership Challenges

The peculiar challenges of leading professionals derive from two interrelated organizational characteristics, which coexist in constant dynamic tension within professional organizations. These are extensive autonomy and contingent authority.

Extensive Autonomy

Autonomy from external control is supposedly a defining condition of a profession and of professionals.[1,2] Traditionally, the professions were entirely

---

1. P. S. Adler, S. W. Kwon, and C. Heckscher. 2008. Professional work: The emergence of collaborative community. *Organization Science* 19(2): 359–76.
2. M. Mazmanian, W. J. Orlikowski, and J. Yates. 2013. The autonomy paradox: The implications of mobile email devices for knowledge professionals. *Organization Science* 27(5): 1337–57.

Box 2.1 What exactly is leadership?

Typically, I begin my leadership interviews by asking professionals to define what the term 'leadership' means to them. I usually get fairly generic responses about 'having a vision', 'creating alignment', 'inspiring followers', the sort of things that business schools teach on executive education programmes. Yet when I ask interviewees to describe what leadership means in their organization, what gradually emerges is an image of something much more subtle and nuanced. It is both a position and a process. Some say leadership is something that *all* professionals in their organization should be doing; others complain that *the* leader is failing to do it entirely.

In fact, my question 'what is leadership?' is a remarkably complex question. After decades of research, leadership scholars still cannot agree on an answer. So it is worth taking a moment to explain what it means in the context of this book. Drucker famously defined a leader as 'someone who has followers', but that definition is far too simplistic for a professional organization, where the concepts of leadership and followership are densely intertwined (see Chapter 3).

In order to explore leadership in this distinctive context, it is more useful to adopt a broader perspective. A good starting point comes from Yukl, who has written one of the best-selling textbooks on leadership. He describes leadership as:

> ...influencing task objectives and strategies, influencing commitment and compliance in task behaviour to achieve these objectives, influencing group maintenance and identification, and influencing the culture of an organisation.[3]

This definition suggests that leadership permeates multiple aspects of work and multiple levels within an organization. Influence can be exercised at the individual and group level, as well as at the organizational and strategic level. It can be exercised by people at the top of the organization with formal management titles, and by people throughout the organization who have no titles at all.

Kets de Vries, another renowned scholar of leadership, focuses on a fundamental aspect of leadership in a professional context: the ability to

(Continued)

---

3. G. Yukl. 1989. Managerial leadership: A review of theory and research. *Journal of Management* 15(2): 251–89. See especially p. 253.

Box 2.1 Continued

reconcile the tension between the interests of the individual and the interests of the collective (see Chapter 4). As he phrases it:

> Leaders inspire people to move beyond personal egotistic motives—to transcend themselves.[4]

All this is not easily done by one individual, which is why leadership in professional organizations is a fundamentally plural phenomenon (as explained in detail later in this chapter), and why it is vital to understand the leadership dynamics of the plural leadership group.

---

self-regulating. Individual professionals, once they had completed their apprenticeship, were supposed to be free to define how they worked, when they worked, and with whom they worked. Gaining this autonomy was a powerful motivating factor during the gruelling years of professional training.

In theory at least, professionals' demand for autonomy is justified by their requirement to preserve the right to make choices about how to apply their specialist technical expertise to the delivery of customized services to their clients. It is perpetuated by the fact that the core-value-creating resources of a professional organization—technical knowledge, client relationships, and reputation—are often proprietary to specific professionals.

Professionals expect autonomy and are frustrated when it is denied them. Lawyers and accountants need to be free to use their professional judgement about how to give the best possible advice, even if that advice is unwelcome and causes the firm to lose a valuable client. Academics need to be able to fail their students without getting a phone call from the Dean asking them to go easy on the child of a wealthy potential donor. Doctors need to be able to prescribe the course of treatment that is right for their patients, rather than what is right for their hospital's finances.

In recent years, much has happened to constrain professional autonomy. External regulation has encroached upon the ability of professions to self-regulate. Within organizations, the concept of professionalism has been

---

4. M. Kets de Vries and K. Balazs. 2011. The shadow side of leadership. In *The SAGE handbook of leadership*, ed. A. Bryman, D. L. Collinson, K. Grint, B. Jackson, and M. Uhl-Bien. London: SAGE Publications, 380–92. See especially p. 385.

redefined to represent a professional's unstinting commitment to serving the needs of their clients,[5,6,7] together with a willingness to sacrifice their own well-being to this end (see Chapter 6). Nevertheless, the expectation and rhetoric of autonomy remains common within professional organizations—if only, sometimes, as a powerful folk memory.

Ultimately, most professionals want to be left alone from 'interference' by their leaders, to do the job they want to do as well as they possibly can. As the practice head quoted at the start of Chapter 1 says about the colleagues he is supposed to be leading: 'Essentially they want to be left alone until it's something that kind of connects with them and then it's: "Why wasn't I consulted?"'

Contingent Authority

This emphasis on extensive autonomy coexists in constant dynamic tension with contingent authority. A leader of professionals may only lead by their consent. Authority is collegial and fragile and deemed to rest with the professional peer group rather than the individual.[8] Even if professionals do not actively resist, they may do so passively by simply ignoring the pronouncements of their leaders.[9] As Mintzberg[10] states, a senior executive in a professional organization 'maintains power only as long as the professionals perceive him or her to be serving their interests effectively'.

Contingent authority is particularly problematic in partnerships which are wholly owned by the senior professionals who work within them.[11] In a partnership, senior executives are elected by their peers to formal

5. F. Anderson-Gough, C. Grey, and K. Robson. 2000. In the name of the client: The service ethic in two professional services firms. *Human Relations* 53: 1151–74.
6. M. A Covaleski, M. W. Dirsmith, J. B. Heian, and S. Samuel. 1998. The calculated and the avowed: Techniques of discipline and struggles over identity in Big Six public accounting firms. *Administrative Science Quarterly* 43: 293–327.
7. E. Freidson. 1984. The changing nature of professional control. *Annual Review of Sociology* 10: 1–20.
8. L. Empson and A. Langley. 2015. Leadership and professionals. In *The Oxford handbook of professional service firms*, ed. L. Empson, D. Muzio, J. Broschak, and B. Hinings. Oxford: Oxford University Press, 163–88.
9. C. R. Hinings, J. Brown, and R. Greenwood. 1991. Change in an autonomous professional organization. *Journal of Management Studies* 28: 376–93.
10. H. Mintzberg. 1989. *Mintzberg on management: Inside our strange world of organizations*. New York: Free Press. See especially p. 181.
11. R. Greenwood, C. R. Hinings, and J. Brown. 1990. 'P²-form' strategic management: Corporate practices in professional partnerships. *Academy of Management Journal* 33: 725–55.

positions of leadership and can be deposed if they fail to retain the support of their fellow partners. While partnership is the prevailing form of governance within established professions such as law and accounting,[12] leadership elections also occur in incorporated professional organizations which mimic partnership governance (see Chapter 4).

Because formal authority is contingent, senior leaders in professional organizations need to be acutely aware of the implicit power dynamics amongst their colleagues. They need to navigate skilfully the covert political processes that permeate their organization, and work out how to strike the appropriate balance between challenging and propitiating powerful prima donna professionals.

Power

Power has been conceptualized in many different ways by many different scholars, but three theoretical approaches are particularly relevant to professionals and professional organizations. Power can be looked upon as something professionals possess, something that influences relationships between professionals, and something that professionals are possessed by.

Power as Something Professionals Possess

The most widely recognized way of conceptualizing power was developed by French and Raven in 1959.[13] They identified six 'bases' of power[14] which an individual can possess.

'Legitimate' power is usually inherent in a formal leadership role. 'Referent' power is personal to the individual and rooted in the respect and affiliations that he or she accumulates over time. In a professional organization, the latter may be far more effective than the former. As a Senior Partner in one of my research studies explains:

---

12. R. Greenwood and L. Empson. 2003. The professional partnership: Relic or exemplary form of governance? *Organization Studies* 24: 909–33.

13. B. H. Raven. 1965. Social influence and power. In *Current studies in social psychology*, ed. I. D. Steiner and M. Fishbein. New York: Holt, Rinehart, Winston, 371–82.

14. French and Raven's original 1959 work identified five bases of power but was updated by Raven in 1965 to include both information and expert power.

You govern by your mandate and your personal credibility and authority, not by virtue of some kind of constitutional power that's given to you. (Senior Partner, Law Firm)

Within a professional organization, referent power is often associated with market success. Professionals who are good at winning work are viewed as role models by their colleagues (see Chapter 3). Role models are able to make their colleagues feel better (or worse) about themselves, by conferring (or withholding) approval. This, in effect, gives them power over their colleagues. As Chapter 6 explains, insecure overachievers are particularly susceptible to referent power as they will work hard to win the approval of a senior colleague they particularly respect.

'Reward' and 'coercive' powers are more commonly described as 'the carrot and the stick'. In many professional organizations, the ultimate carrot is partnership and the ultimate stick is the denial of partnership. In some partnerships, once a professional has made partner, lockstep[15] methods of remuneration limit the extent to which he or she is directly subject to reward or coercive power. As one consultant explains:

> In principle the office practice leader should have a performance discussion with me. But what does that really mean? I am on maximum lockstep. (Partner, Consulting Firm)

In recent years, coercive and reward power have increased substantially in many professional organizations, as lockstep has been modified or abandoned, stringent performance management systems have become widespread, and partner 'culls' have become a routine aspect of successive economic downturns (see Chapter 10). Yet, where coercive and reward power has increased, they are typically not concentrated in the hands of the organization's most senior leaders. Instead, they are often delegated to committees responsible for remuneration and promotion. Thus, the coercive and reward powers of individual leaders are deliberately constrained.

French and Raven identify two other bases of power: 'expertise' and 'information'. As both expertise and information are widely dispersed amongst professionals, they are not obvious sources of power for individual leaders. But a

---

15. Under lockstep, a partner's share of profits is based entirely on the number of years they have been a partner.

skilful leader can make the most of the distinctive expertise and information power that he or she possesses, as explained in the following section.

Power as Something that Influences Relations between Professionals

The resource dependency perspective is most closely associated with the work of Pfeffer and Salancik.[16] They emphasize that all organizations depend on resources to function effectively. Power, therefore, belongs to organizations, and to individuals within organizations, who control access to the most valuable resources. Looked at another way, the people who do not control key resources are at the mercy of those who do.

In professional organizations, the most valuable resources are technical knowledge, client relationships, and reputation. In terms of knowledge, a professional's power will wax and wane depending on demand for his or her specific area of technical knowledge. In an investment bank or law firm, for example, when the mergers market is booming, M&A specialists will be in the ascendancy and may be able to command the highest earnings and influence key leadership appointments. Within academia, a professor who has recently achieved a stream of publications in the most prestigious academic journals can bargain with his or her Dean for a reduced teaching load and access to more resources.

The same applies when it comes to client relationships. The professional who has the closest relationship with the organization's most lucrative client is likely to be very powerful indeed. As one practice head explains:

> You can't really tell people what to do. You can say what you're going to do and then hope people will agree with it . . . and the people you can least tell what to do are those who are most important for the success of the business. Because they are the ones who control the client relationships. (Practice Head, Law Firm)

Reputation can also represent a significant source of individual power within a professional organization. Having a strong external reputation—for being the surgeon who is the best in the country at performing a highly specialized operation, or the architect who wins awards for remarkable buildings—gives

---

16. J. Pfeffer and G. R. Salancik. 1978. *The external control of organizations: A resource dependence perspective.* New York: Harper and Row.

professionals power within their organizations. Such individuals represent a powerful latent force, because they are accorded considerable respect by their colleagues, and are therefore able to mobilize opposition to leadership initiatives. As one Senior Partner explains:

> Charlie is our best-known M&A lawyer. He holds no formal management position in the Corporate practice and he doesn't want one. But he's very influential as he has a significant following among the Corporate partners. He was elected to the Board which has brought him into the fold, so to speak, which is good because these kinds of people can be very difficult when they have power without responsibility. (Senior Partner, Law Firm)

The resources of technical expertise, client relationships, and market reputation are potentially available to all fee-earning professionals. One key resource, however, is the preserve of those who occupy senior leadership positions. On assuming a leadership role, a professional is likely to be highly regarded as an expert in their chosen professional field (see Chapter 3) but relatively ignorant about issues of management. They often respond by forming very close working relationships with the management professionals running functional areas, such as Finance and Human Resources (see Chapter 7), and come to rely heavily upon these individuals' specialist management expertise. In this way, senior leaders are able to exploit a key resource which is not so easily accessible to their professional peers, and thus enhance their relative power.

Power as Something that Professionals Are Possessed By

This is the hardest form of power to understand and to recognize because it is so subtle—we are all subject to it without realizing it. This conceptualization of power is most closely associated with the writings of Foucault.[17] Foucault explores power as something that is diffuse, embodied, and enacted, rather than concentrated, externalized, and possessed. A Foucauldian perspective emphasizes how power can be so deeply embedded in our beliefs and behaviours that we are not aware of it. It is beyond our perception and therefore causes us to discipline ourselves without any deliberate coercion from others.

---

17. See, for example, M. Foucault. 1991. *Discipline and punish: The birth of a prison*. London: Penguin.

This form of power is deeply entrenched in many of the world's most successful professional organizations, which are portrayed as having strong and coherent cultures. It is expressed by one practice head (quoted more fully in Chapter 6) when he talks about his colleagues:

> We are completely independent, but we all march to the same tune without even thinking about it. (Practice Head, Accounting Firm)

In such a context, professionals internalize their organization's disciplinary mechanisms, by engaging in self-monitoring and self-regulating behaviour that conforms to their organizational goals. One intriguing puzzle, therefore, is why do professionals in elite professional organizations believe themselves to be autonomous, whilst simultaneously conforming to, and collaborating with, strong social controls? Chapter 6 explores this theme of social control in depth and explains the potentially damaging consequences for individual professionals.

Politics

As the preceding discussion suggests, power within professional organizations is ambiguous and shifting, and informal sources of power may not correlate directly with the organization's formal hierarchy. This environment is likely to give rise to political behaviours.[18] Politics are particularly prevalent in pluralistic organizations, which are characterized by multiple perspectives, conflicting interests, and ambiguity concerning the power of different individuals and groups—in other words, in a typical professional organization.[19]

In a pluralistic setting, tensions arise because of complex and competing values, cultures, rules, and expectations.[20] For example, in hospitals tensions arise between medical and managerial cultures; in an academic institution, between teaching and research; in investment banks, between trading and

18. C. Parker, R. Dipboye, and S. Jackson. 1995. Perceptions of organizational politics: An investigation of antecedents and consequences. *Journal of Management* 21: 891–912.
19. T. Morris, R. Greenwood, and S. Fairclough. 2010. Decision making in professional service firms. In *Handbook of decision making*, ed. P. Nutt and D. Wilson. Chichester: John Wiley & Sons, 275–306.
20. J.-L. Denis, L. Lamothe, and A. Langley. 2001. The dynamics of collective leadership and strategic change in pluralistic organizations. *Academy of Management Journal* 44: 809–37.

advisory work; in advertising agencies, between creatives and account executives; and in partnerships, between the interests of the individual and the collective (see Chapter 4). In any professional organization, there can be additional tensions between professionals focused on their short-term financial success and professionals concerned with their longer-term legacy, or those who are close to retirement and those at the peak of their productivity.

Reflecting this politicized context, partnerships are governed according to overtly political structures and processes. As a professional in one of my research studies explains, being in a partnership is 'a bit like being part of a political party'. To be admitted to a partnership, professionals must be elected by the partnership as a whole. Thereafter, leadership elections are held for the most senior leadership roles, including membership of the Board. The most hard-fought elections may require prospective leaders to issue 'manifestos', have 'campaign managers', give speeches at 'candidates' debates', and engage in 'run-off elections'. As with political parties, leaders refer to 'the electorate' and their 'constituents', who provide them with 'mandates'.

In these situations, political behaviours, including negotiations and compromises between opposing parties, are essential in order to create consensus. As one accountant explains:

> In the previous election for Senior Partner there was a bit of a power struggle between Peter and Harry who were dominant characters within the organization, but Harry held sway on the basis of support from a number of the more senior partners including the outgoing Senior Partner who had quite a lot of influence.... It was all closed doors—smoke-filled rooms—lots of politicking, etc. etc.—a variety of promises being made to various senior people to get them to support Harry. (Board Member, Accounting Firm)

Political behaviour among professionals, therefore, is not inherently bad—it is an organizational fact of life.[21] It may be most visible in partnerships around the time of leadership elections, but it happens on a day-to-day basis in all forms of professional organizations, as a means of reaching agreement about a plethora of mundane issues. Politics is often portrayed by leadership scholars[22] and professionals alike as a negative and illegitimate

21. J. Silvester. 2008. The good, the bad, and the ugly: Politics and politicians at work. *International Review of Industrial and Organizational Psychology* 23: 107–48.
22. A. P. Ammeter, C. Douglas, W. L. Gardner, W. A. Hochwarter, and G. R. Ferris. 2002. Toward a political theory of leadership. *The Leadership Quarterly* 13: 751–96.

pursuit of self-interest. However, in the context of professional organizations, it is a necessary and positive means of achieving consensus amongst a
collection of powerful professionals.[23] It is the oil that enables the machine
of a professional organization to keep working.

To build consensus, leaders in professional organizations, therefore, need
to be acutely aware of the implicit power structures and shifting networks of
influence among their professional peers. They need to develop sophisticated political skills to navigate and negotiate the invisible networks of
informal power relations which criss-cross their organization. Research
into organizational politics has demonstrated that politically skilled individuals possess four key skills: social astuteness, interpersonal influence, networking ability, and apparent sincerity.[24] With these skills, they can inspire
trust and win the support of colleagues, persuading them that they are acting
in the interests of the organization rather than themselves. Basically, if people
realize you are acting politically, you are doing it wrong.

The inevitability and prevalence of politics in professional organizations is
not normally acknowledged by the professionals who work within them. As
Chapter 3 demonstrates, many professionals, while denying that they are
political, are in fact highly politicized. In general, the words 'power' and
'politics' are carefully avoided in professional organizations, perhaps because
such concepts are inconsistent with a sense of collegiality amongst professional peers. Some professionals would prefer to believe it is not happening.
But it is.

Professionals (and Prima Donnas)

According to the Oxford English Dictionary, a prima donna is a person 'of
great skill and renown, who takes a leading role in a particular community or
field. Also: a self-important or temperamental person.' This definition
encompasses the qualities inherent in many senior professionals. They take
their jobs and themselves tremendously seriously, are driven to achieve

23. D. C. Treadway, W. A. Hochwarter, C. J. Kacmar, and G. R. Ferris. 2005. Political will,
    political skill, and political behavior. *Journal of Organizational Behavior* 26: 229–45.
24. G. R. Ferris, D. C. Treadway, P. L. Perrewe, R. L. Brouer, C. Douglas, and S. Lux. 2007.
    Political skill in organizations. *Journal of Management* 33: 290–320.

excellence in their work, are highly visible and influential within their organizations, and can be very difficult to lead.

The accusation of temperamentalism is a tricky one, as it can be highly gendered (as is the description 'prima donna'). A female professional may be called temperamental when she assertively demands that her colleagues strive for the same standards of excellence that she sets herself, while a male professional behaving in the same way may be praised for being tough on himself and encouraging his colleagues to excel. But male professionals can behave like prima donnas too, as the following comment demonstrates, where a member of the Executive Committee in a global accounting firm is describing his colleagues:

> Bill—his approach to getting his own way was to hurl his toys out of his pram at a moment's notice. And Rudy—I mean he's just like a sort of giant baby. Rudy and Bill, they'd both sit there in ExCo in their nappies throwing rattles and toys around the place. (ExCo Member, Accounting Firm)

While this is perhaps an extreme example, a colleague's comment in the same firm suggests this kind of behaviour is not unusual:

> I spend the vast bulk of my time just trying to resolve internecine conflicts between partners. And it's not big conflicts, it's not, 'We think the direction of the travel of the firm and its vision is wrong', it's things like, 'He won't give me his two members of staff. He's being protective.' Or, 'She wasn't very nice to me.' (Client Sector Head, Accounting Firm)

Rather than rush to judgement about prima donna professionals, it is worth taking time to understand what may lie behind this kind of behaviour and the more generally 'challenging' behaviour which professionals exhibit on a day-to-day basis.

Kets de Vries's[25,26] psychoanalytically based leadership research sheds valuable light on this phenomenon. He identifies two distinct personality types which often rise to leadership positions: narcissists and insecure over-achievers. Superficially, they may appear similar. They are likely to do well in a professional organization because they are attracted by high-status occupations, are intensely ambitious, have a strong need for recognition, and will work tirelessly to achieve their goals.

25. Kets de Vries and Balazs 2011.
26. M. Kets de Vries. 2012. Star performers: Paradoxes wrapped up in enigmas. *Organizational Dynamics* 41(3): 173–82.

According to Kets de Vries, a degree of narcissism is valuable to anyone who hopes to rise to the top of an organization. Constructive narcissists, he argues, are outgoing, very confident, and function well under pressure. 'The strength, and even inflexibility, of a narcissistic leader's worldview gives followers something to identify with'.[27] Constructive narcissists have the necessary self-mastery to be able to deal with their 'powerful feelings of envy, jealousy, rage, and vindictiveness, and direct their energy towards more constructive behavior'.[28] However, if they lack this capacity, they may become excessively demanding, egotistical, or aggressive. They may become fixated on issues of power, status, prestige, and superiority. Destructive narcissists 'are under the impression that rules are for others... and are unable to handle negative feedback'.[29]

Whereas the narcissist may enjoy exceptionally high levels of self-confidence, the insecure overachiever is at the opposite end of the spectrum. An insecure overachiever perpetually doubts what they know, yet is compulsively driven to succeed.[30] 'With each milestone passed and accolade bestowed, they tell themselves, "I was lucky, I fooled everyone this time, but will my luck hold?"'[31] Or, as a lawyer in one of my research studies explains about his colleagues:

> People at the peak of their career, who are outstanding, are also unbelievably insecure, unbelievably until you understand where they're coming from, which is, 'I've just won the biggest case in this country. Now what do I do?' (Partner, Law Firm)

The insecure overachiever is attracted by the high status and financial rewards which professional organizations offer. At the same time, as explained in Chapter 6, the intensely competitive and insecure working environment prevalent in many professional organizations fuels their sense of insecurity and drives them to ever more intensive patterns of work. Such individuals are, therefore, susceptible to burnout, and are particularly convenient targets for exploitation by the professional organizations that employ them.

---

27. Kets de Vries and Balazs 2011. See especially p. 289.
28. Kets de Vries 2012. See especially p. 176.
29. Ibid., p. 177.
30. A. Michel. 2007. A distributed cognition perspective on newcomers' change processes: The management of cognitive uncertainty in two investment banks. *Administrative Science Quarterly* 52: 507–57.
31. Kets de Vries 2012. See especially p. 177.

The insecure overachiever's susceptibility to displays of prima-donna-like behaviour may therefore stem from overwork—they may be so exhausted and stressed that they have lost their capacity to self-manage (see Chapter 6 for a detailed analysis of the phenomenon of overwork). This underlying vulnerability can be exacerbated by an organizational culture which tolerates such behaviours, and which fails to deal effectively with the powerful professionals who are 'acting out'. As one junior in a global accounting firm explains:[32]

> There are people whose behaviour is not normal: aggressive, mean people.... I have in mind a manager who often works until midnight and he asks the same from his team. People are being yelled at like rotten fish all day for anything and everything. (Junior, Accounting Firm)

Caught as they are between narcissists and insecure overachievers, and perhaps struggling to manage their own innate tendencies towards either personality type, the hackneyed phrase 'herding cats' does not even begin to capture the complexity of the challenge facing leaders of professional organizations.

Plural Leadership

'Power, politics, and prima donnas'—what does all this mean for leadership in a professional context? Despite their distinctiveness, professional organizations have received very little attention from leadership scholars, perhaps because leadership is so difficult to study when it is not possible to draw clear distinctions between leaders and followers. As an accountant I interviewed makes clear, amongst the partners in his firm 'frankly nobody has to follow anyone'. Or, as the Senior Partner quoted at the start of Chapter 3 explains, in his organization 'leadership sort of happens'. If the leaders themselves believe that 'leadership sort of happens', it is not surprising that there has been very little rigorous, theoretically grounded, and empirically based scholarly research into leadership in professional organizations.[33] How can you study such an amorphous phenomenon?

32. See I. Lupu and L. Empson. 2015. *Illusio* and overwork: Playing the game in the accounting field. *Accounting, Auditing, and Accountability Journal* 28(8): 1310–40.
33. Empson and Langley 2015.

Fortunately, a developing and important area of research has the potential to provide valuable insights. In recent years, there has been growing interest among leadership scholars in what has variously been termed collective, distributed, or shared leadership. These somewhat different approaches have been brought together under the umbrella term of 'plural leadership'.[34] A plural approach to leadership questions traditional assumptions that leadership is top-down, hierarchical, and equivalent to formal supervisory roles.[35]

It represents a reaction against individualized and heroic conceptualizations of leadership developed in conventional bureaucratic contexts.[36] As organizations in developed economies become more 'knowledge-based', conventional command-and-control leadership models become anachronistic, so a different approach to leadership must be developed.[37,38] Plural leadership theory points us in the right direction.

From a plural perspective, leadership is not necessarily something that an individual does or a quality that an individual possesses, but is a process of interaction among organizational members seeking to influence each other. In this plural approach to leadership, leadership roles are shared amongst multiple actors, and authority relationships are ambiguous and potentially contested.

Unlike most conventional leadership research, a plural conceptualization of leadership does not focus on the traits and behaviours of individual leaders. Instead, it views leadership as a collective process, unfolding over time and arising from the actions and interactions of an extended leadership group. Leadership, therefore, is not something that is done by people but something that happens between people seeking to influence each other. As a result, it can be more temporary, more insecure, and more subject to negotiation than conventional notions of leadership.

34. J.-L. Denis, A. Langley, and V. Sergi. 2012. Leadership in the plural. *Academy of Management Annals* 6: 211–83.
35. D. S. DeRue and S. J. Ashford. 2010. Who will lead and who will follow? A social process of leadership identity construction in organizations. *Academy of Management Review* 354: 627–47.
36. M. C. Bligh, J. C. Kohles, and R. Pillai. 2011. Romancing leadership: Past, present, and future. *The Leadership Quarterly* 22: 1058–77.
37. M. Uhl-Bien, R. E. Riggio, K. B. Lowe, and M. K. Carsten. 2014. Followership theory: A review and research agenda. *The Leadership Quarterly* 25: 83–104.
38. M. Uhl-Bien, R. Marion, and B. McKelvey. 2007. Complexity leadership theory: Shifting leadership from the industrial age to the knowledge era. *The Leadership Quarterly* 18: 298–318.

However, if all the senior professionals within an organization are seeking to influence each other, does this mean that everyone is a leader, or that no one is? The frustrating answer is: yes, and yes, but only up to a point. Any senior professional, who has attracted their own following of junior colleagues and senior clients, is a leader in the sense that they have the capacity to exert considerable influence both inside and outside their organization. And while there may be several hundred 'leaders' in a large professional organization, no single individual is *the* leader. So, who is in charge?

Conclusions: Leadership Constellation

Conventional organization charts, which express formal hierarchical power structures, are of only limited use in the context of professional organizations. Organograms describe the formal authority structure but do not express who actually has power or reveal anything about how leadership actually happens. I have therefore developed the concept of the leadership constellation[39,40,41] to express a professional organization's informal power structure (Figure 2.1).

The leadership constellation is, by definition, a plural conceptualization of leadership. It expresses the informal power structure that overlaps with, and sits alongside, the formal authority structure. In Figure 2.1, leadership is represented by the arrows that connect individuals within the constellation as much as by the individuals themselves. The key is to discover how these individuals build consensus and work together to influence the rest of their colleagues.

The individuals who comprise the leadership constellation do not form a leadership team in any explicit sense because the constellation as a whole has no formally defined boundaries or overt identity within the organization. The hierarchy within the constellation is opaque to outsiders, as roles and relationships are negotiated among insiders on an ad hoc basis. Individuals may see themselves as leaders because they have important-sounding titles

39. The term was first referred to by Denis et al. (1996), based on Hodgson et al.'s (1965) concept of the executive role constellation, but it has not previously been operationalized.
40. J.-L. Denis, A. Langley, and L. Cazale. 1996. Leadership and strategic change under ambiguity. *Organization Studies* 17(4): 673–700.
41. R. Hodgson, D. Levinson, and A. Zaleznik. 1965. *The executive role constellation*. Boston: Harvard University Press.

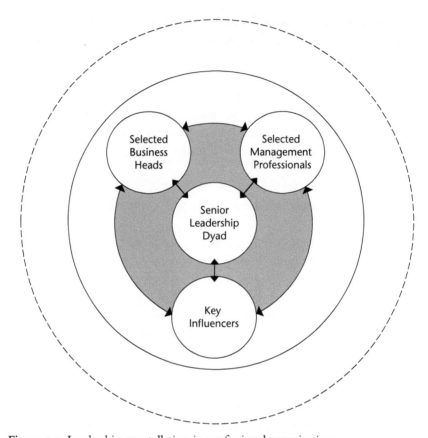

Figure 2.1 Leadership constellation in professional organizations

Source: Previously published in L. Empson. 2015. Leadership, power, and politics in law firms. In *Leadership for lawyers*, ed. R. Normand-Hochman. London: Globe Law and Business, 89–102.

on the Board or Executive Committee, but may have no significant position in the leadership constellation because they are not recognized or accepted as leaders by their colleagues. Similarly, individuals may be part of the leadership constellation without having a formal title, or without appearing particularly prominently on an organogram.

In the context of a professional organization, the key elements of the leadership constellation are:

Leadership dyad—professional organizations are often led by two individuals. The terms used for these roles, and the responsibilities associated with them, vary considerably across professional organizations, but are likely to be Managing Partner and Senior Partner, or Chair and Chief Executive, or some hybrid combination of these terms. How precisely these roles are defined will vary according to the organization and the individuals who occupy these roles (see Chapter 5 for a detailed examination of the leadership dyad).

Heads of major businesses—these professionals are in charge of the most important client-facing areas and may include practices, offices, and client sectors. They are likely to be members of the Executive Committee, but not all members of ExCo will play an equally prominent role in the leadership constellation. For example, the leadership constellation might include the head of the New York but not the Toronto office, the head of the Audit but not the Tax practice, the head of the Financial Services sector but not Oil and Gas. On the organization's organogram, however, each one of these office, practice, and sector heads might appear to have equivalent status.

Senior management professionals—these may include the COO and other Directors of business services functions such as Finance, Human Resource Management, and Marketing. By working closely with the leadership dyad, these individuals may move into positions of considerable informal power (see Chapter 7 for a detailed analysis of the rise of the management professional). Yet professionals are often not particularly aware of these individuals in so-called 'support' functions and have very little sense of how much influence they wield within the leadership constellation.

Key influencers—these individuals may have no formal leadership role but have considerable informal power, derived from their client relationships, valuable technical knowledge, and strong reputations. They may, for example, have previously held significant formal leadership roles and have now stepped back to focus on client work, yet retain a strong following among their colleagues. They may have been elected to the Board, reflecting the regard in which they are held by their peers. Or they may have been co-opted onto the Board by the leadership dyad, to bring them 'inside the fold' and minimize their disruptive potential. However, not all Board members will be key influencers.

It is worth noting who is missing from the leadership constellation: external non-executive Board members. Many professional organizations do not have Boards, or may have something called a Board which functions in place of an Executive Committee. External members, if they are involved at all, are likely to be relegated to an Advisory Board. This insularity is a significant vulnerability in many professional organizations and inconsistent with widely established views on good governance.

The concept of the leadership constellation has important implications for leaders, for those who wish to become leaders, and for those who wish to influence leaders in professional organizations. It is important to work out who is part of the leadership constellation, and how they relate to each other. It is particularly important to distinguish between those people who think they matter, and those who actually do. This will not be immediately obvious, as power and influence in professional organizations are often exercised indirectly and discreetly (see Chapter 3).

To map the power relations in a professional organization it is necessary to seek out multiple perspectives. Crises and major change initiatives are particularly helpful in revealing hidden power structures—who is involved and who is excluded, and in what sequence and at what stage they become involved. Chapter 10 explains details of how I performed this analysis in one organization, and the map of the leadership constellation I developed.

Whether you are a member of the leadership dyad about to launch a major change initiative, a candidate for election wishing to build a network for support, a rank-and-file professional wanting to gain support for a pet project, an external supplier wanting to close a major deal, or an academic commencing a major research study, mapping the leadership constellation can help you to maximize your impact. It can prevent you from falling foul of the hidden power dynamics within a professional organization.

3

Leadership Dynamics
Co-Constructing an Unstable Equilibrium

It's not telling them what to do; it's actually just coming up with the prompts and ideas to maximize the business and get the best out of people. So leadership sort of happens.

(Senior Partner, Law Firm)

It's not about following in that sense. It's about leaders enabling and directing, giving people outlets. Because frankly nobody has to follow anyone.

(Partner, Accounting Firm)

Introduction

The Senior Partner of one of the world's leading law firms says that 'leadership sort of happens'. A partner in an equally pre-eminent accounting firm says that 'nobody has to follow anyone'. It sounds slightly shambolic—not very professional, frankly. Yet both of these firms have achieved and sustained an elite global status. What is going on? This chapter sets out to explain in detail how leadership actually happens in a professional organization—how people become part of the leadership constellation and what they actually do once they get there.[1]

The phenomenon of plural leadership sheds some light on the puzzle of how leadership 'sort of happens' in professional organizations. As Chapter 2 explains, in recent years leadership scholars have begun to

---

1. The analysis and conceptual model contained in this chapter are based on work I have done with my colleague, Johan Alvehus.

examine leadership as a collective phenomenon that is distributed or shared among multiple individuals.[2] In other words, leadership is something that happens between people, something that is co-constructed through inter-action. But this does not necessarily mean that leadership 'sort of happens'.

By looking at leadership as something that is created through interactions among professionals, we can start to understand how it is fluid and unstable, changing and adapting as relations between professionals change and adapt. In spite of the quotations at the start of this chapter, there *is* a logic to how leadership happens in professional organizations, even if that logic is not necessarily apparent to the professionals themselves.

By carefully piecing together the insights of over a hundred leaders, this chapter maps the plural leadership dynamics of professional organizations, and identifies the three microdynamics in which professionals collectively engage as they co-construct leadership. The model of the leadership con-stellation presented in Figure 2.1 (Chapter 2) emphasizes that leadership is represented by the arrows that connect individuals within the constella-tion as much as by the individuals themselves. The model developed in this chapter (Figure 3.1) seeks to explain those arrows. It challenges the assertion that leadership in professional organizations 'sort of happens'; it is in fact the result of a complex and highly nuanced set of interactions among peers. But it is an unstable equilibrium. The leaders who misjudge the subtleties of these interactions will quickly discover that 'nobody has to follow' them.

Rethinking Followership

As Chapter 2 explains, plural leadership research is a good place to start when exploring the dynamics of leadership in professional organizations, but it only gets us so far. This rapidly developing body of theory typically takes the formal authority of leaders for granted but neglects the power dynamics which underlie plural leadership.[3]

---

2. J.-L. Denis, A. Langley, and V. Sergi. 2012. Leadership in the plural. *Academy of Management Annals* 6: 211–83.
3. S. Chreim. 2015. The (non)distribution of leadership roles: Considering leadership practices and configurations. *Human Relations* 68: 517–43.

To really understand what is going on with the leaders quoted at the start of this chapter, we need to pay greater attention to the underlying power dynamics that influence the emergence of plural leadership within professional organizations. And in order to understand these, we need to develop a more subtle conceptualization of followership. After all, how someone leads is inextricably bound up with how others follow.

There is a substantial body of research on followership but, unfortunately, much of it is not relevant to professional organizations. Traditional studies of followership look upon it as a role, something fixed. They assume that the people being studied are either leaders or followers—never both at the same time, or even at different times. These studies contain the implicit assumption that leader–follower relationships are given;[4] existing research does not look beyond this to understand how these relationships form and evolve.

Recent studies, by scholars such as Uhl-Bien, suggest a new view of followership that is more ambiguous and nuanced.[5] Drucker's assertion that 'leaders must by definition have followers' (see Chapter 2) turns out to be incorrect, or at least very unsophisticated. Instead, this emerging body of scholarship emphasizes the need to develop a more dialectical understanding of leader–follower relations, to recognize how leaders and followers coexist in interaction, and to examine the complex dynamics which guide these interactions.

If we examine followership alongside plural leadership, we can start to understand how leadership emerges as a relational process, co-created by leaders and followers.[6] Leadership is not something that one person does to others—it is something that leaders and followers create together. It follows, therefore, that leader and follower relations are not predetermined by established hierarchies but are negotiated among colleagues. This dynamic starts to sound more like what is happening in professional organizations.

DeRue and Ashford,[7] who have done interesting theoretical work on the relationship between leadership and followership, seek to explain the

4. M. K. Carsten, M. Uhl-Bien, B. J. West, J. L. Patera, and R. McGregor. 2010. Exploring social constructions of followership: A qualitative study. *The Leadership Quarterly* 21: 543–62.
5. M. Uhl-Bien, R. E. Riggio, K. B. Lowe, and M. K. Carsten. 2014. Followership theory: A review and research agenda. *The Leadership Quarterly* 25: 83–104.
6. G. T. Fairhurst and M. Uhl-Bien. 2012. Organizational discourse analysis (ODA): Examining leadership as a relational process. *The Leadership Quarterly* 23: 1043–62.
7. D. S. DeRue and S. J. Ashford. 2010. Who will lead and who will follow? A social process of leadership identity construction in organizations. *Academy of Management Review* 354: 627–47.

microdynamics involved in an individual coming to see themselves, and being seen by others, as a leader or follower. They talk about how individuals in organizations grant and claim the identities of leader and follower to each other.

Collinson[8] goes further, arguing for a much more subtle and nuanced understanding of both leadership and followership. He suggests that leader and follower identities are not homogeneous but 'blurred, multiple, ambiguous, and contradictory'.[9] Or, as the professionals quoted at the start of this chapter assert, leadership does 'sort of happen' but 'nobody has to follow anyone'.

Research Study

The broad question guiding the analysis was: *how is plural leadership constructed among professional peers?* The data come from 102 interviews I conducted with senior professionals in fifteen countries. Interviewees were drawn from three firms in the accounting, consulting, and legal sectors.

Each firm is ranked in the top four globally within its respective sector. Two firms are partnerships. One is legally a corporation but mimics a partnership by electing leaders, calling senior professionals 'partners', and adopting a lockstep method of remuneration (see Chapter 4 for an explanation of how some corporations deliberately mimic partnerships). Methods of compensation vary. In one firm a substantial component of compensation is based on individual performance; another operates a modified lockstep system; a third maintains a pure lockstep system (i.e. the leaders in these firms potentially have access to different levels of reward and coercive power—see Chapter 2).

The variations between the organizations are highlighted here simply to emphasize the fact that they make no significant difference to the underlying leadership dynamics. As a result, the phenomena identified are broadly applicable across professional organizations in general.

I conducted preliminary interviews with the firms' senior leadership dyads (Senior and Managing Partner, or Chair and CEO) and thereafter employed a

8. D. Collinson. 2006. Rethinking followership: A post-structuralist analysis of follower identities. *The Leadership Quarterly* 17: 179–89.
9. D. Collinson. 2005. Dialectics of leadership. *Human Relations* 58: 1419–42.

'snowball' method of sampling[10] to identify those involved in the leadership constellation. This process prompted me to interview a further thirty to forty professionals in each firm, including heads of practices, geographic regions, market sectors, and business services functions (i.e. HR, Finance, Marketing).

For the analysis, I worked closely with my colleague Johan Alvehus. We examined how individuals rise to positions of influence within the leadership constellation and how they exercise leadership once they get there. We were initially inspired by the plural leadership literature presented in Chapter 2, but as the emphasis on the ambiguous and contested nature of power dynamics emerged from our analysis, we turned to the literature on followership, specifically the work of DeRue and Ashford, Uhl-Bien, and Collinson.

Ultimately, we identified three microdynamics and developed a model of the co-construction of leadership dynamics among professional peers (Figure 3.1), which forms the basis of the analysis that follows.

Co-Constructing Leadership among Professional Peers

The model shown in Figure 3.1 identifies three distinct yet interrelated microdynamics: legitimizing, negotiating, and manoeuvring. Each microdynamic involves the interaction of two distinct elements.

Legitimizing involves a professional succeeding in the market while his or her peers (rather than 'followers') are inferring that he or she has leadership ability. Through legitimizing, peers raise one of their own to senior leadership status, granting leadership identity but not necessarily leadership authority. Leadership authority is claimed and granted by professional peers negotiating and manoeuvring.

Negotiating involves a professional asserting control while his or her colleagues are exercising autonomy. Professionals will permit a peer to assert control, but only as long as this does not impinge too far on their own autonomy.

Manoeuvring involves a professional behaving politically while colleagues are perceiving that he or she has integrity. Professionals need to make trade-offs and strike bargains in order to build consensus among powerful peers.

---

10. This is a non-probability sampling technique where interviewees are asked to nominate or recruit individuals for subsequent interviews. It is often used to reveal and access hidden populations.

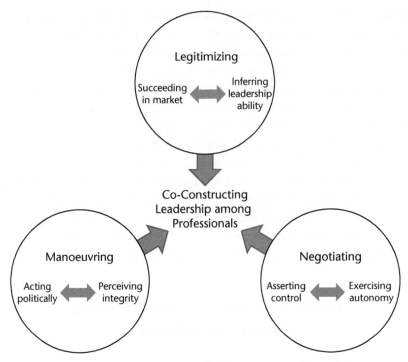

Figure 3.1 Co-constructing leadership among professional peers

However, this political behaviour must be subtle and seen to be in the interests of the organization rather than the individual.

Legitimizing: Succeeding in the Market/ Inferring Leadership Ability

> Your credibility is tied up with how successful you've been as a professional, so that's the starting point for people who end up in leadership positions. It's being a successful practitioner so that you've won the respect of the people around you. It doesn't necessarily mean you're a good leader. (Practice Head, Law Firm)

Many professionals are appointed rather than elected to leadership positions. In addition to holding elections for the most senior leadership roles, some partnerships also hold elections for practice heads. More commonly, however, senior executives 'take soundings' from among the key influencers in a practice, to identify the individual they are most likely to accept as the head of their practice.

So how does a professional win the respect of his or her colleagues in order to have the legitimacy to lead them? The answer is, through succeeding in the market. This success prompts a professional's peers to infer that he or she has leadership ability. According to interviewees, to win the respect necessary to lead effectively, professionals need to be 'strong performers in the market' and 'outstanding with clients'; 'everything else is icing on the cake'. As one professional explains:

> You always generate respect if you are a heavy hitter. If you bring in lots of business you will always generate respect. (Partner, Law Firm)

A professional also needs to be proficient at the more 'technical' aspects of professional work, such as quality of advice, in order to establish visibility and credentials within a professional organization. Yet professional skill is most highly valued by colleagues when it is translated into commercial success. Only then do they see it as an indicator of fitness for leadership.

Why should someone who is good at building relationships with clients and winning substantial amounts of business be any good at leading a professional organization? Superficially, these activities seem to have relatively little to do with each other. There are three related explanations.

Measuring the Ambiguous

Because of the ambiguous nature of professional work (see Chapter 6), professionals may struggle to evaluate exactly what their peers are doing, particularly when they have different specialist expertise or work in different client sectors. So, lacking any better measure of quality, market success comes to symbolize professional proficiency. As one interviewee explains: 'In the end all that we do is ultimately directed towards our clients.' By selling a lot of work, aspiring leaders demonstrate that they are not simply technically expert but also have a broader understanding of their clients' needs. By implication, this suggests that they also have the commercial acumen needed to lead their peers to commercial success. As a consultant explains:

> You can't be a leader without having credibility as a practitioner in this firm. . . . You have to have a demonstrated track record of having delivered, of being somebody who can not only propose but also dispose. (Office Head, Consulting Firm)

Of course, in the more highly regulated areas of professional work, such as audit, there are more objective external measures of quality, but the same dynamic applies in this sector also.

> I've dealt with some of our most difficult audits. So I've been the partner on [major client] having won that. I'm also still currently the partner on [major client] and that's not the easiest one either. And even now I've become head of the audit practice, I'm just going onto [major client]. . . . So if I put my little ego hat on for a moment I was sort of, you know, seen to be a good partner. You know, one of the top partners, I suppose, and one that can get out there and win work. (Head of Audit Practice, Accounting Firm)

The assumption is that professionals who understand their clients' business will be well qualified to lead their own. This inference is, of course, no more than a good guess—a proxy for more direct evidence of leadership ability.

Feeding and Leading

Professionals value a colleague's success in the market because ultimately it makes them richer too. In a lockstep firm, the link between individual performance and collective enrichment is most obvious, but the same principle applies in organizations which adopt more individualized systems of remuneration. Someone who is successful at bringing in business creates a halo effect for his or her colleagues, whether directly by passing on add-itional work or indirectly by bringing reputational benefits to the organiza-tion as a whole. As one practice head explains: 'I created opportunities for other partners, I was successful. They enjoyed working with the clients I brought to the firm.' According to another:

> People were drawn to me. I had followers before I went into a leadership role because I was the lead partner on [Company X], which was a big client for the firm. So I created opportunities for people, I was successful, they enjoyed working with the client. So all those things, I think, create followers. (Practice Head, Accounting Firm)

Ultimately, those who prove they can 'feed' their colleagues are also deemed to be qualified to lead them.

Role Modelling

Being successful in the market also has strong symbolic qualities. If a professional is seen to be willing to push themselves to their limit, they earn the right to ask their colleagues to do the same (see Chapter 6 for details of how leaders can exacerbate the problem of overwork). As one interviewee phrases it:

> I think that professional service practitioners . . . will accept almost unlimited decision making and authority from someone that they think understands the things they are going through. (Chair, Accounting Firm)

This role modelling harks back to the concept of referent power (see Chapter 2). As another interviewee describes:

> I did more billable hours than any other practice group head. . . . I always find if you ask people to do something, you get a lot more respect if they think, 'Well, *he's* doing it,' so therefore they follow that. (Practice Head, Law Firm)

A professional must continue to achieve success in the market, even after they have been accepted as a leader by their peers. The practice head quoted above goes on to contrast his own experience with that of a fellow practice head:

> Bob, who's very, very good, made a classic mistake of cutting right back on his practice and becoming full-time management. And that doesn't work in a firm like ours. You do lose credibility doing that. You have to be able to show you can still cut it. (Practice Head, Law Firm)

Whereas legitimizing is concerned with how an individual professional is 'raised up' from among his or her peers and gains the legitimacy to lead them, the second microdynamic, negotiating, explains how individuals sustain their authority to lead once they get there.

Negotiating: Asserting Control/ Exercising Autonomy

> Being Chairman is like walking a tightrope of helping my partners feel like owners, helping them feel involved, helping them be engaged, not dominating them, not getting out in front, not having a huge ego which makes them feel like the Chairman's kind of off on his own trip. At the same time being strong and providing them with a sense of confidence that we're going somewhere. (Chair, Consulting Firm)

This comment captures the complexity of a leader's ongoing day-to-day negotiations, of enabling colleagues to exercise their professional autonomy whilst ensuring that a necessary degree of control is maintained, of knowing when to say 'no' and 'yes', as explained below:

> Even though all the partners are your peers...there do need to be tough things done or decisions made on where we're going to invest, that sort of thing...knowing when you have to step in and say 'no', 'yes'. (Practice Head, Accounting Firm)

Chapter 2 emphasizes that in many professional organizations, increasingly stringent management systems constrain professionals' activities, yet there is still a vestigial remnant of professional autonomy in even the most 'corporate' of professional organizations. One COO, who worked in the corporate sector before joining a large accounting firm, contrasts his experience of working in these two environments, and explains how he attempts to 'walk the tightrope':

> When I was in a public company, I did a shareholder roadshow once a quarter and met shareholders for an hour, then I'd go away till the next quarter. Here, the shareholders are in the building every single day.... So the way I try and reconcile that is I say to them: 'One day a quarter I'm accountable to you, you are my shareholders, if you want to exit me, fire me, dock my pay, that's fine. But eighty-nine days of the quarter you just need to go and do the job you've been asked to do. (COO, Accounting Firm)

This COO acknowledges, however, that his approach is not always successful. In spite of increasingly stringent managerial controls, professionals consistently claim the right to be autonomous, and emphasize the importance of that autonomy to them. As Chapter 6 explains, even those professionals who conform enthusiastically to strong social controls can retain a strong belief in their own autonomy.

It is important to recognize, therefore, that autonomy is a relative, not an objective, concept. Within some organizations, professional autonomy may be no more than a mythical relic from a bygone era, yet leaders will still need to be seen to honour that relic. This is demonstrated by the two contrasting comments from interviewees in the same organization: an office head and the Chairman.

> The CEO and Chairman, Board of Directors, Executive Committee etc.... a lot of those positions are really coordinating or communicating...but definitely not controlling, not managing, not policing—no not that kind of thing. (Office Head, Consulting Firm)

> We're all leaders.... That's the narrative, that's part of the story and that's exactly what I say and that's what I expect them to say. But when we went

through the global financial crisis, guess what: there was no argument. When the pressure is on, they expect me to lead. (Chair, Consulting Firm)

Professionals tend to resent their leaders' attempts to control them personally, whilst encouraging their leaders to control their colleagues.

> Partners always ask for more accountability, but it's someone else's accountability. It's: 'I want everyone to be accountable, but not me.' (Practice Head, Accounting Firm)

Leaders regularly need to assert control over colleagues who are seeking to exercise autonomy. They need to judge carefully when to do this, who to do it to, and exactly how much control to exert. As a Chair explains: 'Partners say, "You're too tight, get looser." So you get looser and they say, "It's chaotic, get tighter."' This can be frustrating.

> At times I'd just like to say, 'You know something, just go and do it, because we haven't got time to debate it; just do it.' But that's not our culture. (Practice Head, Accounting Firm)

Negotiating is concerned with how leaders explicitly assert control; manoeuvring explains what is happening in parallel at a more covert and political level.

Manoeuvring: Behaving Politically/ Perceiving Integrity

> I think the political types in this firm are playing too many games, getting too clever for their own good, constantly thinking about tactics. But actually I do that all the time with my clients.... My last transaction, there were seven different stakeholder groups, all with complex demands, all wanting their own way, and my job was to get everybody across the line without them punching each other....I am really good at working out strategically how to move something forward. I feel passionately about the firm and I think there is a difference between me and the real political game players here, who are not always doing it for the common good. (Board Member, Accounting Firm)

This lengthy and nuanced quote captures the complexity and subtlety of the third microdynamic, manoeuvring. In order to be accepted by their peers as leaders, professionals must engage in subtle political behaviours, whilst appearing to be apolitical and acting in the best interests of the organization as a whole.

Manoeuvring is particularly complex because of the contradictory beliefs that professionals hold about the nature of politics. As explained in detail in this section, they decry political behaviours whilst explicitly creating intensely political environments. As a result, professionals must possess sophisticated political skills in order to lead effectively.

The pluralistic nature of professional organizations creates enhanced levels of organizational politics (see Chapter 2). Professional organizations which elect their leaders explicitly adopt the language and processes of political parties. Even leaders in non-elected positions use the language of politics, as one practice head demonstrates:

> The role involves us being seen as acting as the servants of the partners. We have our constituents—when they email us or call us we have to call back and we have to help them, be seen to be helpful. (Practice Head, Law Firm)

Professionals abhor political behaviour, yet their leaders must engage in subtle political behaviour, whilst being perceived to act with integrity.

Abhorrence of Overt Political Behaviour

When interviewing professionals, I did not ask them directly about politics, yet many raised the topic unprompted. They were keen to volunteer: 'I hate politics'. They like to think that their colleagues 'are not in the business of politics'. A professional's reputation within their organization can be damaged if he or she is seen to be politically 'pushy' or 'ambitious', if they are viewed as 'leading for their own advantage and just grabbing opportunities for themselves'. As a COO explains:

> There are people who are clearly very ambitious in the firm, who will say from quite an early stage to you, particularly over a beer or over a meal or over a chat [slams hand on table], 'Do you think I'm in the frame to be Managing Partner or Senior Partner? What is it I need to do along the way?'.... And they're regarded as quite pushy, and will be more political in their views in terms of what they think people will want to hear and what they think people will want to vote for. (COO, Law Firm)

But what exactly does 'political' mean in this context? The professionals I interviewed appear to have a fairly crude or naive conceptualization of political behaviour—which is probably why they think it does not occur in their organizations. They regard organizational politics as self-serving, a means by which an individual advances his or her own interests rather than the interests of the organization as a whole.

> To me, politics smacks of alliance-building in the corridors, in offices behind the scenes. It smacks of people engineering agendas, which creep up on the firm and deliver a fait accompli or behave in ways that become disruptive. Or politics could manifest as someone undermining another person. I would like to think we don't have those behaviours in this firm. (Chair, Consulting Firm)

This Chairman likes to think politics is rare in his organization. However, the following comment from one of his colleagues reveals intensely political behaviours, suggesting that they are in fact the 'norm'.

> There was a time at a partner conference when I thought somebody was getting lynched. We were having a formal vote.... There were two or three people with a personal agenda, a particular dislike for an individual.... They were trying to scuttle this person.... It was like fighting in public. I mean, the way this firm operates it should all be resolved before you ever go in the room. (Office Head, Consulting Firm)

This interviewee is arguing, in effect, that while there may be debates and formal votes at partner conferences, they should be highly ritualistic because consensus has already been brokered through a series of ad hoc discussions with key decision makers. While the interviewee sees this as much more appropriate and less 'political' than using the partner meetings to 'fight in public', he is nevertheless advocating highly political behaviour.

Within professional organizations, politics is at work every day—it is the oil that lubricates the interactions of professionals and enables them to broker a consensus. So politics, as with autonomy, is a highly subjective concept in professional organizations.

Dependence on Subtle Political Behaviour

Within a plural leadership context, a leader needs to be able to build and sustain consensus among his or her colleagues, to make trade-offs between competing interest groups, and to offer incentives to individuals in private to persuade them to lend their support in public. Leaders need to deploy these subtle political behaviours in different ways, for different colleagues, at different times, as the following two quotes from the same individual demonstrate:

> This is about dealing with adults, very bright adults, okay, and consequently I think the consummate leadership skill in this firm is the ability to influence change, and to drive change through influence rather than by telling. (ExCo Member, Accounting Firm)

> With my colleagues I apply the same skills as I do with clients, to arbitrate. To be able to hold up a mirror and say, 'Guys, you look like two kids scrapping in the playground. Is that really what we want? I mean we're all partners, for goodness' sake.' (ExCo Member, Accounting Firm)

This professional sees his colleagues simultaneously as 'very bright adults' and 'kids scrapping in the playground'. Like the professional quoted at the start of this chapter, he also sees clear parallels between the interpersonal skills he deploys with his clients and with his partners as he arbitrates and influences. He can engage in political behaviours with his colleagues, yet still be perceived as apolitical, because he is seen as acting in the best interests of the organization rather than (or perhaps as well as) his own interests.

Perception of Integrity

How is it possible for a professional to rise to the very top, to be elected Senior Partner of a global law firm, and yet not be 'a player'?

> Sometimes my sense would be [Senior Partner] doesn't necessarily always understand how influential he is. He's very modest about it, quite self-effacing, and he himself doesn't attach such great importance to some of those things that might be under the heading of 'creeping'—as in, slightly sinister. He is not himself a player in that way at all. . . . It's simply because his own motivations in this world are so, I think, very genuine and clean. (Head of HR, Law Firm)

Skilful professionals persuade their peers that they are apolitical by emphasizing that they are ambitious for the organization as a whole rather than for themselves personally. They may of course also be ambitious for themselves personally, but they explain that they are motivated by something bigger than that—the desire to do their very best for their organization and their colleagues. Whether or not their ambition for the organization is greater than their personal ambition is not the point—all that matters is that their colleagues believe that it is. Reflecting this heroic self-sacrificing view of leadership, one interviewee describes how a colleague used to 'come in on

his white horse' at partner conferences—the man on the white horse was
subsequently elected Chair.

> He didn't say a lot at partner conferences. But on some key discussions he was
> the compelling speaker.... He would come in on his white horse and say,
> 'Well, this is what I think,' and do it very well and with a good ability to link
> the discussion that had been happening to some prime value of the firm. (Head
> of Market Sector, Consulting Firm)

The Director of HR in a law firm reconciles the apparent irony of colleagues
denigrating political behaviour whilst privileging political skill by articulating a
subtler conceptualization of politics than is typically presented by fee-earning
professionals. This may reflect the fact that management professionals, who
occupy full-time functional rather than fee-earning roles, require particularly
sophisticated political skills to function effectively within professional organizations (see Chapter 7).

> It is important to distinguish between the sort of political ego which doesn't
> work, and political savviness, which is absolutely essential. And that savviness is
> born out of empathy and the ability to see and absorb and understand what is
> spoken and unspoken, and just what goes on sort of implicitly. I think is critical
> in this organization.... Without it, you are in real trouble because if you don't
> have it you can't have influence. (Director of HR, Law Firm)

Individuals operating in a highly politicized environment who do not appear
to have to work politically to keep their position may in fact—consciously
or not—be deploying highly sophisticated political skills in order to influence their colleagues, to fulfil their personal ambitions or their ambitions for
the firm. Chapter 2 identifies four key political skills[11]—social astuteness,
interpersonal influence, networking ability, and apparent sincerity—that are
widely recognized in studies of political leadership. The concept of apparent
sincerity does not imply that leaders are 'faking it'. It is not possible to crawl
inside a leader's head or heart and determine their fundamental truth. All
that matters in this context is how colleagues perceive their leader's behaviour because that is what determines their response. So, far from being
apolitical, successful leaders of professional organizations are highly politically skilled—or at least work very closely with someone who is (see
Chapter 5 on the leadership dyad).

---

11. G. R. Ferris, D. C. Treadway, P. L. Perrewe, R. L., Brouer, C. Douglas, and S. Lux. 2007.
    Political skill in organizations. *Journal of Management* 33: 290–320.

This is another reason why professionals infer that those who succeed in the market will also have the ability to lead them. The political skills of social astuteness, interpersonal influence, networking ability, and apparent sincerity are directly relevant to the management of client relationships. Professionals intuitively understand that a colleague who is particularly skilled at managing their clients will probably also be skilled at dealing with the complex and competing demands of their professional colleagues.

Having won the trust of their colleagues, a leader must behave consistently in order to retain that trust. As one practice head explains: 'If you're seen as being slippery, just saying things to be highly political, you lose a lot of the trust.' This consistency is, therefore, integral to the perception of integrity.

> The one who does leadership more naturally, partners will recognize that, and he is more likely to sustain the role. And the others are more likely to crash and burn. (ExCo Member, Accounting Firm)

Reluctant Leaders and Autonomous Followers

Many senior leaders in professional organizations talk in terms of their reluctance to take on a leadership role. As one interviewee describes it: 'It's something the partners ask you to do.' Another explains why he put himself forward for election:

> I realized I was fed up with lying awake at night feeling angry with the guy who was running my practice. When he put himself up for re-election, I decided I had to stand against him. (Practice Head, Law Firm)

Interviewees who have taken on senior leadership roles describe the conflict they experience between their desire to continue with their fee-earning work (the successful professional's 'first love') and their desire to bring about change within their organization (which inevitably takes them away from spending time with clients).

> The happiest times of my working life are when I'm with my clients.... Actually, I get a real buzz out of being in their offices rather than mine. I find when I'm in my office, I'm doing admin, internal meetings. And what I love is to be with clients. (Practice Head, Accounting Firm)

A Senior Partner remembers how he used to be a 'deal junkie' when he was doing transaction work full time and admits that he still misses the deals: a deal 'reinforces the ego' while 'nobody will tell you how great you are' as Senior Partner. Or, as an office Managing Partner explains:

> I say to the partners—I'm your servant leader and frankly if you don't want me in this role I'm more than happy just to be a partner and focus on clients because that's what we all love to do best. (Office Managing Partner, Consulting Firm)

Taken together, the three microdynamics of leadership help to explain why so many interviewees talk in terms of their reluctance to take on a leadership role.

Legitimizing means that leaders in professional organizations must be, or at least appear to be, reluctant to move away from day-to-day client work. Only once they have excelled as a fee-earning professional (i.e. they can act as an idealized role model) do their colleagues grant them legitimacy, allowing them to step back from—but not entirely abandon—their client work, and take on a leadership role.

Negotiating suggests that this reluctance may also stem from an understandable hesitation in taking on a very challenging role. Leaders need to assert control whilst enabling autonomy among their professional colleagues. They are seen as responsible for the success of the organization and are accountable to their colleagues for delivering that success, but lack the formal authority they need to deliver it.

Manoeuvring suggests that when professionals appear eager for power, and are seen as behaving politically to achieve power, their colleagues will not be willing to accord them power. In order to gain power, professionals need to appear hesitant to take on a leadership role. They need to convince their colleagues that they are only willing to do so because they believe they have even more to offer the organization in a senior leadership role than as a full-time client-facing professional.

A parallel phenomenon coexists alongside the reluctant leader: the autonomous follower. Professionals may grant leadership identities to their peers without necessarily claiming follower identities for themselves. This may not seem to make much sense initially—how is it possible to recognize someone as your leader if you are not willing to be their follower? It is all a matter of timing. Inherent in legitimizing, negotiating, and manoeuvring is the fact that 'followers' retain the right of veto over their leaders. They may be willing to accept the identity of follower but only on a temporary and contingent basis.

Conclusions: An Unstable Equilibrium

Each of the three microdynamics that collectively constitute the co-construction of leadership (Figure 3.1) represents an unstable equilibrium. In terms of legitimizing, it is not enough simply to have won business in the past. If professionals want to retain the respect of their colleagues, they need to keep winning business, even while they are engaged in highly demanding leadership roles. But now market success is defined more broadly. Failing to succeed with major strategic initiatives, or simply presiding over a significant decline in profits, may cause leaders to lose their legitimacy, so that their colleagues are no longer willing to grant them a leadership identity.

In terms of negotiating, the complex balancing act referred to by one professional as 'walking the tightrope' also represents an unstable equilibrium. If the leaders are 'too tight' or 'too loose' they risk losing their balance; in other words if they try to exert too much or too little control they risk losing their legitimacy to lead and their colleagues will no longer grant them leadership authority.

In terms of manoeuvring, professionals will no longer grant a colleague leadership authority if they perceive that he or she is behaving politically and not acting with integrity. Yet behaviours seen by one professional as highly political may be perceived by another as evidence of leadership ability. It rather depends on whether the leader's actions are advancing or undermining that professional's interests—we tend to look more favourably on the motivation of those who are helping rather than hindering us. Manoeuvring, in effect, involves making finely tuned judgements about which professionals to privilege and which to disadvantage. Misjudge this and the equilibrium is destabilized.

Negotiating and manoeuvring do not exist in isolation but are inter-related. Their inherent instability is therefore amplified. A small disturbance in any one may produce a large change in the leadership dynamics overall. This may result in a leader losing the respect of his or her peers, becoming ineffective, and even being deposed. Authority in a professional organization is always contested and contingent, and consequently represents a delicate balancing act.

Legitimizing and negotiating, for example, are interrelated because a professional's ability to 'walk the tightrope' between autonomy and control will be influenced by whether they continue to succeed in the market. If the organization is doing well, professionals will be content with their leaders and are more likely to infer that they have leadership ability, granting them the authority they need to continue to deliver that success. But if the organization is struggling, then the leader may lose the authority they need to assert control.

There is also a connection between legitimizing and manoeuvring which serves to amplify the instability. Leaders need to develop and maintain a strong external reputation for themselves personally to win the respect of their peers. However, once they become leader they must not be suspected of being overly preoccupied with managing their own public image. When they engage in high-level networking with senior clients and policymakers, and when they appear in the media, they must be seen by their colleagues to be promoting the organization rather than themselves. This becomes particularly important if leaders wish to retain legitimacy as their term of office draws to an end, and when they start to consider their role outside the organization, as colleagues will be quick to question their motives for engaging in this kind of high-level networking.

Negotiating and manoeuvring are also interrelated because manoeuvring is a more covert expression of negotiating. A professional who struggles to assert control directly may try instead to achieve their leadership objectives by behaving politically. However, when a leader is deemed to be acting politically, they are likely to lose their ability to assert control. They may simultaneously lose their capacity to negotiate and manoeuvre effectively—at which point they become highly vulnerable to being deposed.

This chapter has emphasized that leadership in a professional organization is not simply something that an individual does, or a quality that an individual possesses. It is something that is co-constructed among professional peers. It is therefore unstable and shifting. Whereas leadership in conventional organizations is typically portrayed as something which drives the firm forward, in a professional organization leaders must expend a great deal of effort just to maintain an equilibrium.

Leadership and followership are at best temporary and negotiated positions, requiring continuous interactions among professional peers, to both grant and claim the identity and authority of leaders and followers. The most effective leaders of professional organizations are those who intuitively understand this delicate equilibrium and work relentlessly and imperceptibly to maintain it.

The good news for leaders of professional organizations is that you do not have to do it on your own. You are part of a leadership constellation, working together to co-construct leadership. If it feels lonely at the top, this is probably because you are not doing it right.

4

Leadership and Governance
Reconciling the Individual with the Collective

The special nature of a partnership is that you've got a commitment and buy-in that is so special. People overachieve the whole time.... They feel that being a partner is very special and very empowering. So you have these amazing people who really feel they can sort of take on the world and feel part of a club, part of a very, very, very special club. And I think in a way that's really what partnership means to me.... It's quite a personal and emotional thing.

(Practice Head, Law Firm)

Introduction

Chapter 2 focused on leadership dynamics within the plural leadership group. This chapter expands this focus, to explore the dynamics which govern the interactions of professionals more generally, and to examine the role of leaders in creating and perpetuating a sense of partnership among senior professionals. What does it mean to 'feel part of a club, part of a very, very, very special club' of people who 'can sort of take on the world'?[1]

As the opening quotation suggests, the ethos of partnership represents a powerful means of motivating and securing the commitment of autonomous professionals. In recent years, many professional organizations have

---

1. This chapter is a new edition, updated and substantially revised to incorporate significant new data, of the chapter that first appeared as L. Empson. 2007. Surviving and thriving in a changing world: The special nature of partnership. In *Managing the modern law firm: New challenges, new perspectives*, ed. L. Empson. Oxford: Oxford University Press, 10–36.

abandoned partnership as a legal form and become incorporated. Yet some corporations in the professional services sector seek to mimic the organizational aspects of partnership.[2] At the same time, some partnerships no longer function as partnerships in any meaningful sense, whilst remaining a partnership in legal form.[3] This chapter will argue that the partnership as an ethos (rather than as a legal form) represents a highly effective means of reconciling the interests of professionals as individuals and professionals as a collective.

To expand upon the argument introduced in Chapter 1, professional organizations embody a delicate balance between the interests of the individual and the interests of the collective. There may be several hundred senior professionals working inside a large professional organization. At any moment, these individuals may stop thinking of themselves as part of the collective and start acting in accordance with their self-interests.

To complicate matters further, each senior professional may themselves simultaneously embody multiple and potentially competing objectives, from maximizing their personal income to maximizing their autonomy, or from maximizing their professional experience to maximizing their client's experience. When they vociferously assert their right to simultaneously pursue apparently inconsistent objectives, they may display prima-donna-like behaviour. The politically skilled leader must persuade these potential prima donnas that their individual interests are consistent with the interests of the collective. Leaders therefore need to develop a sophisticated understanding of how the partnership ethos is created and sustained within their organization, to understand the scope that they have for influencing the partnership dynamics, and the potential unintended consequences of their actions.

This chapter begins by identifying the economic and sociological factors which explain why partnership remains the optimal legal form of governance for professionals. It identifies what exactly professionals mean

---

2. L. Empson and C. Chapman. 2006. Partnership versus corporation: Implications of alternative forms of governance in professional service firms. *Research in the Sociology of Organizations* 24: 139–70.

3. For example, in 2002, Judge Posner argued that the partners of Sidley Austin Brown & Wood could be deemed to be employees rather than self-employed partners. Whilst they had shared in the profits and had unlimited personal liability for the debts of the firm, Posner argued that they had been 'at the mercy' of a small, unelected and self-perpetuating executive committee which could 'fire them, promote them, demote them, raise their pay, lower their pay, and so forth'. Equal Employment Opportunities Commission v. Sidley Austin Brown & Wood, 315 F.3d 696 (7th Cir. 2002).

by the term 'partnership' and goes beyond the basic legal definition to define the ethos of partnership. It identifies and analyses how the interests of the individual are reconciled with the interests of the collective through the interaction of socialization processes, management systems, and governance structures. It demonstrates how it is possible for valuable aspects of the partnership ethos to survive and thrive within alternative legal forms, specifically the publicly quoted corporation, and examines the implications for leaders in this context.

Why Partnership Works

A partnership is distinguished from alternative legal forms of governance by two key characteristics.[4] First, ownership is confined to an elite group of professionals within the organization. Second, partners share unlimited personal liability for the actions of their colleagues. Within the established professions such as law, accounting, and general medical practices, partnership has traditionally been viewed as the only legitimate mode of organizing. Among the aspiring professions (e.g. consulting and investment banking) firms historically often chose to organize themselves as partnerships, thus assuming the mantle of professionalism that it conveyed.

In the past twenty years, however, there has been a notable decline in the prevalence of partnership. This is due to a combination of factors,[5] including increasing size and complexity, increasing demand for capital, increasing commodification and litigation, and changing social trends.[6] As Figure 4.1 demonstrates, almost all of the fifty largest law firms are now organized as limited liability partnerships (LLP), and most of the fifty largest consulting firms are private or publicly quoted companies.

As the quotation at the start of this chapter demonstrates, professionals can become emotional about partnership. Beyond the hot emotional rhetoric, however, there is a fairly cool piece of logic. In the following analysis, I draw together (in highly summarized and simplified form) more than fifty years of

---

4. This is beyond the basic fact that the firm does not have a legal identity independent from its partners.
5. Empson 2007.
6. R. Greenwood and L. Empson. 2003. The professional partnership: Relic or exemplary form of governance? *Organization Studies* 24: 909–33.

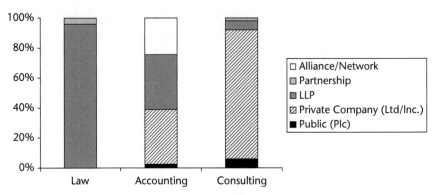

Figure 4.1 Legal forms of governance in large law, accounting, and consulting firms

sociology and economics research into the professions and professional organizations, to identify exactly why partnership works.

Governance in all organizations is concerned with three central questions. First, who controls the actions of the firm (i.e. power)? Second, for what purpose and for whose benefit does the firm act (i.e. benefit)? Third, who is held accountable for the consequences of these actions (i.e. accountability)? Ultimately, partnership works in professional organizations because it is the optimal method of reconciling the competing interests of three sets of stakeholders: professionals, owners, and their clients (see Figure 4.2), thus bringing together and reconciling questions of power, benefit, and accountability. Each of these stakeholder groups is discussed in turn in the next three sections.

Professionals

As Chapter 2 explains, professionals expect and enjoy high levels of personal autonomy within their working environment.[7,8] Problems can arise when this is denied them.[9,10] This emphasis on autonomy derives in part from the

7. W. Heydebrand. 1973. Autonomy, complexity, and non-bureaucratic coordination in professional organizations. In *Comparative organizations: The results of empirical research*, ed. W. Heydebrand. Englewood Cliffs, NJ: Prentice Hall, 158–89.

8. P. Meiksins and J. Watson. 1989. Professional autonomy and organizational constraint: The case of engineers. *The Sociological Quarterly* 30(4): 561–85.

9. J. Raelin. 1985. *Clash of cultures: Managers managing professionals*. Boston, MA: Harvard Business School Press.

10. J. Sorenson and T. Sorenson. 1974. The conflict of professionals in bureaucratic organizations. *Administrative Science Quarterly* 19(1): 98–106.

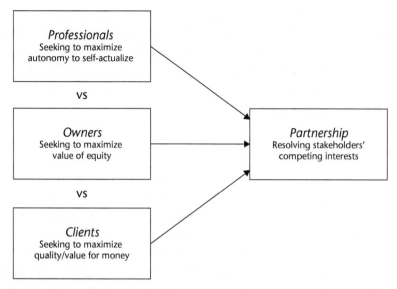

Figure 4.2 Reconciling stakeholders' competing interests in professional organizations

nature of professional work. In order to deliver a customized service of the appropriate quality, expert workers must be free to exercise their independent judgement. The desire for autonomy may go even further. Professionals seek opportunities to self-actualize (i.e. to pursue personal fulfilment), for example, by taking on assignments which they find intellectually rewarding, or which satisfy their altruistic impulses. Maximizing income is not necessarily a professional's primary objective; their motivations are likely more complex than that.

A sociological perspective suggests that partnership is an effective governance mechanism for delivering the degree of autonomy required to motivate senior professionals. In a partnership, ownership is confined to an elite group of professionals within the organization. Typically, partners retain the right to vote on key management decisions and elect representatives from among their ranks to perform senior leadership roles on a fixed-term basis.[11,12] Within this

11. M. Dirsmith, J. Heian, and M. Covaleski. 1997. Structure and agency in an institutionalised setting: The application and social transformation of control in the Big 6. *Accounting, Organizations and Society* 22(1): 1–27.
12. P. Tolbert and R. Stern. 1991. Organizations of professionals: Governance structures in large law firms. In *Research in the sociology of organizations, Vol. 8: Organizations and professions*, ed. P. Tolbert and S. Barley. London: JAI Press, 97–118.

context, partners may have considerable scope to pursue their individual objectives[13] (for example, to satisfy their professional pride by delivering a superior quality of service to clients). Consequently, partners are not necessarily required to focus exclusively on commercial imperatives. Whilst this may satisfy their desire as professionals to self-actualize through their work, it may not satisfy their desire as owners to accumulate wealth.

Owners

A property rights perspective emphasizes that, in professional organizations, it is not clear who owns the most critical assets—the fee earners, or the 'shareholders'.[14] The key income-generating assets (i.e. resources) are technical knowledge, client relationships, and reputation. As Chapter 2 explains, these may be proprietary to (or at least strongly associated with) individuals and may represent a potentially significant source of power and income for these professionals. There is a clear incentive for a professional to protect rather than share these assets, thus limiting the possibility of maximizing the value of the organization. Property rights theory argues that, when the key income-generating assets are proprietary to individuals, they should share in the ownership of the organization and participate directly in decision making. This implies a partnership form of governance.[15]

An agency theory perspective, which explores the costs associated with different governance structures, recognizes that it can be difficult and costly to apply formal controls to the monitoring of non-routine activities such as the provision of professional services.[16] This is because professionals are offering complex and intangible services. At the same time, informal monitoring is limited by the fact that their leaders may not share their specialist expertise and are unlikely to be directly involved in the more technical aspects of their work. The partnership form of governance emphasizes informal practices of mutual and self-monitoring, which are backed up by

13. R. Greenwood, C. R., Hinings, and J. Brown. 1990. 'P²-form' strategic management: Corporate practices in professional partnerships. *Academy of Management Journal* 33: 725–55.
14. For the sake of simplicity, the term 'owner' rather than 'shareholder' is used generically in this chapter to describe the owners/shareholders of all professional service firms, whether corporate or partnership.
15. O. Hart and J. Moore. 1990. Property rights and the nature of the firm. *Journal of Political Economy* 98(6): 1119–58.
16. M. C. Jensen and W. H. Meckling. 1976. Theory of the firm: Managerial behaviour, agency costs, and ownership structure. *Journal of Financial Economics* 3(4): 305–60.

unlimited personal liability. These will be more effective than formalized managerial controls at minimizing 'free-riding' and 'shirking'.[17,18]

Overall, therefore, in professional organizations the interests of the owners are best served when they are aligned with the interests of the professionals. The partnership form of governance is designed to achieve this. Both sets of stakeholders (i.e. owners and professionals) may still represent competing interests. However, by combining the roles in each partner, the partnership structure ensures that the tension is ultimately reconciled at both an individual and organizational level.

Clients

Just as leaders of a professional organization need to balance the competing interests of owners and professionals, so too must they balance the competing interests of owners and clients. Given the distinctive characteristics of professional work, the client must be certain that he or she can trust the professional to focus on maximizing quality of service rather than on maximizing profits.

When clients approach a professional organization they may not fully understand the nature of their problem and cannot sample the service prior to purchase. This puts the professional in a position of considerable power relative to their client. The client's trust in the professional will be based upon a complex set of factors, such as personal relationship and organizational reputation;[19,20] the partnership form of governance has traditionally represented an important source of reassurance. Unlimited personal liability, combined with the emphasis on internal ownership, ensures that partners share their clients' financial interests in maintaining quality standards and are not expected to prioritize the interests of external shareholders over those of their clients.[21]

17. E. Fama and M. Jensen. 1983. Separation of ownership and control. *Journal of Law and Economics* 26: 301–25.
18. A. Leibowitz and R. Tollison. 1980. Free-riding, shirking, and team production in legal partnerships. *Economic Inquiry* 18(3): 380–94.
19. M. Alvesson. 2001. Knowledge work: Ambiguity, image, and identity. *Human Relations* 54(7): 863–86.
20. J. M. Podolny. 1993. A status-based model of market competition. *American Journal of Sociology* 98(4): 829–72.
21. W. Shafer, D. Lowe, and T. Fogarty. 2002. The effects of corporate ownership on public accountants' professionalism and ethics. *Accounting Horizons* 16: 109–25.

Partners may, of course, choose to prioritize their own interests over those of their clients, but the intensive inculcation of standards of professionalism through formal training and informal socialization supposedly militates against such a tendency.[22,23] The protracted system of promotion to partner is designed to ensure that an individual's professionalism can be trusted by clients and partners alike.[24,25]

Partnership, therefore, appears to be the legal optimal form of governance for professional organizations. But it seems unlikely that the lawyer quoted at the start of this chapter would feel so committed to—and get so emotional about—a legal construct. Distinguishing between partnership as an ethos and partnership as a legal form opens up two possibilities. The first is that partnerships can continue to operate as a legal form long after the partnership ethos has ceased to exist in any meaningful sense. The second is that publicly quoted corporations can embody the most meaningful and valuable aspects of the partnership ethos, whilst avoiding the legal ramifications of partnership.

Research Study

The question guiding my analysis was: *how is the ethos of partnership created and sustained among professionals and what is the role of leaders in this context?* The data in this chapter comes from two studies I conducted on governance and leadership (the former study was with my colleague Chris Chapman). The total data set comprises 317 interviews within the law, accounting, and consulting sectors.

For the purposes of this chapter, I have cited data from two 'extreme' contexts. At one end of the spectrum is a relatively traditional law firm partnership. At the time of the study, it had recently converted to LLP status so partners had gone through a period of careful reflection on the nature of

22. A. Sharma. 1997. Professional as agent: Knowledge asymmetry in agency exchange. *Academy of Management Review* 22(3): 758–98.
23. P. Tolbert. 1988. Institutional sources of organizational culture in major law firms. In *Institutional patterns and organizations: Culture and environment*, ed. L. Zucker. Cambridge, MA: Ballinger Press, 101–13.
24. F. Anderson-Gough, C. Grey, and K. Robson. 1998. *Making up accountants: The organizational and professional socialization of trainee chartered accountants*. Aldershot: Ashgate Publishing.
25. M. Galanter and T. Palay. 1991. *Tournament of lawyers: The transformation of the big law firm*. Chicago, IL: University of Chicago Press.

partnership as part of their conversion to LLP. At the other end of the spectrum are two consulting firms which are legally corporations but which mimic partnerships.

The firms vary considerably in terms of size (from fifty to over 500 partners), geographic spread (from one to thirty-three countries), methods of growth (from primarily organic to merger-driven), and remuneration (from pure lockstep to performance-related). It is all the more significant, therefore, that the analysis reveals a remarkable degree of consistency across the firms in terms of how the partnership ethos is articulated and how it has been created and sustained.

In the research study I began by asking interviewees, 'What does partnership mean to you?' and, by analysing their responses, developed a framework which identified the dynamics of partnership (see Figure 4.3).

Dynamics of Partnership

As a legal form, the partnership is highly geographically and institutionally specific. However, when professionals talk about what partnership means to them, they are not referring to the legal form of partnership but to its 'ethos' (i.e. defined by the Oxford English Dictionary as the 'characteristics, beliefs and behaviours of a community'). It is this ethos of partnership that inspires strong sentiments.

Partnership Ethos

The two legal features of collective ownership and unlimited personal liability represent the foundations upon which the partnership ethos is constructed. As owners of the firm, partners have a clear imperative to maximize their individual autonomy. They are effectively shareholders, and what is the point of a firm if it is not to serve the interests of its shareholders? This individualistic impulse is tempered by unlimited personal liability, which binds all partners together by making them individually liable for the actions of their colleagues (though the partners I interviewed were keen to stress that becoming an LLP or a corporation did not constitute a licence for individualism). Partners, therefore, have a clear financial imperative to operate collectively and to monitor and support each other, both at a personal and professional level.

This tension between individualism and collectivism is fundamental to understanding the dynamics of partnership. The legal form of partnership creates the tension; the ethos of partnership reconciles that tension.

In some partnerships, the balance may be tipped strongly towards individualism—partners are free to pursue their personal priorities, whether they are income maximization or self-actualization. In such an environment, partners can make their own lifestyle choices. Rather than argue that the partnership ethos is absent in such firms, it is more accurate to recognize that the partners have chosen to strike the balance between individualism and collectivism in such a way that favours the individual. This articulation of the partnership ethos may resonate most strongly with professionals working in 'eat what you kill' partnerships, such as some US law firms.

In other partnerships, the balance may be tipped strongly toward the interests of the collective (i.e. the firm). The senior leadership will have a clear mandate from the partners to manage the firm on their behalf for their common financial gain. In such firms, constraints on individual partner autonomy may be quite extensive, with clearly defined rules within which partners must operate, clear performance targets, and serious penalties for failing to achieve these targets. This articulation of the partnership ethos may resonate most strongly with partners working in Big Four accounting firm partnerships, where the pressures of scale and regulation have encouraged the development of a more explicitly 'corporate' approach (see Chapter 8).

Regardless of where the leaders have struck the balance, in each of the organizations in this study there remains a strong and dynamic tension between the interests of the individual and the interests of the collective. The leaders of these firms are in effect engaged in a constant struggle to identify and reconcile the tension between the individual and the collective. In this context, a commonly understood partnership ethos represents a powerful unifying force. It counteracts the potentially self-serving impulses that drive each professional individually.

In firms with many long-serving partners, this sense of collectivity is associated with strong personal relationships. This may partly reflect the long hours worked together over the years and the absence of opportunities to build relationships outside work.

> One of the things my wife always says: 'All your best friends are your partners—you've got hardly any friends who aren't your partners.' I always

say, 'Rubbish, what about X and Y?' —and she says, 'But when did you last see them?' (Practice Head, Law Firm)

When personal friendship is not practical or possible, strong social norms nevertheless result in strong bonds of mutual trust. A partner in an accounting firm, struggling to express the extent of his trust and respect for his colleagues, explains it as follows: 'I would be happy to introduce any of my partners to my wife.' Another interviewee expresses this same sentiment somewhat differently:

> The most important thing to a refugee like me who has got kicked out of their country is their passport. Without that, you don't exist. I trust my colleagues completely and I would trust any of them with my passport. That is an amazing thing to say. (Practice Head, Consulting Firm)

Rather like brothers and sisters in a family, the expectation of mutual support is not necessarily associated with harmonious relationships. But the common bond of partnership holds the partners together in an obligation to each other, even if that obligation may sometimes seem irksome.

> The partners really do look out for one another. I might be working flat out day and night but if one of the others comes in to my office and says: 'Look, I've got a personal issue. I need to drop this hot potato and go and deal with it,' I will take it on. (Salaried Partner, Law Firm)

> The sense of community can become strained at times but it is strained in a constructive way. You've got several hundred individuals, each has their own ideas and their own ego—there are difficult and sometime abrasive people in any organization such as this—but if you can harness their skills it can be fantastically effective. (Salaried Partner, Law Firm)

When I asked the partners in all of the firms I studied to explain what partnership meant to them, they sometimes reverted to literary references. The ones I heard most frequently were 'One for all and all for one' (*The Three Musketeers*, Alexandre Dumas) and 'band of brothers' (*Henry V*, William Shakespeare). It is worth noting that both references are military in origin and are, by definition, exclusively male. Whether it is the Three Musketeers' rallying cry or Henry V's speech to his troops on the eve of the Battle of Agincourt, both references embody the sense of a collection of individuals coming together to defeat a common enemy. The Three Musketeers and the English army at Agincourt are famous for winning fabulous victories against seemingly impossible odds. If this is what partnership really means, no wonder it is something professionals prize so highly.

Figure 4.3 Dynamics of partnership

While the partnership ethos is clearly associated with partnership as a legal form, it is not explained by it. Three additional elements help create and sustain the partnership ethos and define where the balance is struck between the interests of the individual and the collective. These are the socialization processes, the management systems, and the governance structures. The dynamic interaction of these concepts, and the centrality of leadership to creating and sustaining them, is encapsulated in Figure 4.3.

Socialization Processes

The dictionary definition of 'to socialize' is 'to prepare for life in society' (Oxford English Dictionary). Within a partnership, socialization is the process by which an individual is evaluated and prepared to join the society of partners. The process begins in the initial recruitment phase at university, where interviewers may be asked to consider whether they could imagine the candidate as a potential partner of the firm. One consulting company (which is not legally a partnership but refers to senior professionals as partners) goes so far as to describe junior recruits as 'pre-partners'. This firm offers potential recruits up to forty interviews before making an offer, during which time interviewers are evaluating whether people 'fit' in terms of their attitudes, values, and behaviours. They recognize, however, that they are perhaps too effective at screening out candidates who do not fit.

> One of the big difficulties we're struggling with at the moment is that we hire too many people who are too similar. So everybody has the same thought patterns—we're very bad at recruiting dissonant thinkers. (Office Head, Consulting Firm)

Once recruited, socialization follows the traditional apprenticeship model. The junior professional observes the partners and learns the appropriate technical and interpersonal skills. During the process of socialization, a professional is developing the requisite technical skills to become a partner. Whilst these skills are essential, they are not sufficient. It is the personal qualities of the professional, specifically the extent to which he or she is valued by clients and colleagues, which represent the deciding factors.

> You may be working with a lawyer over a ten-year period. We spend a lot of time working in groups together and on the road so you see what people are really like. Do they have good client skills? How are they at mentoring the juniors? Can they hold their own over dinner? Can they have a few beers in the bar and make sense the next day? Have they got the intellectual stamina to keep going through two or three all-nighters? Can they withstand criticism? Are they able to take the knocks? (Practice Head, Law Firm)

Throughout this apprenticeship period, the potential partners are learning to subsume their own identity into that of the profession, the organization, and ultimately the partner group. When they make partner, the sense of pride in their achievement is phenomenal.

> How did I feel the day I made partner? I was over the moon. It was something I had worked for eight years to achieve and I had achieved it as quickly as I had dared to think possible. It was a real landmark in my career. So, yeah, I was ecstatic. I still do cherish that achievement. I know it's not like winning gold at the Olympics, but it's the closest I am ever going to get to it. (Partner, Law Firm)

This process of socialization is fundamental to the partnership ethos, which requires the interests of the individual to be reconciled with those of the collective. The individual must demonstrate that he or she has the necessary confidence and strength of character to exercise independent judgement and to behave with authority towards clients. At the same time, the prospective partner must show that he or she can be trusted to act in accordance with the wishes of the partnership as a whole.

Through the process of socialization, the professional learns in effect to become self-regulating. The lawyer who told me: 'I became a lawyer because I never wanted to have a boss' is perhaps unaware of the extent to which he will have internalized an extensive set of norms through his professional and organizational training and is, therefore, constrained in his capacity to exercise truly independent judgement. These norms do not seem oppressive to him because they have become an integral part of his own identity (see Chapter 6 for a detailed discussion of social control within professional organizations). This attitude, in an extreme form, is summed up by a partner in a consulting firm.

> No partners have left us in the past fourteen years.... We cannot live in the outside world—we're like animals in a zoo. In the wild we probably wouldn't be that good because we have been so well trained for this environment. (Office Head, Consulting Firm)

Management Systems

Traditionally, partners were exempt from rigorous performance management systems but these have become increasingly common in recent years. Regardless of the formal systems, the innate drive of most professionals and their sense of commitment to the partnership, ensure that they continue to generate and maximize profits on behalf of the firm (see Chapter 6 on the phenomenon of the insecure overachiever). As one partner explains:

> Do I feel pressure to bring in work? Yes I do. I think I have a responsibility to the firm to keep feeding the machine, and I personally take that responsibility very seriously and I do go out and get work. But I don't think the machine is forcing me to do that. No I don't. I think it comes from inside. It comes from a sort of desire to prove myself and the only way I can really prove myself, once I have become a partner, is to keep bringing in the work. (Partner, Law Firm)

In order to be elected to the partnership, a professional must therefore demonstrate his or her ability to be self-regulating. This is backed up by informal peer pressure and formal systems for evaluating, rewarding, and sanctioning partners. Together, these help determine the nature of the partnership ethos and how the balance is struck between the interests of the individual and the collective.

The lockstep system is the tangible embodiment of the desire to reconcile the interests of the individual with the interests of the collective. Under lockstep, profits are shared amongst the partners on the basis of time served rather than individual contribution in a given year. The effect of lockstep on a firm's ethos is explained as follows:

Our founder used to say, 'We're all in it together and we all succeed.' People say we're a kind of communistic, socialist system, both in terms of financial distribution and the way we make decisions—and I think there's an element of truth in this. We're like a commune. (Chair, Consulting Firm)

The extreme alternative of lockstep, 'eat what you kill', generates a very different kind of ethos, as explained by the Managing Director of another consulting firm.

Our consultants are like Clint Eastwood in *High Plains Drifter*. We go out into the outside world and clean up. Then we bring the carcass back to the office for our colleagues to gnaw on whatever we have left them. (European Managing Director, Consulting Firm)

Whilst lockstep may help to ensure that the interests of the individual coincide with those of the collective, when it is allowed to operate without sanction it can become a licence for individualism as partners free-ride on the effort of their peers. The intense socialization process prior to partnership is intended to guard against this behaviour, but cannot prevent it.

I had a partner come into my office recently, saying: 'I am sick to death of getting in the office at 7:30 every morning and watching X walk in at 9:10 and leave at 5:00 after doing bugger all, all day. I want him out. Get him out of here because he is pissing me off and if he doesn't go soon, I will.' (Practice Head, Law Firm)

Traditionally partnerships have dealt subtly and informally with underperforming partners. As the Senior Partner of a consulting firm explains:

There is a limit to what I can do because I need to respect their rights as a partner. So I put it to them very diplomatically and subtly that people would appreciate it if they did this or stopped doing that. Or, do they realize that this is what people think about them, and what are they going to do about it? If somebody has dug their feet in, I don't think I've got the right to try and force them to do something. This is delicate stuff. . . . I need to use a mixture of encouragement and suggestion without causing emotional upset. (Senior Partner, Consulting Firm)

With flagrant underperformers, partners signal their displeasure with their colleagues in much the same way that schoolchildren marginalize and ostracize their peers who do not conform to their norms of behaviour.

> It's usually the judgement of the peer group which is the most lethal, not anything that the management does. I mean, management might put questions into the frame but it's when the peer group gives up on someone that he is really sunk. (Partner, Law Firm)

When partners have 'grown up' together, they will understand the subtle ways in which they are being punished and are likely to feel shame at being excluded from the group. With a less stable and more heterogeneous partner group, such informal processes are less likely to prove effective. More formalized systems of evaluation and sanction become necessary. As one law firm partner reflects somewhat nostalgically:

> When we were a smaller firm you could get rid of partners by saying: 'You've lost the confidence of your peers, old boy. You either piss off now and we'll give you a year's money and be nice to you, or you can stay and we'll make it bloody uncomfortable for you.' ... It isn't so simple nowadays. (Partner, Law Firm)

Governance Structures

Whereas the partner management systems define how the partners are managed by their leaders, the governance structures define how the leaders are managed by their partners. In a publicly quoted corporation, leaders must act in the interests of shareholders who delegate authority to them to build and sustain shareholder value. The priorities of governance are, therefore, relatively unambiguous. Not so in a partnership, where the 'shareholders' or owners are working within the firm. The following comment from a lawyer caricatures the differences in leaders' authority between a corporate and a partnership structure.

> In a normal corporate hierarchy where, in theory at least, there is no questioning of authority—'He's my boss, he can tell me what to do whether I like it or not, I've got to do it or I can get fired'—I'm assuming that's the basic corporate premise, right?—but in a partnership it's, 'I don't like what you're telling me and I'm not going to do it, so you can just bugger off.' (Practice Head, Law Firm)

Leadership in this context may need to be subtle and indirect, guiding partners towards an understanding of how their individual interests can be reconciled with those of the collective.

The key is to understand the currents that flow around this place. The surface may be fairly wave-free—four-foot waves, five-foot waves—but it's the currents going backwards and forwards underneath that you really need to be aware of. Every now and then a big wave will break and cause the place to change. That's something that is primarily in the hands of the leadership team. They need to create enough waves going in the right direction for people to say, 'Okay, if that's what we've got to do then let's just get on with it.' (Partner, Law Firm)

The ability of senior leaders to exercise effective leadership in a partnership is severely hampered by the contingent nature of their authority and the ambiguous governance structures within which they typically operate. They have been elected by a majority of their peers and can be deposed by them at any time. As a practice head explains:

It's like I'm the eldest brother. I'm not the dad; there is no mum and dad. It's like I've got to the top because I'm the oldest or the tallest or whatever, but I'm still their brother. (Practice Head, Law Firm)

An individual leader's authority will derive from a complex mix of informal and formal sources of power (see Chapters 2 and 3). In terms of formal governance structures, my studies have identified three components which are particularly important in determining the nature and extent of authority in a partnership.

The first is formally delegated authority—specifically, which issues require a full partnership vote and what size majority is required for key decisions? Which decisions can be decided by the Managing Partner and his or her team? The second is the process by which the leadership team is selected. Is the Managing Partner able to nominate or select practice heads? Is he or she required to work with whomever the partners in that practice choose to elect? The third key component of the governance structure is the delineation of roles of Managing and Senior Partner (see Chapter 5). Specifically, to what extent is anyone formally tasked with monitoring the actions of the Managing and Senior Partners on behalf of the partnership?

Earlier in this chapter the phrases 'One for all and all for one' and 'band of brothers' were presented as expressions of the partnership ethos. It is worth remembering that, while the English knights at Agincourt submitted to the authority of their inspirational leader, the Three Musketeers were an extremely heterogeneous and ill-disciplined collection of individuals who won through because of their remarkable skills with the sword. Some professional organizations resemble the Three Musketeers; others have more in common with Henry V and his knights. A partnership ethos may operate very powerfully and effectively in either context.

There were only Three Musketeers (and D'Artagnan), whereas the English knights at Agincourt numbered 900. There is a risk that very large partnerships may end up encompassing the weaknesses of both the partnership and corporate structures (i.e. insufficient discipline and excessive bureaucracy). If a large partnership must inevitably adopt more 'corporate' practices, should large partnerships simply bow to the inevitable and opt for incorporation?

Imitating Partnership

Anecdotal evidence from the investment banking, accounting, and advertising sectors suggests that the flotation of professional organizations has had damaging consequences for clients, professional staff, owners, and even society as a whole.[26,27,28] In recent years, management writers[29] have exhorted corporations outside the professional services sector to emulate professional partnerships. They see such firms as embodying many characteristics essential for operating within the knowledge-based economy. Within the professional sector, some corporations deliberately imitate aspects of partnership, to try to create and sustain the ethos of partnership within a corporate form.

McKinsey & Company, for example, was incorporated in the 1950s, but to the outside world and to the consultants within it, still embodies many of the qualities of a partnership. As Marvin Bower (Managing Director 1950–67, described on McKinsey's website as 'the soul of McKinsey') said: 'We find it takes intensive and continuous effort to preserve the real and useful partnership spirit.'[30] McKinsey does not rely simply on the 'spiritual' approach but seeks also to mimic the structure of a partnership. For

26. P. Augur. 2000. *The death of gentlemanly capitalism.* London: Penguin.
27. Shafer et al. 2002.
28. A. Von Nordenflycht. 2007. Is public ownership bad for professional service firms? Ad agency ownership, performance, and creativity. *Academy of Management Journal* 50(2): 429–45.
29. B. Gerson. 2005. The limits of professional behaviour. *Harvard Business Review* 83 (April): 14–16.
30. M. Bower. 1997. *Will to lead: Running a business with a network of leaders.* Boston, MA: Harvard Business School Press. See especially p. 59.

example, the Managing Director is elected by a large group of the most senior 'partners'. The term 'partner' is still used informally within McKinsey because, as Bower states, 'even though it may not be legally accurate it can bring out some of the best qualities in people'.[31] Whether McKinsey is genuinely behaving like a partnership is not the issue—what matters is that it has created the impression of partnership amongst its clients and professional staff because it is 'useful' in business terms. McKinsey has succeeded in 'imitating' partnership.

McKinsey was once a partnership, albeit more than half a century ago, and has remained privately owned. Is it possible to create and sustain a partnership ethos within a publicly quoted firm with no history of partnership? My research suggests that the answer is yes, up to a point—but it is not easy.

One consulting firm ('Company') I studied had floated on the New York Stock Exchange in 2000 (for full details of this study see Empson and Chapman[32]). Although Company had never been a partnership, its shareholding structure closely resembled one at the time of the flotation (i.e. IPO). Shares were held internally by a broad cross-section of employees, with no individual owning more than 1.5 per cent. Post-IPO, 50 per cent of Company transferred to external investors.

Reflecting attitudes associated with traditional professional partnerships, the CEO recalls a time prior to the IPO:

> I remember eight years ago having conversations with people who would say things like, 'Do we really need to be in business to make a profit? Aren't we here to serve our clients?' (CEO, Consulting Company)

Preparation for the IPO prompted a more overt emphasis on commerciality and a drive for growth and revenue enhancement, which became stronger post-IPO. These changes are subtle, however, designed to encourage professionals to develop a more explicit focus on cost control and revenue growth. A practice head explains how management has sought to contain the impact of the IPO:

> There's been less change than one would imagine. We've been maintaining a balance between long- and short-term benefiting employees and benefiting shareholders and so far that's turned out very well. . . . I thought the recession would test it, but the CEO told the analysts that we were reserving a fair

31. Ibid. See especially p. 60.
32. Empson and Chapman 2006.

amount of profits for the bonus pool—the reaction from the analysts was, 'Good, your product is your employees and if you try to pay out too much in dividends you blow the whole thing.' (Practice Head, Consulting Company)

Just as in a partnership, the CEO has recognized the inherent tension between the interests of the individual and the interests of the collective. However, in Company the 'collective' has been expanded to embrace external shareholders. The CEO recognizes his responsibility to act in the interests of the shareholders, but he also knows that he must first build consensus among his colleagues.

> We don't have a classic management structure that says 'you shall'. The CEO creates opportunities and platforms for new ideas, but he very rarely says 'you shall'—he says, 'You should listen to what John has to say about XYZ', but he will rarely ever say, 'We're going to do this programme'—it doesn't work like that. So it becomes a very time-consuming process of selling your ideas to people. (Head of Business Services, Consulting Company)

The painstaking process of consensus building, so familiar to leaders within partnerships, is embedded within Company's organization structure. Company is structured as a matrix, with each member responsible to dual reporting lines of practice and geography. All key decisions require approval from both sides of the matrix. Where agreement on key issues cannot be reached between peers, the decision is moved up to the next level of the matrix. Interviewees argue that better-quality decisions are made after careful consultation and consensus building. However, as often happens in a partnership, there is frustration about the time taken to reach decisions. By substituting the word 'partnership' for 'matrix' in the following comments, it is possible to see how the matrix structure in Company imitates some of the best and worst aspects of a partnership.

> The nice thing about the matrix is that you can bounce decisions back and forth, very freely and openly. It is not like you have to hide anything. . . . In the matrix we know we are all in this together. (Practice Head, Consulting Company)

> I have laid off senior people and it has been ferociously difficult. The quantitative information on them was categorical. In other words, there was no ambiguity about whether they were terrible or not or whether we were losing money on them, but it still took months, and in one case years, to get rid of a person because of the inherent conservatism of the matrix. (Practice Head, Consulting Company)

Whilst the matrix prevents professionals from acting unilaterally with regard to internal issues, professionals have considerable autonomy with regard to client issues (e.g. which clients to serve and how to deliver the service).

> There is a certain amount of flea-market mentality here. Each senior consultant has their own booth at the flea market, renting space from the flea-market operator. (Practice Head, Consulting Company)

> This place gives me room. It is very trusting. It relies on my entrepreneurial spirit to move forward. . . . This place lets you use your brain cells and lets you try; it gives you the opportunity to sell, to persuade. (Functional Head, Consulting Company)

For these consultants, the autonomy they prize is not about resisting managerial control but about acting entrepreneurially—in other words, the freedom to make money any way they like. The leaders of Company have recognized that as long as their professionals are left alone to serve their clients, they will accept many of the constraints associated with being part of a large corporation.

Conclusions: Leadership, the Individual, and the Collective

This chapter argues that it is possible for professionals to imitate the most valuable aspects of a partnership without necessarily being restricted by its legal form. However, for this process to be effective, professionals and their leaders must be strongly committed to the partnership ethos and work actively to create and sustain it. Incorporation and flotation may not automatically destroy the partnership ethos, but they certainly do not encourage its survival. The partnership ethos can survive within the challenging contemporary context in which professional organizations must compete, but only under certain conditions.

At the heart of the partner dynamics framework (Figure 4.3) is the word 'leadership', reflecting the fact that the leaders of the firm are integral to defining the balance between the interests of the individual and the collective.

Leaders of professional organizations must develop a sophisticated and subtle understanding of what exactly the partnership ethos means within their particular organization—in other words, where the balance should be drawn between the interests of the individual and the interests of the collective. Once they are clear about this, leaders need to develop and apply their management systems, governance structures, and socialization processes to ensure that this ethos adapts and survives.

Whilst the partnership ethos reconciles the tension between individualism and collectivism, the precise manner in which it is manifested and enacted within a professional organization will be determined by a complex combination of firm-specific factors. These will include the competitive environment within which the organization must operate and its relative position within it; the historically derived expectations of the senior professionals and the differing factions among them; and the relative influence of these factions and their importance to the future of the firm. Taking all this into account, leaders need to arrive at a clear understanding of the collective interests of the partners and communicate these coherently and consistently so that they become the established 'truth' within the firm and an integral part of the partnership ethos.

Whilst the partnership ethos can meld a disparate group of senior professionals into a collective entity, the exclusivity which makes it attractive to those within the partnership serves to exclude, and potentially alienate, those outside the partnership. Perceptions of the partnership ethos may vary considerably within the firm, between junior and senior professionals, between professionals and support staff, as well as externally with clients and with potential recruits. Do salaried partners, for example, feel included or excluded from the partnership? Do the women who make it to partnership remain excluded from the inner circle of male leaders? Do junior professionals understand the partnership ethos and do they aspire to be partners? Does the partnership ethos relegate high-quality management professionals in senior business services roles to the status of second-class citizens (see Chapter 7)? Are junior staff expected to tolerate extreme and inappropriate behaviours from partners who view themselves as unaccountable owners of the firm? (see Chapter 6). Are clients and potential recruits aware of the partnership ethos and do they understand its significance?

By addressing these questions carefully, leaders can develop a clearer understanding of what partnership means to their key stakeholders. What has it meant traditionally? What is challenging traditional attitudes? What aspects of partnership are vital to preserve? How can the partnership ethos adapt to the changing competitive marketplace? With this foundation in place, the next step for leaders is to understand how their organization's management systems, governance structures, and socialization processes can be managed to ensure that the most valued aspects of partnership are retained and the more anachronistic aspects of partnership are done away with.

There is much, therefore, that leaders of professional organizations can do to protect and develop the partnership ethos, whether they choose to retain the partnership in its legal form or to move towards incorporation or flotation. The key is to recognize what exactly the partnership ethos means in the context of their own organization, what is threatening it, and specifically how it can remain valuable in a changing competitive context. As a partnership grows, and its structures, systems, and socialization processes evolve, senior leaders are responsible to their stakeholders to ensure that such changes support, rather than undermine, the partnership ethos. The ethos of partnership and professionalism are inextricably connected; it is in the interests of professionals, their organizations, and society as a whole that both remain robust.

PART II

Leadership and Individuals

5

Leadership Dyads

The Ideal Leader Is Two People

Empson:	Who's in charge here?
Senior Partner (Firm X):	[Pause.] Well I suppose I am, I mean in a way, I mean I think, but it's difficult to answer that question.
Empson:	Who's in charge here?
Managing Partner (Firm X):	Hmmm. You want one name or you want . . . ?
Empson:	I just want your view of what the truth is.
Managing Partner:	[Pause.] I think it's the two of us actually. We rarely disagree. It's instinctive.

Introduction

The dual leadership model, or leadership dyad, is common in professional organizations. Often it is clear who is in charge, but sometimes it is left deliberately ambiguous, as in the above examples from an elite global professional organization.[1,2] While this kind of arrangement is most typically found at the very top, leadership dyads can occur throughout a professional organization. There are, for example, multiple joint practice heads in the leadership constellation mapped in Figure 10.1 and described in detail in Chapter 10.

Over the years, I have observed many different combinations and permutations of leadership dyads within leadership constellations. In the

---

1. My thanks to Wendellyn Reid for her very helpful comments on an early draft of this chapter.
2. Given the extremely sensitive nature of the issues in this chapter, I have not identified which sector any quotations are drawn from, to ensure total anonymity.

following analysis the terms Senior and Managing Partner are used, but professional organizations, whether partnerships or corporations,[3] also deploy the terms Chair and Chief Executive, or hybrid combinations such as Chair and Managing Partner. The terms themselves have little inherent meaning—they are merely signifiers—because the roles are defined very differently in different professional organizations. Sometimes individuals are jointly elected to these dyads; sometimes separately and at different times; sometimes one is elected by the partnership and the other is appointed by the Board. Regardless of what they are called or how they got there, what matters is how each combination of individuals develops a modus operandi within the leadership dyad.

This chapter asks whether leadership dyads can be effective and, if so, how they work in practice. It presents a framework derived from my research which identifies and analyses four different leadership dyads that occur in professional organizations: Intuitive Collaboration, Structured Coordination, Negotiated Cohabitation, and Careful Cooperation. It explains why each of these dyads can be effective, in very different ways and for very different reasons. It argues that it is notionally possible for one individual to be in charge of a professional organization, and to embody and reconcile the inherent tension between the individual and collective, but it is much easier when two are involved—a leadership dyad. It demonstrates how even the most discordant dyads can be effective if their members are able to embody, express, and repeatedly resolve the conflict which permeates the organization as a whole. This chapter examines the serious consequences when leadership dyads break down and suggests what leaders can do if they become involved in a dysfunctional dyad.

Leadership Dyads: When Two Is Better than One

Co-leadership is widespread in certain sectors, where it has developed as a response to pluralism.[4] As Chapter 2 explains, in a pluralistic setting[5] tensions

3. As Chapter 4 explains, the formal legal distinctions of partnership and corporation may disguise similarities in the informal power dynamics.
4. E. Gibeau, W. Reid, and A. Langley. 2015. Co-leadership: Contexts, configurations and conditions'. In *The Routledge companion to leadership*, ed. J. Storey, J. Hartley, J.-L. Denis, P. 't Hart, and D. Ulrich. London: Routledge, 225–40.
5. J.-L. Denis, L. Lamothe, and A. Langley. 2001. The dynamics of collective leadership and strategic change in pluralistic organizations. *Academy of Management Journal* 44: 809–37.

arise because of complex and competing values, cultures, rules, and expect-ations. Chief among these in a professional organization is the tension between the interests of the individual and the collective (see Chapter 4). Co-leadership represents an effective mechanism for reconciling, or at least managing, these tensions.

Concern for People vs Concern for Production

The highly influential behavioural studies of leadership in the 1960s char-acterized leaders on two broad dimensions: concern for people versus concern for production. Leadership styles were defined in terms of their relative positions on what was termed a managerial 'grid'.[6] In a professional organization, however, the distinction between concern for people and concern for production is highly problematic as the people are the machine of production. Consequently, the ideal leader of a professional organization must excel on both dimensions simultaneously.

Concern for production implies that leaders view the organization as a reified entity. In other words, they focus on the abstraction of the organ-ization as if it were a concrete and singular thing rather than a collection of individuals. In terms of the partnership dynamics referred to in Chapter 4, such leaders focus on the interests of the collective by emphasizing issues such as strategy and operational performance, to ensure short-term profit-ability and long-term growth for the organization as a whole. They aim to identify, articulate, and advance a coherent set of clearly prioritized object-ives and to focus on driving the organization forward by initiating and implementing change.

By contrast, concern for people implies that leaders are less focused on the organization as a reified entity but instead view it more as a collection of individuals, for whom they have a duty of care. In terms of the partnership dynamics referred to in Chapter 4, this implies that leaders are custodians of the interests of the individual rather than the collective, and are therefore more focused on addressing and resolving the disaggre-gated and pluralistic nature of the organization, by emphasizing issues such as culture and governance.

6. See, for example, R. Blake and J. Mouton. 1964. *The managerial grid: The key to leadership excellence*. Houston: Gulf Publishing Co.

In a professional organization, very few individuals are likely to be able to address concerns for people and production simultaneously and effectively. It typically takes two to do this, with both members of the dyad focusing on one or the other. The more intensely one individual focuses on production, the more the other will need to focus on people. My analysis suggests that the members of the dyad may not agree this division of labour explicitly or even recognize that this is what they are doing. But when the dyad is functioning effectively, simply by playing to their respective strengths, the members of the dyad are able to work this out between them.

The idea that it may take two to lead a complex organization is not confined to the professional sector, so it is worth considering briefly how it operates more broadly in order to establish how it differs in a professional context. Previous research has addressed this issue from two distinct perspectives, as explored in the next two sections.

Chair/Chief Executive Split in Corporations

In Europe it has long been established practice within conventional corporations to separate the role of Chair and Chief Executive.[7] In the UK, the separation of roles is enshrined in the UK Corporate Governance Code.[8] In the US, however, the practice is for one individual to occupy both roles.[9] Post Sarbanes-Oxley, however, corporations in the US have come under increasing pressure from activist shareholders. As a result, currently 40 per cent of S&P 500 corporations now split the Chair and Chief Executive roles.

The conventional view is that combining the role of Chief Executive and Chair promotes unity of leadership and organizational effectiveness.[10] However, these benefits are potentially outweighed by the need to ensure that managers act at all times in the interests of shareholders rather than in their

7. For a detailed analysis of comparative governance research, see R. Aguilera and G. Jackson. 2010. Comparative and international corporate governance. *Academy of Management Annals* 4(1): 485–556.
8. Financial Reporting Council. 2016. The UK corporate governance code. London: Financial Reporting Council. <https://www.frc.org.uk/Our-Work/Publications/Corporate-Governance/UK-Corporate-Governance-Code-April-2016.pdf>.
9. R. Krause, M. Semandi, and A. Cannella. 2014. CEO duality: A review and research agenda. *Academy of Management Annals* 40(1): 256–86.
10. H. Fayol. 1949. *General and industrial management.* London: Pitman.

own self-interests. Splitting the roles of Chair and CEO is supposed to prevent the interests of the principals from being subjugated to those of their agents.[11]

However, these arguments from corporate governance theory do not apply directly to privately held professional organizations, where the roles of principal and agent are combined. In most professional organizations, the most senior fee-earners inside the firm also own the majority of the equity. As a result, they are well-placed to provide effective oversight of the individuals they select to occupy leadership positions.

While the leadership dyad within a professional organization may resemble the separate roles of Chair and Chief Executive in a conventional corporation, it must contend with very different power dynamics. This applies equally to those professional organizations which are partnerships and those which are corporations, because the dyad is shaped by the idiosyncrasies of the individuals who occupy the roles, as much as by the organization's formal legal and governance arrangements.

Co-Leadership

Within the leadership literature there is an important strand of research which examines co-leadership.[12] Co-leadership, as the term suggests, involves two individuals sharing leadership on a roughly equal basis—they are at least nominally equal partners.[13] Their roles may be distinct but their power is much the same. It is this phenomenon of co-leadership that is being expressed by the Managing and Senior Partner quoted at the start of this chapter, who struggle to answer my deceptively simple question: who's in charge? With the Chair/Chief Executive split in conventional corporations, the Chair is in charge of the Board to which the Chief Executive reports. With co-leadership, the distinction between roles and the authority associated with those roles is more complicated.

Previous studies have pointed to the inherent fragility of co-leadership, founded as it is on the amorphous concept of trust. These studies cite the

11. E. Fama and M. Jensen. 1983. Separation of ownership and control. *Journal of Law and Economics* 26: 301–25.

12. For a comprehensive review of research into this phenomenon, see J.-L. Denis, A. Langley, and V. Sergi. 2012. Leadership in the plural. *Academy of Management Annals* 6: 211–83.

13. J. Alvarez and S. Svejenova. 2005. *Sharing executive power: Roles and relationships at the top.* Cambridge: Cambridge University Press.

potential for confusion, conflict, ambiguity, and lack of accountability. They argue that such arrangements are likely to be incoherent and ineffective, and may ultimately fail. For example, Denis, Lamothe, and Langley's[14] study of leadership constellations in hospitals found that, while each leader had a distinctive domain with clearly defined roles and responsibilities, they nevertheless needed to engage in sustained emotional labour to create and maintain an effective collaboration. Similarly, Reid and Karambayya's[15,16] studies of dual leadership in arts organizations found that the leadership dyad becomes an arena for balancing and negotiating tensions inherent in differing conceptualizations of the organization's purpose and priorities. When the dyad does not contain the conflict between artistic and commercial imperatives, it spills out into the organization, with potentially damaging implications for individual leaders and the organization more generally.

Scholars of dual leadership, such as Denis et al.[17] and Hodgson et al.,[18] have argued that conflict can be minimized by creating clearly differentiated, specialized, and complementary roles and responsibilities. However, Gronn[19] has suggested that, far from exacerbating conflict, ambiguity within a shared role space may be a means of avoiding it. His numerous studies of leadership in the educational sector have highlighted a much looser plural leadership dynamic based on 'intuitive working relationships' or 'intuitive mutual adjustment'. According to Gronn and Hamilton,[20] such ambiguous dynamics reflect the unspoken and implicit understandings that emerge over time, as two or more organizational members negotiate their power relationships. Gronn and colleagues argue that, in such an environment, leadership roles are open-ended 'emotional spaces' and must be negotiated

14. Denis et al. 2001.
15. W. Reid and R. Karambayya. 2009. Impact of dual executive leadership dynamics in creative organizations. *Human Relations* 62(7): 1073–112.
16. W. Reid and R. Karambayya. 2015. The shadow of history: Situated dynamics of trust in dual executive leadership. *Leadership* 12(5): 609–31.
17. Denis et al. 2001.
18. R. Hodgson, D. Levinson, and A. Zaleznik. 1965. *The executive role constellation*. Boston, MA: Harvard University Press.
19. See Gronn's series of studies, beginning with P. Gronn. 2002. Distributed leadership as a unit of analysis. *The Leadership Quarterly* 13: 423–52.
20. P. Gronn and A. Hamilton. 2004. 'A bit more life in the leadership': Co-principalship as distributed leadership practice. *Leadership and Policy in Schools* 3(1): 3–35.

with colleagues on a day-to-day basis, with a concomitant increase in political activity associated with such arrangements.

Research Study

For the purposes of this chapter, the question guiding my analysis was: *in professional organizations, can leadership dyads be effective and, if so, how do they work in practice?*

During the past twenty years I have researched and worked closely with a great many senior leaders and leadership dyads. To address the question above, I identified those organizations where leaders had talked to me at length about their relationships with each other, or where their colleagues had discussed the leaders' relationships. I returned to my interview transcripts and also examined the observational notes I had made at meetings and events where I had been particularly struck by the relational dynamics of the leadership dyad. I narrowed my focus onto those accounting, consulting, and law firms whose leadership dyads embodied particularly distinctive or extreme characteristics. From this analysis I developed the leadership dyads framework (see Figure 5.1).

Inspired by the work of Denis et al.,[21] the framework highlights the significance of the degree of separation and overlap in the members of the leadership dyads' respective roles. Building on the work of Reid and Karambayya,[22] it also emphasizes the extent to which their relationship is harmonious or discordant. The studies of Denis et al. and Hodgson et al.[23] have both suggested that overlapping roles will lead inevitably to conflict. My analysis challenges this assertion.

Foundational Assumptions

The framework is based on three foundational assumptions, relating to conflict, power, and history, as explained in the following sections.

21. Denis, Lamothe, and Langley 2001.
22. Reid and Karambayya 2009, 2015.
23. Hodgson, Levinson, and Zaleznik 1965.

Conflict is Inherent and Healthy

Extending Reid and Karambayya's argument, my framework is built on the assumption that the leadership dyad should embody and resolve organizational conflict. Here it is important to distinguish between organizational conflict and personal conflict. The former is inherent in professional organizations and arises from their pluralistic nature and the tension between the individual and the collective which permeates them. The latter is specific to individuals and is grounded in personality differences between members of the leadership dyad which would likely exist independent of any organizational conflict.

In embodying the organizational conflict, members of the leadership dyad reduce the extent to which this conflict is enacted within their organization—so that the conflict does not 'leach out' into the leadership constellation more broadly or to the professionals as a whole. Having addressed this organizational-level conflict between themselves, the members of the leadership dyad may present a negotiated solution and united front to their colleagues. This is vital if they are to succeed in building consensus across the leadership constellation and throughout the organization. Effective leadership dyads should be able to do this repeatedly and continuously, over a range of issues and in a variety of contexts.

By logical extension, ineffective leadership dyads can be ineffective in three distinct ways. First, they may fail to manage and contain the organizational conflict. They may successfully embody that conflict but the personal conflict may be so intense that they are prevented from engaging meaningfully with the organizational sources of conflict. Instead, because they are unable to resolve their personal conflict, it will permeate the organization as a whole. Individuals within the leadership constellation will become co-opted into managing and enacting this conflict.

Second, they may avoid conflict and thus fail to address or resolve the tension inherent in the organization.

Third, they may be so much in accord at a personal level that they fail to recognize or embody the organizational conflict, which may become more acute as a result. By living in a harmonious cocoon, they risk becoming disconnected from the concerns and anxieties of the rest of the leadership constellation and may fundamentally misjudge the mood of the organization as a whole (see Chapter 8).

Informal Power is as Important as Formal Authority

As Chapter 2 explains, a professional's power within their organization is made up of a complex combination of factors. To understand the leadership dyad, two broad types of power are significant. The first is the formal authority embodied in their role. The second is the informal power, such as the mandate gained from their election and how they are currently viewed by their colleagues.[24]

One member of the leadership dyad may have more formal authority than the other, but this is not necessarily an accurate indicator of their relative informal power. For example, in one organization I studied, the Managing Partner was required to report to a Board that was chaired by a Senior Partner. However, as the Board and Senior Partner were viewed as ineffective by the rest of the partnership, the Managing Partner was relatively more powerful.

One means of minimizing potential conflict between the Managing and Senior Partner is for the latter to select the former, rather than for them both to be elected. By logical extension, however, this approach presents a different kind of problem from the dual election model, as it potentially limits the informal power of the Managing Partner. Appointees may lack legitimacy within the leadership constellation, and among their colleagues more generally, and may struggle to assert authority over them. To quote one of my interviewees, they risk being seen as the elected leader's 'poodle'. This problem is less likely to arise if the Senior Partner selects a colleague who has gained a high level of legitimacy amongst their peers. However, in this scenario, the Senior Partner's power may be diminished as a result.

History Matters

The concept of path dependency refers to how the set of decisions one faces in any given circumstance is limited by the decisions made in the past, even though past circumstances may no longer be relevant. In this context, an organization's current leadership dyad will be influenced by a variety of

24. Other examples include the referent power and legitimacy they have gained from their previous success in the market (see Chapters 2 and 3), and the social capital they have gained from their dense network of social ties within the organization (see Chapter 7).

historical factors, such as the organization's previous leaders, its governance structures, and its cultural norms.

In terms of the impact of previous leaders, Reid and Karambayya's[25] study of plural leadership demonstrates how the current leadership dyad is shaped by the 'shadow of history'. When electing a Managing or Senior Partner, professionals will be mindful of previous leadership dyads, and may seek to replicate particularly effective previous combinations. As demonstrated in the following analysis, if there is a legacy of dysfunctional dyads, the new incumbents may try hard to avoid their predecessors' mistakes, by making particular efforts to establish consensus.

The functioning of the dyad will also be influenced by the governance structures and practices that the leadership dyad inherits, such as the Executive Committee or Board. Is there, for example, a history of the Board exerting effective oversight of the Managing Partner, or have they traditionally acted more as an Advisory Board? Governance structures and practices concerning the election and selection of the Managing and Senior Partner will also be highly relevant. For example, in some professional organizations elections are held, but there is a general understanding that these are preceded by 'taking soundings' so that a single uncontested candidate for Managing or Senior Partner emerges.

Cultural norms will determine the permissible arenas for conflict among members of the leadership dyad and the leadership constellation more generally, and the permissible forms of political activity. So, for example, in some professional organizations political behaviour may be deemed appropriate when it is deployed to build consensus, but dysfunctional when used to undermine the other member of the dyad. In other words, how a leader may 'appear apolitical' is in itself a cultural construct. Conflict between professionals may be deemed permissible when conducted 'in the name of the client', but dysfunctional when a professional is seen as acting in his or her own interests.

Leadership Dyads Framework

Figure 5.1 represents the leadership dyads framework I have developed through my research across a range of professional organizations.

25. Reid and Karambayya 2015.

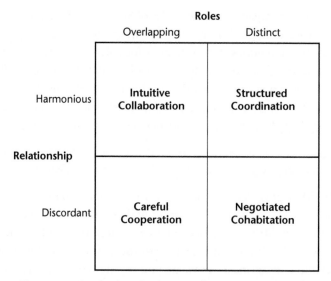

Figure 5.1 Leadership dyads in professional organizations

The framework encompasses two dimensions: structural roles and personal relationships. From this I have derived four distinct leadership dyads which I have termed: Intuitive Collaboration, Structured Coordination, Negotiated Cohabitation, and Careful Cooperation.

We may intuitively assume that separate roles and harmonious relationships will always be optimal (i.e. Structured Coordination is ideal). However, as the following analysis demonstrates, all four leadership dyads can be both effective and ineffective. The key is to recognize which dyad is being enacted, identify if it is fit for purpose, and consider whether a more appropriate dyad might be adopted.

The following sections examine each of the four dyads in turn. The examples are of relatively effective dyads but the chapter goes on to examine dysfunctional dyads, and to illustrate the serious consequences when dyads break down.

Intuitive Collaboration

The Senior and Managing Partners quoted at the start of this chapter represent an extreme example of the Intuitive Collaboration dyad. Here the relationship is so harmonious that roles overlap almost entirely (top left quadrant of

Figure 5.1). In this organization, the roles of Senior and Managing Partner are not defined or distinguished (so that both, in effect, have equal power). Reflecting the ambiguous distribution of formal power, they both struggle with my question, 'Who's in charge?'. Others within the leadership constellation believe that the Senior Partner has more informal power than the Managing Partner—he is 'clearly the leader'—but recognize that they 'merge very happily across the boundaries'. As the Senior Partner comments:

> Sometimes it's not necessary to say who is in charge for it to be obvious. Stating it, even privately, might upset a delicate balance. (Senior Partner)

While the Managing Partner is notionally more concerned with day-to-day operational issues and the Senior Partner with longer-term strategic issues, in practice there is little distinction between their roles. In an attempt to achieve some clarity around role demarcation, I asked individuals within the leadership constellation: 'How do you decide which of them to send an email to?' Interviewees say that they typically send an email to both the Senior and Managing Partner, that typically both reply, and typically both agree. However, as the Senior Partner explains:

> Behind the scenes there may have been a ferociously intense consultation between us to agree a common response—even agreement about who should reply to the email first. (Senior Partner)

In other words, within the Intuitive Collaboration dyad, considerable thought must be given to how members maintain the image of a naturally occurring and happy union to the rest of the leadership constellation. In this way, the Senior and Managing Partner are displaying a finely tuned political sensibility (i.e. they are acting politically while appearing apolitical), both in terms of how they influence each other and in how they work together to influence the organization as a whole.

While their shared role space is ambiguous, the members of the dyad operate particularly well together. According to the Managing Partner: 'it's instinctive'. As one practice head states, the Managing and Senior Partner 'instinctively feel broadly the same about important decisions'. As another explains, 'The current model works particularly well with these two because they're great friends.' In other words, the relationship is generally harmonious and conflict is minimized.

The Managing and Senior Partner had not worked together prior to their election. Immediately afterwards, however, they were united by the need to resolve a fundamental threat to the firm (see Chapter 10) and their relationship was forged in the crucible of this organizational crisis. To some extent, their harmonious relationship also reflected their deliberate choice. Disturbed by examples of the discordant relationship between previous Senior and Managing Partners, they decided to make a particular effort to ensure their own relationship was harmonious.

Where there is considerable harmony in terms of personal relationship and considerable overlap in terms of role, it is worth considering: what is the point of having two leaders? Is Intuitive Collaboration simply a glorified job share? As the primary purpose of the leadership dyad is to embody and enact conflict within the partnership, Intuitive Collaboration contains the inherent risk that this harmonious relationship will become 'groupthink', with both individuals in such complete accord that they are unable to identify important issues and fail to take account of conflict within the partnership. In the example described above, this risk is alleviated by the fact that practice heads and Board members are elected and their electoral mandates give them the informal power to challenge each other effectively. The conflict is, therefore, enacted and contained within the leadership constellation.

Structured Coordination

In the Structured Coordination dyad (top right quadrant of Figure 5.1), the members have distinct roles and the relationship is relatively harmonious.

Some years ago, I was giving a speech at the partner conference of a leading international professional service firm. Standing on the platform, I looked out at several hundred partners, seated in rows and divided by a central aisle. In the front row on the right-hand side of the aisle sat the Senior Partner, amusing and urbane, surrounded by a group of friends, laughing, excited, and talking quite loudly. In the front row on the left-hand side of the aisle sat the Managing Partner. His row was empty except for him and no one sat in the row immediately behind him. He was entirely alone.

The Managing Partner had been elected on the platform of international expansion and many partners were enthusiastic about his vision for building a highly profitable global firm. However, there was a conflict within the partnership. As the drive for profitability intensified, many partners had been asked to leave and other partners knew that they might soon be asked to do the same.

The Managing Partner was feared and resented by those partners who felt most threatened by the restructuring. They believed that he alone wielded the axe when sacking partners. In fact, it was the Senior Partner, as Chair of the Board, who had ultimately approved the programme of partner departures. However, because the original strategy of global expansion had been devised by the Managing Partner, the Senior Partner was not so closely associated with the increased pressure on performance, and therefore remained popular with the partners.

The Managing Partner was not a man who needed to be liked. This was one of his great strengths but also potentially his greatest vulnerability. He was able to pursue his vision for building a global firm without being particularly upset by the intense and very public criticism he received from many of his partners. Fortunately, unlike many leaders who do not count emotional intelligence as one of their strengths, the Managing Partner recognized his limitations (a level of self-awareness which is in itself an indication of emotional intelligence). He knew that in order to carry off his plans, he needed his ebullient and popular Senior Partner to balance and dilute his tough and uncompromising approach to leadership. In other words, the Senior Partner could focus on the interests of the individual partners whilst the Managing Partner was free to focus on the interests of the collective (as he defined them).

They worked closely together to ensure that the Senior Partner could interpret the Managing Partner's terse statements, reassure the 'average' partners who feared for their jobs, and help those who were asked to leave to do so with dignity. Alongside their formally distinct roles, the Managing and Senior Partner had developed informal roles which were also distinct and complementary. The Senior Partner was able to warn the Managing Partner when he was driving the partners too hard, alert him to the more serious signs of partner discontent, and remind him of the need to maintain strong affiliations with the key influencers in the organization. Whilst the Managing Partner was content to sit alone, he recognized the importance of never becoming isolated. The personal friendship between the Senior and Managing Partner, and the great respect they had for each other professionally, meant that they could work together effectively. This combination of distinct roles and harmonious relationship enabled them to enact Structured Coordination effectively.

The Structured Coordination dyad can be highly effective, but can also go badly wrong, as outlined later in this chapter. This particular example was successful because the Senior and Managing Partner recognized each other's strengths and were happy to compensate for each other's weaknesses. They did not explicitly define their relative roles as 'concern for production' and 'concern for people', but that in effect was what was happening. The Senior Partner recognized that, as well as managing relations with the partners, he also needed to manage the Managing Partner. By playing the informal role of coach and interpreter, he helped to minimize potential conflict between the Managing Partner and the partnership as a whole.

Negotiated Cohabitation

In the Negotiated Cohabitation dyad (bottom right quadrant of Figure 5.1), the roles are also distinct but, in contrast to the Structured Coordination dyad, the relationship between the Managing and Senior Partner is relatively discordant.

Superficially, this leadership dyad may appear to have broken down entirely. Like an unhappy married couple trying to coexist under the same roof 'for the sake of the children', harmony is maintained by minimizing the contact they have with each other and by establishing clearly demarcated roles. Negotiated Cohabitation may in fact represent a pragmatic and highly effective response to a difficult situation, as the following example demonstrates.

I began working with one firm when the Managing Partner was just beginning his third term of office. The Managing Partner was relatively young, highly ambitious, and energetic. He was a charismatic and complex individual, popular with many partners but personally disliked by a sizeable proportion of his colleagues. He could be quick to anger and brutally offensive. He was something of a prima donna in his own right. The partners had elected and re-elected him on three separate occasions because they realized he could help them re-establish their position as market leaders.

By contrast, the Senior Partner was older and quieter, highly trusted and respected by partners as a man of integrity and modesty. When, for example, older partners at the top of lockstep were asked to accept a cut in equity to reflect their declining level of fee income, it was the Senior Partner who volunteered for the deepest cut in equity.

This example has much in common with the previous dyad (Structured Coordination). The Managing and Senior Partners' roles were clearly

delineated and both notionally had equivalent power. A sizeable proportion of the partnership were uncomfortable with the Managing Partner.
Third, the Senior and Managing Partner were committed to bringing
about a substantial improvement in the firm's competitive position. And
there was conflict within the partnership, between those partners who
were content with their level of earnings and those who aspired for more
and resented those partners whom they perceived to be free-riding.

The key distinction between the Structured Coordination dyad and the
Negotiated Cohabitation dyad is that, in the latter case, the personal relationship between Managing and Senior Partner was extremely discordant.
I observed one private meeting where the Managing Partner proposed an
initiative that would involve further substantial intensification of partner
performance management. The Senior Partner was clear that the partners
needed more time to adjust to the previous round of changes.

The Managing and Senior Partner argued for over an hour and, as both
men refused to give way, the debate became more and more heated and the
criticism more personal. Always the first to escalate a conflict, the Managing
Partner rose from his chair, adopting a challenging posture, and threatened
to resign if the Senior Partner did not give way. The Senior Partner
remained quietly spoken and unemotional throughout. By the end of the
meeting they had agreed to delay the initiative for six months. The next time
I spoke to the Senior Partner he told me:

> After a meeting like that with [the Managing Partner] I always want to take a
> shower. I feel like he has poured a warm bucket of **** all over me. (Senior
> Partner)

The Senior Partner realized that the Managing Partner needed an outlet for
his anger towards his partners and had decided that it was part of his role as
Senior Partner to bear the brunt of that anger. The attitude which prompted
him to volunteer for the largest cut in equity also led him to bear the conflict
for the partnership as a whole. He accepted the democratic will of the
partners to repeatedly elect this Managing Partner, and believed his duty
to the partnership was to contain his colleague's dysfunctional behaviour. In
other words, remaining committed to this highly discordant relationship
with the Managing Partner was a significant and distinctive aspect of the
Senior Partner's role in this particular manifestation of Negotiated
Cohabitation.

The Negotiated Cohabitation dyad can seem dysfunctional to an outsider and to the members of the dyad themselves. However, as this example shows, it may be highly effective when a professional organization is grappling with a complex conflict amongst different factions of professionals. Sometimes it is the only pragmatic solution. For example, when one leader is proving too ineffective or too autocratic, partners may not want to engage in the highly political process of removing an elected incumbent. They may prefer to 'rebalance' the incumbent, by forcing him or her to accept another individual within the leadership constellation as a co-leader.

Careful Cooperation

The fourth leadership dyad, Careful Cooperation, involves a discordant personal relationship and overlapping roles (bottom left quadrant of Figure 5.1).

In one firm I studied, the Senior Partner intervened strongly in the work of the Managing Partner. The Managing Partner was notionally less powerful, as the Senior Partner chaired both the Board and Executive Committee. So, as well as not having a clearly defined role, the Managing Partner did not have distinct formal authority within the governance structure. Being recently elected and less well-embedded within the leadership constellation of the firm, he also had less informal power than the Senior Partner.

As a result, according to the Director of HR, the Managing Partner was 'slightly repressed' by the Senior Partner. As a Board member explains:

> It was frustrating because there were several things where we'd actually like to have known what [the Managing Partner] was thinking. But, right or wrong, he took the view that he shouldn't show any disloyalty to [the Senior Partner]. (Board Member)

The Managing Partner was aware of the potential risks of challenging the Senior Partner, who had instigated the removal of the previous Managing Partner because 'they didn't agree on anything'. The relationship between the current Senior and Managing Partner was not harmonious but was not allowed to become discordant—in other words it was a Careful Cooperation. As the Managing Partner explains:

I felt the firm could not afford another split between the Senior and Managing Partner. The partners were unlikely to forgive us if we got them into that position . . . another internecine struggle would probably end up taking both of us down. (Managing Partner)

Contrast this with the discordant relationship in the previous example, Negotiated Cohabitation. There the Managing and Senior Partner fought relentlessly; because they had equal power, neither was ultimately able to land a knockout blow. In this example of Careful Cooperation, the balance of power is unequal and therefore the discordant relationship remains repressed. As a result:

Some big issues were left unaddressed or skirted around. We both privately understood we would not be able to agree on them. (Managing Partner)

The Senior Partner, deploying the finely honed political skills which had enabled him to organize the overthrow of the previously elected Managing Partner, used other individuals within the leadership constellation to manage conflict with the current Managing Partner. As a practice head explains:

I would go and see [the Managing Partner] and say, 'Look, you know [the Senior Partner] has asked me to talk to you about this.' Usually he would give way because he was very keen not to allow any dissent to show outside. But there were some things where I would have to turn round to [the Senior Partner] and say, 'Look, you know that's something between the two of you, I really can't get involved in that.' (Practice Head)

The Managing and Senior Partners struggled sometimes to communicate effectively, both with each other and with the rest of the leadership constellation. As another practice head explains:

There was inconsistent thinking. If you asked one for their view and then went to the other, it could be the opposite. Or they'd do things without telling each other. (Practice Head)

In spite of the Managing and Senior Partners' attempts to conceal the tensions in their relationship, some individuals within the leadership constellation were fully aware of it.

If it was something [the Senior Partner] was completely adamant on and [the Managing Partner] wasn't prepared to fight him about it, he would say '[the Senior Partner] has asked me to do this' and the code was understood by everyone. (Practice Head)

The Senior and Managing Partner managed to develop a modus operandi of Careful Cooperation, to retain the outward impression of behaving apolitically. However, this created political work for others within the leadership constellation. Partners needed to become skilled at decoding the language through which the Managing and Senior Partner expressed their unresolved conflict, and to act as a buffer between the members of the leadership dyad.

While it was far from ideal, this Careful Cooperation dyad was effective. The Senior Partner and Managing Partner were able to work together, carefully and cautiously, but effectively nonetheless. They did not repeat the political battles of the previous incumbents and remained in position to the end of their terms of office. The Managing Partner was not damaged by being 'repressed' by the Senior Partner and was ultimately rewarded by the rest of the partnership for his careful handling of the relationship. When the Senior Partner retired, the Managing Partner was elected to replace him.

Under certain circumstances, Careful Cooperation may be the only available dyad: for example, because two ill-matched individuals are elected to the roles following a merger. When this happens, the challenge is to ensure that incumbents make the best of a potentially dysfunctional dyad.

Dysfunctional Dyads

In a dysfunctional dyad, the conflict inherent in a pluralistic professional organization is not effectively contained or resolved by the dyad. Instead it leaches out into the leadership constellation and the organization more generally. This may happen because an interpersonal conflict within the dyad exacerbates the conflict in the organization, or because the members of the dyad shy away from expressing any conflict between themselves.

In one organization I studied, for example, the founder had invited a long-standing colleague to become the firm's first Managing Partner, to take over the day-to-day running of the business from him. The founder regularly undermined the Managing Partner's initiatives in front of other partners. In another professional organization I studied, the Managing Partner was very jealous of his Senior Partner. On discovering that the Senior Partner was to receive a lifetime achievement award at the profession's top awards ceremony, the Managing Partner withdrew his firm from participating in the event.

The following two examples represent very different permutations of power and conflict and were resolved in very different ways.

Equal Power/Focused Conflict

Following a global merger, two individuals were appointed by the global leadership to become co-leaders of the newly combined UK practice. Their roles were not clearly defined. The global leadership hoped that these individuals would role-model integration to their colleagues through their personal collaboration.

However, their interpersonal conflict proved ferocious. As one Vice President explains: 'They were at each other's throats non-stop.' Though technically a Careful Cooperation dyad (overlapping roles and discordant relationship), they were unable to engage constructively with each other. Their roles remained undefined and overlapping as neither member of the dyad was prepared to concede ground to the other. As another Vice President explains:

> They had worked all their lives to become office head. Suddenly they got their wish but realized that they had no real authority. They had to share power with each other. It was disastrous for both of them. (Vice President)

The global leadership of the firm recognized that the intense nature of the interpersonal conflict between the UK heads was exacerbating rather than resolving the inherent conflict between the merging firms. They replaced one of them with a colleague who was less personally ambitious and was happy to work closely with his co-leader to ensure the merger was a success. The new dyad rapidly developed into Intuitive Collaboration.

Unequal Power/Distributed Conflict

In the second example, the Senior Partner was clearly more powerful, having appointed the Managing Partner. While their relationship was harmonious, the conflict within the leadership constellation was ferocious and the political behaviours extreme.

The Senior Partner was intensively preoccupied with building and integrating the firm's global network. He therefore delegated the day-to-day running of the UK business to the Managing Partner, who bore the brunt of partner discontent in the regular Executive Committee (ExCo) meetings. As one ExCo member explains:

> I saw the anger of the partnership coming through ExCo members—the legacy of the last three years of the UK business not getting the attention we deserved. I saw the anger directed towards [the Senior Partner] for not being there in the meeting or leading the UK. And I saw the naked ambition of some ExCo members who could see the problems as a chance for their own advancement, to replace the Senior Partner at the next election—and to ensure that the Managing Partner was discredited as a potential Senior Partner candidate. (ExCo Member)

The partners as a whole tended to shy away from conflict, so ExCo members struggled to deal with the intensely political and prima-donna-like behaviour of their colleagues within the leadership constellation. A delegation of ExCo members approached the Senior Partner and asked him to intervene, but the Senior Partner also had a strong preference for avoiding conflict.

> We talked to him about it, and he said, 'OK, I'm going to take charge of this. . . . I'm going to bang heads together. This is unacceptable.' But that didn't happen. (ExCo Member)

The Senior Partner failed to support the Managing Partner, by failing to confront the behaviours of certain individuals and by undermining him when he tried to remove them from ExCo.

> All the people who'd been thrown off ExCo went to [the Senior Partner] and said 'This is completely unacceptable. We're not doing this.' And so the decision was reversed and by the next meeting they were all back on ExCo. (ExCo Member)

Throughout, the Senior and Managing Partner maintained a harmonious relationship so this could be described as a Structured Coordination dyad. However, unlike the example of Structured Coordination discussed earlier, it proved ineffective for two reasons. First, the apparently harmonious relationship reflected an imbalance of power. Unlike the Senior Partner, the Managing Partner was not elected and therefore lacked a mandate from the partnership. Instead, he had been appointed by the Senior Partner and, as he was dependent upon his patronage, felt unable to challenge the Senior Partner forcefully. Second, the Senior Partner maintained an extreme distinction between his role and the Managing Partner's that he was in effect abrogating responsibility for supporting the Managing Partner.

As a result, the inherent conflict within the partnership was not resolved within the leadership dyad but externalized to the leadership constellation as a whole. Rather than bring the conflict to a head with the Senior Partner, the Managing Partner himself began to act out the conflict within the leadership constellation. As one ExCo member explained:

> [The Managing Partner] would lose his temper in ExCo on a reasonably regular basis…and some ExCo members would deliberately rile him. (ExCo Member)

The conflict within the leadership constellation therefore remained unresolved until the Senior Partner's term of office came to an end and the partnership elected a new Senior Partner.

Singles and Triads

Whilst this chapter has asserted that it takes two to lead a professional organization, it is worth acknowledging other configurations that can be successful.

Some professional organizations are led by a single powerful leader, who does not work particularly closely with any one individual within the leadership constellation. I have observed three distinct manifestations of this which I term 'cyborgs', 'parents', and 'headteachers', reflecting how these individuals are referred to within their own organizations.

The 'cyborg' leader, identified by Muhr[26] in her study of professionals, is someone who demonstrates an 'almost superhuman' capacity for hard work. They attract followers who seek to emulate them and win their approval as the cyborg leader possesses considerable referent power (see Chapter 2). One Managing Partner I studied was reputed to sleep for only two hours a night. Whether or not this was true, the point is that his colleagues proudly reported this 'fact' to me. Individual founders are often referred to as 'fathers' of their firm, assuming they are male. Chapter 8 outlines the difficulties such

---

26. S. L. Muhr. 2010. The leader as cyborg: Norm-setting, intimidation and mechanistic superiority. In *Metaphors we lead by: Understanding leadership in the real world*, ed. M. Alvesson and A. Spicer. London: Routledge, 138–61.

organizations have when attempting to grow beyond the potentially benign yet autocratic approach to leadership this implies. Sometimes a founder is replaced by another individual who replicates this model of leadership. As one such leader I studied explains:

> Alexander used to run this place like a headmaster runs a school. I have replicated that. Partners get sent to me if there is a problem. So I am their tough headmaster but also their father–protector. (Managing Partner)

Any of these individuals, whether 'parent', 'headteacher', or 'cyborg', may function as a single leader, but their effectiveness will be very context-specific.

A few studies of plural leadership have examined leadership triads in professional settings.[27] Chapter 7 looks at what happens when a third individual is added to the mix—such as a Chief Operating Officer (COO) or Chief Financial Officer (CFO)—to work alongside the Managing and Senior Partner. Chapter 8 describes a firm which is run by three founders.

Notionally, a leadership triad is an effective response to the conflict inherent in a pluralistic professional organization. According to relational systems theory, as developed by Bowen,[28] a triad can encompass more tension than a dyad because tension can shift around the three members. Whilst spreading this tension can help to create stability, it also enables its members to avoid conflict. This may be a useful expediency; if there is an intractable interpersonal conflict within a leadership dyad, a third member can be introduced as a buffer to cope with, if not resolve, the crisis.

However, it is not an ideal long-term solution. Relational systems theory emphasizes that within a triad there will always be two insiders and one outsider. Someone is always uncomfortable in a triad and pushing for change.[29] If tension develops between the two insiders, the most uncomfortable one will move closer to the outsider. For example, the challenge for the COO or CFO, as discussed in Chapter 7, is how to secure his or her position in the triad without splitting the Managing Partner from the Senior Partner, or being used as a tool to absorb the conflict that the Managing and Senior Partner should be resolving between themselves.

27. See, for example, Hodgson et al.'s 1965 study of a psychiatric hospital led by three psychiatrists, or Alvarez and Svejenova 2005.
28. M. E. Kerr and M. Bowen. 1988. *Family evaluation*. New York: W. W. Norton & Company.
29. M. E. Kerr. 2000. One family's story: A primer on Bowen theory. The Bowen Center for the Study of the Family. <http://www.thebowencenter.org>, accessed 6 October 2016.

Conclusions: Dyads as Champions

As this chapter has demonstrated, senior leadership dyads are widespread in the professional sector and can represent a highly effective method of containing and resolving the conflicts inherent within pluralistic organizations. The members of the leadership dyad can be seen as 'champions' of opposing 'armies', fighting battles with each other to spare the lives of the conflicting factions of professionals (and the conflicting priorities they represent). The organizational context determines the nature of the battleground and the permissible weapons and tactics. When the champions fail to engage in combat, the conflicts are not resolved and the armies they represent become drawn into the battle. By contrast, when the champions' conflict is personalized, they engage in combat for their own sakes and fail to fulfil their responsibilities to the professionals they represent.

The chapter identified four distinct dyads, based on two dimensions: the extent to which structural roles are overlapping or distinct, and the extent to which personal relationships are harmonious or discordant. Four distinct leadership dyads were derived from these two dimensions: Intuitive Collaboration, Structured Coordination, Negotiated Cohabitation, and Careful Cooperation. Each of these can be effective, depending on the individuals involved and the context within which they are operating. With this in mind, there are five important issues for leaders of professional organizations to consider.

First, when a conflict between leaders becomes particularly fraught, it is worth analysing whether this is simply due to a clash of personalities or whether it represents important 'data' about the firm. A difficult colleague may be playing an important role in expressing the views of a key constituency of professionals, and this view ought to be understood and addressed. The leadership dyad may be internalizing a conflict that is being experienced more generally among the wider professional group.

Second, it is possible for the same two individuals to enact different dyads, according to different issues. A harmonious relationship with distinct roles may become more discordant and less clearly differentiated when both members of the dyad care passionately about a particular issue. It is even notionally possible for two members to experience all four types of dyad while working together. If the relationship is particularly unstable, it will be helpful to identify which of the different dyads are being played out within the relationship and the kinds of issues that give rise to these different dynamics.

Third, it is not always necessary for both members of the dyad to be mindful of the need to address and resolve their conflict. One member may be more highly sensitized to this issue and more politically skilful than the other, willing to make compromises for the sake of longer-term objectives. Conflict can be effectively managed, even if it is never resolved.

Fourth, while it is normal to shy away from spending time with a person we dislike or disagree with, in the context of a discordant dyad it may be advisable to spend more rather than less time together. The underlying conflicts will be manifested repeatedly in many different guises so it may be necessary to return again and again to the underlying issues in order to confront and, at least temporarily, resolve them. One dyad I studied calibrated their disagreements in terms of the number of bottles of wine they needed to drink together before they could reach an agreement.

Finally, the full extent of these conflicts generally remains hidden—from the outside world, the professionals within the organization, and even individuals within the leadership constellation. Such conflicts reflect badly on both members of the leadership dyad, so there is a strong incentive to keep them concealed. Like a marriage, no one else can fully understand what goes on inside a leadership dyad. However unpleasant the conflict may feel to the members of the leadership dyad, they may derive comfort from knowing that it is likely to be just as bad or even worse for some of their competitors. At times of acute stress, it can help a lot to realize you are 'normal'.

In conclusion, it is important for members of a leadership dyad to recognize the inherent conflict within a pluralistic professional organization and seek to embody rather than shy away from it. Depending on their personalities, the conflict between the members of the leadership dyad may be ferocious at times. But by having these fights in private and in moving towards a consensus, they are helping to reduce the conflict experienced by the organization as a whole. Those leaders who have the wisdom to understand and articulate the conflict, and the courage to embody and address that conflict, will perform the ultimate act of leadership within their organization.

6

Leading Insecure Overachievers
The Comforts of Social Control

Our partners are insecure overachievers. Partners are earning over £800,000 a year and the average guy here will be thinking, 'God, I'm not worth it,' and that keeps them motivated to prove that they are.

(Managing Partner, Law Firm)

I believe that most of my colleagues are insecure overachievers. I have two colleagues in particular that always want to be at top of the league because, deep down, they're very insecure. They feel that I will say to them, 'Sorry. You're not performing. You have to leave.'...So I say, 'Are you crazy? Why don't you go home earlier and think about your family?' And they say, 'No, no, no, no, I have to work.'

(Office Head, Consulting Firm)

Introduction

So far, this book has focused on leaders and leadership at a senior level within professional organizations. This chapter focuses on individual professionals, the rank-and-file fee earners, who represent the lifeblood of these firms.[1] As Chapter 2 explains, the prima-donna-like behaviour that some senior professionals display may simply result from an uncomfortable combination of sustained overwork and intense insecurity. Under conditions of extreme overwork, senior professionals may lose their ability to manage their emotions and behaviours. If they experience extreme overwork over a sustained period, they may even sacrifice their physical and mental health

---

1. My thanks to Sara Louise Muhr for her very helpful comments on this chapter.

(see Michel,[2] for a landmark study of the impact of overwork on investment bankers). This chapter looks at the role that insecurity plays in elite professional organizations. It examines the relationship between insecurity, social control, and overwork, and explores the implications for leaders of professionals.

I was introduced to the concept of the insecure overachiever by the Director of HR of one of the world's leading accounting firms. She explained the firm's policy of deliberately seeking out graduate recruits who fitted this profile. The firm looked for individuals with a track record of exceptional achievement on multiple dimensions throughout their school and university careers. She emphasized that, for these individuals to be suitable recruits, they needed to be motivated by a profound sense of insecurity, which the firm could identify through psychometric tests and interviews. For example, the question, 'What are your weaknesses?' might elicit the 'correct' response, 'I am too much of a perfectionist' or 'I drive myself too hard'. She explained that, for insecure overachievers, a job offer from her firm provided them with the comfort of knowing: 'You are special because we want you to be one of us.' In other words, being a professional within this elite organization would become an important part of their identity.

Once these individuals joined, the Director of HR explained, the firm would deliberately maximize competition and uncertainty among new recruits by pursuing an aggressive up-or-out policy. Those who survived the cull were spurred on to ever-higher levels of performance to maximize their chances of surviving the following year's cull. In effect, the annual cull amplified the insecure individuals' 'imposter syndrome', because it activated their fear of being found to be less good than their peer group. To counteract this imposter syndrome they needed to retain the identity anchor that the firm represented to them. The fear of losing that identity thus became a powerful control mechanism, helping the firm ensure that its professionals conformed and complied with the pressures it placed upon them.

I suggested to the Director of HR of this elite professional organization that she was like a drug dealer, deliberately seeking out vulnerable people and getting them hooked on the high-status identity the firm represented, to

2. A. Michel. 2011. Transcending socialization: A nine-year ethnography of the body's role in organizational control and knowledge workers' transformation. *Administrative Science Quarterly* 56(3): 325–68.

ensure that recruits would submit to the intense demands placed upon them. She emphasized the symbiotic relationship between her firm and these individuals. The insecure overachievers needed to demonstrate success. Her firm was helping them to fulfil that need. And everyone got extremely rich as a result—at least those who survived the culls.

The firm is not an isolated example among elite professional organizations. Firms such as McKinsey and Goldman Sachs are explicit about their policy of recruiting and promoting insecure overachievers.[3,4] Even if individuals do not fit this profile when they are recruited, the elite professional organizations engage in what Michel has termed 'uncertainty amplification',[5] to exacerbate and exploit recruits' latent insecurities. Therefore, while certain professionals may be more vulnerable than others to this form of exploitation, it is very much an organizational-level phenomenon.

This chapter examines the origins of insecurity among professionals and explains how their organizations amplify and exploit this insecurity. It explores how elite professional organizations offer insecure overachievers the security of exceptional psychic as well as financial rewards: i.e. how professionals enjoy the comforts of being associated with an elite organization and how they are able to incorporate this elite status into their own identity to counteract their sense of insecurity. It demonstrates how the 'comforting' social control mechanisms embodied in strong cultures can translate into cult-like conformity among senior professionals. It explores the dark side of social control and its most typical manifestation—overwork. It asks: why do senior professionals in many elite professional organizations, who notionally enjoy a high degree of autonomy, 'choose' to exercise their autonomy by overworking to such an extent that they potentially risk their personal relationships and physical and mental health? It concludes by examining the responsibilities of leaders in this context.

I know from my experience of teaching senior professionals and MBA students that, for some professionals, what follows will be quite challenging because it will call into question deeply held beliefs about themselves and their organizations. Others will find it helps them to see themselves, their careers, and their organizations in a new light. Even those professionals who

3. S. Mandis. 2013. *What happened to Goldman Sachs: An insider's story of organizational drift and its unintended consequences.* Boston: Harvard Business Review Press.
4. M. Hill. 2011. Inside McKinsey. *Financial Times*, 25 November. <http://www.ft.com/cms/s/2/0d506e0e-1583-11e1-b9b8-00144feabdc0.html>, accessed 25 April 2015.
5. Michel 2011.

do not recognize themselves will probably recognize some of their colleagues or friends. The question for leaders of professional organizations is: what is your responsibility to the insecure overachievers in your organization and does your organizational culture represent an appropriate degree of social control?

Research Study

For the purposes of this chapter I began with two broad questions to guide my analysis: *what role does insecurity play in successful professional organizations?* And *what are the implications for leaders in this context?*

I went back over twenty-five years of my research interview transcripts, focusing on accounting, consulting, and law firms where the theme of insecurity featured most strongly, whether at a professional, organizational, or individual level. I never explicitly asked about this issue in my interviews, which made interviewees' unprompted references to insecurity all the more significant. All of these firms were at the pinnacle of their professional sector, whether in consulting, law, or accounting. While the Magic Circle lawyers seemed most likely to describe themselves as insecure (see Daicoff[6] for a fascinating study of the psychological profiles of lawyers), Big Four accountants and consultants were more likely to speak about the insecurities of their colleagues.

Having looked at insecurity at an individual level, I then sought to understand the symbiotic relationship between insecure individuals and professional organizations. Here I focused on the phenomenon of social control, reflecting the insights I had been given by the Director of HR referred to at the start of this chapter, but also inspired by the work of O'Reilly and Chatman,[7] Tourish,[8] and Willmott.[9] Building on the work of Foucault,[10] as described in Chapter 2, these scholars have done valuable

6. S. Daicoff. 2004. *Lawyer, know thyself: A psychological analysis of personality strengths and weaknesses.* Washington, DC: American Psychological Association Books.
7. C. O'Reilly and J. Chatman. 1996. Culture as social control: Corporations, cults, and commitment. *Research in Organizational Behaviour* 18: 157–200.
8. D. Tourish. 2011. Leadership and cults. In *The SAGE handbook of leadership*, ed. A. Bryman, D. L. Collinson, B. Jackson, and M. Uhl-Bien. London: SAGE Publications, 215–29.
9. H. Willmott. 1993. Strength is ignorance; slavery is freedom: Managing culture in modern organizations. *Journal of Management Studies* 30(4): 515–52.
10. M. Foucault. 1991. *Discipline and punish: The birth of a prison.* London: Penguin.

work in highlighting the phenomenon of social control in organizations more generally.

The chapter incorporates data from a wide range of elite professional organizations. In most of the elite firms in my research, the majority of staff were recruited directly from university and intensively socialized thereafter. One firm I studied, however, focused exclusively on lateral hires, yet had been able to replicate the phenomenon of social control amongst its highly experienced recruits. I, therefore, concentrated my analysis on this extreme case as it brought the mechanisms of social control into particularly sharp focus. In this firm I conducted interviews with thirty-three senior professionals in sixteen offices around the world, including the firm's entire senior leadership group.

I then developed my analysis to explore the dark side of social control in professional organizations, the phenomenon of overwork. Here I focused primarily on a separate piece of analysis I had developed with a colleague, Ioana Lupu,[11] which drew upon interviews with thirty-three accountants, the majority of whom came from Big Four accounting firms. Through this analysis I wanted to understand how and why professionals continue to perceive themselves as autonomous whilst engaging in intensive overwork.

Origins of Insecurity in Professional Organizations

The insecurity that is endemic in many professional organizations results from the interaction of three forms of insecurity: professional, organizational, and individual. Regardless of their individual predisposition to insecurity, professionals are likely to feel insecure for a variety of profession-wide and organization-specific factors.

Professional

The nature of professional work is inherently ambiguous, bringing with it an enhanced insecurity. Professionals are essentially dealing with intangible

---

11. I. Lupu and L. Empson. 2015. *Illusio* and overwork: Playing the game in the accounting field. *Accounting, Auditing, and Accountability Journal* 28(8): 1310–40.

inputs and outputs, applying their specialist technical knowledge to the creation of customized solutions to clients' problems.[12] While the outcome may be tangible (e.g. a completed merger, a complex surgical operation, a newly constructed building), it may take time for clients to be certain whether or not it was a success (i.e. a credence-based model of service acquisition).[13] It is, therefore, difficult to evaluate either the quality or worth of both inputs and outputs. Those within elite professional organizations must therefore project an impressive organizational image and individual identity to build clients' trust, and to justify the fees they are charging.[14] As the lawyer quoted at the start of this chapter emphasizes, the intangibility and cost of the service they are offering exacerbates professionals' sense of insecurity.

Clients approach elite professional organizations to deal with their most complex and important problems, and expect professionals to justify the high fees they charge by delivering innovative and customized solutions.[15] As professionals rise through the organizational ranks, they gain in experience and expertise, but the breadth of responsibility they assume for resolving increasingly complex problems increases commensurably. As a result, they are unlikely ever to achieve a sense of mastery of their work; even if they follow the technical expert career track, they will have to assume ever greater responsibility for advising on increasingly specialized topics. One interviewee, from a specialist change-management consulting firm, explains:

> It was quite frightening when I joined because I didn't know all the answers. Even now, every new job I win, I can't do on Day One. (Vice President, Consulting Firm)

The constant challenge of learning is an important motivation for high-achieving professionals, but brings with it the perpetual insecurity of not knowing. This is one of the factors that makes professional work

12. L. Empson, D. Muzio, J. Broschak, and B. Hinings. 2015. Researching professional service firms: An introduction and overview. In *The Oxford handbook of professional service firms*, ed. L. Empson, D. Muzio, J. Broschak, and B. Hinings. Oxford: Oxford University Press, 1–24.

13. W. Harvey and V. Mitchell. 2015. Marketing and reputation within professional service firms. In *The Oxford handbook of professional service firms*, ed. L. Empson, D. Muzio, J. Broschak, and B. Hinings. Oxford: Oxford University Press, 279–304.

14. M. Alvesson. 2001. Knowledge work: Ambiguity, image, and identity. *Human Relations* 54(7): 863–86.

15. Empson, Muzio, Broschak, and Hinings 2015.

so interesting and fulfilling, but also so insecure.[16] As Clarke et al.'s[17] study of academics demonstrates, high levels of insecurity may be bound up with a sense of professional vocation and an all-absorbing 'love' for one's work.

Organizational

The up-or-out tournament model of promotion[18] exacerbates the insecurity inherent in professional work. Typically, the leverage model ensures that a large number of professionals compete for a progressively smaller number of positions, and at each stage are subject to a rigorous cull of underperformers.[19] Whilst encouraged to espouse the rhetoric of teamwork and cooperation, professionals are pitted against each other in an explicit battle for survival of the fittest (quite literally, as the phenomenon privileges the most physically healthy).[20] As one accountant explains:

> They [the partners] are all in competition with each other. It's unbelievable, we are supposed to be what they call one firm, but in reality we don't function as one firm. They try to steal each other's turf. (Manager, Accounting Firm)

This inherent insecurity may be exacerbated by the opacity of the promotion process, which leaves individuals searching for 'signs of grace' that they are 'one of the elect' in a process which has been likened to 'organizational Calvinism'.[21]

Whilst partnership may seem like the ultimate prize in many professional organizations, it does not represent an end to that insecurity, particularly in elite firms. As a Director of HR explains:

16. S. L. Muhr, M. Pedersen, and M. Alvesson. 2012. Workload, aspiration, and fun: Problems of balancing self-exploitation and self-exploration in work life. In *Managing human resources by exploiting and exploring people's potentials*, ed. M. Holmqvist and A. Spicer. Research in the Sociology of Organizations 37. Bingley: Emerald Group Publishing Limited, 193–220.

17. C. Clarke, D. Knights, and C. Jarvis. 2012. A labour of love? Academics in business schools. *Scandinavian Journal of Management* 28(1): 5–15.

18. M. Galanter and T. Palay. 1991. *Tournament of lawyers: The transformation of the Big Law firm*. Chicago: University of Chicago Press.

19. F. Anderson-Gough, C. Grey, and K. Robson. 1998. *Making up accountants: The organizational and professional socialization of trainee chartered accountants*. Aldershot: Ashgate Publishing.

20. Michel 2011.

21. C. Grey. 1994. Organizational Calvinism: Insecurity and labour power in a professional labour process. Paper presented at the 13th International Labour Process Conference.

It's almost impossible for anyone to become a passenger in this firm, *especially* once they have made partner. It is very hard to find a corner to shirk in. (HR Director, Accounting Firm)

Or, as a partner in an elite law firm puts it:

As an individual partner we're walking a precipice every day of the week. We do not know where the next piece of business is coming from. (Partner, Law Firm)

Of course, most elite professional organizations will have built up a fairly stable core business which offers them a degree of protection from the vagaries of the economic cycle, but senior professionals are still likely to feel very exposed at an individual level. They are the most expensive assets within their organization, so once they are seen as unproductive, they become vulnerable to being 'disposed of'. Under these conditions, peer pressure may be more effective than formal performance monitoring and management. As a partner quoted in Chapter 4 states: 'It's usually the judgement of the peer group which is the most lethal.'

Winning and retaining the respect of peers is vital for professionals. In practical terms, it ensures they will be referred work and remunerated accordingly. In psychological terms, it reinforces their sense of identity—their precarious sense of self is reinforced by seeing themselves reflected back positively through the perceptions of their colleagues. As another interviewee explains:

I want to succeed. I want my peers to think I'm good—maybe that's my own insecurity. I want that status. I like it when a fellow partner acknowledges me as someone who is doing something really well. It's important to me, very important. (Partner, Law Firm)

The exceptionally high level of income associated with senior positions in many elite professional organizations means that senior professionals must constantly demonstrate they are 'worth it'. For an insecure overachiever this is particularly problematic. On the one hand their (over)achievement within an elite firm is evidence that they are 'worth it', yet their insecurity persuades them that, in reality, they are not. The ambiguity surrounding the evaluation of the outputs of professional work, coupled with the degree of uncertainty about the sustainability of performance, exacerbates insecurity among senior professionals in elite organizations.

I just come in here and *work as hard as I can all the time*. I feel like I'm doing a good job, but it's hard to measure. Right now, if you were to look at my business, you would say, 'Peter, you're slow,' but ask me three months ago and you'd say, 'Wow, Peter, you're really doing well.' And that's the nature of what we do: it's feast or famine. And we all tend to be such insecure people that *we're all scared all the time*. (Practice Head, Law Firm)

Individual

The third form of insecurity is inherent in the kinds of people who are attracted to the challenge and status offered by elite professional organizations: insecure overachievers. Of course, it is possible to be highly successful in a professional organization without fitting this profile. For example, Kets de Vries,[22,23] who presents a psychoanalytic perspective on organizations (see Chapter 2), emphasizes the extreme self-confidence of constructive narcissists who rise to the top of professional organizations. More generally, however, elite professional organizations are adept at amplifying whatever innate insecurities a professional possesses.

The term 'insecure overachiever' combines observable behaviour (achievement) with a subjective judgement about that behaviour (*over*achievement) and inferences about motivation (insecurity). The concept of the insecure overachiever is more frequently deployed subjectively by professionals themselves rather than objectively by psychologists, but it is closely related to the psychology-based concept of the imposter syndrome.[24] (See Chapter 2 for a detailed explanation and interpretation.)

As Berglas[25] argues, the insecure overachiever is a highly intelligent, 'fiercely ambitious', and 'wildly capable' individual, who is driven by a profound sense of their own inadequacy, stemming typically from experiences of insecurity in childhood. These experiences may encompass psychological, financial, and physical insecurity. For example, children who experience sudden and

22. M. Kets de Vries and K. Balazs. 2011. The shadow side of leadership. In *The SAGE handbook of leadership*, ed. A. Bryman, D. L. Collinson, K. Grint, B. Jackson, and M. Uhl-Bien. London: SAGE Publications, 380–92.
23. M. Kets de Vries. 2012. Star performers: Paradoxes wrapped up in enigmas. *Organizational Dynamics* 41(3): 173–82.
24. P. Clance and S. Imes. 1978. The imposter phenomenon in high-achieving women: Dynamics and therapeutic intervention. *Psychotherapy: Theory, Research and Practice* 15(3): 241–7.
25. S. Berglas. 2006. How to keep 'A' players productive. *Harvard Business Review* 84(9) September: 1–9.

unexpected poverty may find that as adults they are never able to earn enough to overcome their fear that this will happen again.[26]

Often the insecurity has its origins in parental practices. As Kets de Vries[27] explains, children whose parents are 'overinvested' in their achievements and are lacking in human warmth are more likely to become insecure over-achievers, believing that their parents will notice and value them more when they are excelling. This attitude may persist as a motivating factor long after they have left home and have achieved exceptional professional success because they have internalized this insecurity as part of their identity.

Michel's study of investment bankers refers to the 'constant fear-driven narrative'[28] that motivates behaviours. This research, along with other research conducted in the investment banking,[29] accounting,[30] and consulting sectors,[31] emphasizes the importance of appearing confident at all times and demonstrating an unshakeable belief in one's own ability, to inspire confidence in clients and colleagues.

It is notable that almost all Kets de Vries's examples of insecure over-achievers are drawn from the professions—specifically medicine, engineer-ing, consulting, and investment banking. Academia is particularly prone to this phenomenon.[32] As Kets de Vries puts it, for insecure overachievers grappling with their imposter syndrome, success is worse than meaningless because it increases the risk of their inadequacies being exposed. This, he argues, 'is the flipside of giftedness which causes many talented, hardwork-ing, and capable leaders . . . to believe that they don't deserve their success'.[33] Or as a partner in one of my studies explains:

> Our partners are looking for reassurance all the time. It is ridiculous. Some of the partners who are most clearly insecure are some of the very best people we have. (Managing Partner, Law Firm)

26. Lupu and Empson 2015.
27. M. Kets de Vries. 2005. The dangers of feeling like a fake. *Harvard Business Review* 83(9) September: 108–16.
28. Michel 2011.
29. J. Moore, L. Higham, A. Mountford-Zimdars, L. Ashley, V. Birkett, J. Duberley, and E. Kenny. 2016. Socio-economic diversity in life sciences and investment banking. London: Social Mobility Commission. <https://www.gov.uk/government/uploads/system/uploads/attachment_data/file/549994/Socio-economic_diversity_in_life_sciences_and_investment_banking.pdf>.
30. Grey 1994.
31. Alvesson 2001.
32. D. Knights and C. Clarke. 2014. It's a bittersweet symphony, this life: Fragile academic selves and insecure identities at work. *Organization Studies* 35(3): 335–57.
33. Kets de Vries 2005. See especially p. 2.

Such individuals make ideal recruits to elite professional organizations. Those who survive the culls are likely to rise to the heights of their firms, assuming they don't burn out along the way (see the discussion of overwork later in this chapter). As the Chair of a consulting firm explains: 'A lot of us are very insecure overachievers. I am and I think the best of us are. I think it's a good thing because I don't think we ever sit back.' He goes on to argue:

> My theory is that the best client relationship builders in our firm are insecure. They are so hell-bent on making their clients feel good about them, that they work overtime. Clients feel their passion and respond to that. (Chair, Consulting Firm)

There is, therefore, a symbiotic relationship between insecure overachieving individuals and elite professional organizations. Being chosen by and promoted within an elite professional organization provides huge reassurance for insecure overachievers because the high status of the organization becomes an integral part of their own identity. As an accountant explains:

> When I go to a client meeting I feel supremely assured because I know that I am offering the best tax services that are available in the business, and I have been shaped by and successful within an exceptionally demanding environment. (Practice Head, Accounting Firm)

The reassurance associated with being part of an elite professional organization was explained graphically to me by a partner in a Magic Circle law firm. He told the story of a friend who had become a trainee at the law firm Slaughter and May (often considered to be the most elite of the Magic Circle, or in a class of its own).[34] His first week in the office a colleague told him: 'When you are in a meeting with a lawyer from another law firm and they pull a gun on you, just remember you work for Slaughter and May and that means you have one extra bullet in your gun.' On recounting this story about his friend, the Magic Circle partner added wistfully: 'I wish I had the confidence that comes from working at Slaughter and May.'

In other words, the elite identity of the firm becomes inextricably bound up with the identity of the insecure overachiever—this is the essence of the symbiotic relationship between the professional and their organization, which in turn helps to explain the phenomenon of social control. Given

---

34. R. Moloney. 2016. The long read: The numbers game at Slaughter and May. <https://www.thelawyer.com/issues/6-june-2016/the-numbers-game-at-slaughter-may/>, accessed 19 October 2016.

the right combination of circumstances, it is a phenomenon to which any professional may succumb.

The Comforts of Social Control

Social control comes from the knowledge that someone who matters to us is paying close attention to what we are doing and will tell us if our behaviour is appropriate or inappropriate. In an organizational context, unquestioned norms of beliefs and behaviour become so deeply embedded within the culture that individuals do not recognize the extent to which they 'voluntarily' self-discipline themselves (as Chapter 2 explains, this represents a Foucauldian conceptualization of power). Focusing on professional contexts, Kunda[35] has shown how some engineers, consultants, investment bankers, and lawyers 'choose' to work up to 120 hours per week.

As O'Reilly and Chatman[36] explain, 'the paradox is that strong social control systems often result in positive feelings of solidarity and a greater sense of autonomy.' Willmott,[37] in his classic study of 'corporate culturism', explains how employees are led to understand that identification with the organization's values will ensure their autonomy. Adler et al.[38] suggest that, where there is much ambiguity and pressure for achievement, 'culture-strengthening' programmes represent 'an irrational yet also very real attraction because of their promise of freedom from insecurity'. In other words, elite professional organizations provide a fertile environment for social control.

The autonomy/control paradox is encapsulated in the following comment from the Head of the Audit practice in an elite accounting firm quoted earlier in this book:

> As a partner I have a huge amount of personal independence. No one tells me what to do. . . . I do what I want, but the things I want are likely to help the firm because that is the way I have been trained. At one level we are completely independent, but we all march to the same tune without even thinking about it. (Partner, Accounting Firm)

---

35. G. Kunda. 1992. *Engineering culture: Control and commitment in a high-tech corporation*. Philadelphia: Temple University Press.
36. O'Reilly and Chatman 1996: 198.
37. Willmott 1993: 518.
38. P. S. Adler, S. W. Kwon, and C. Heckscher. 2008. Professional work: The emergence of collaborative community. *Organization Science* 19(2): 359–76. See especially p. 360.

This partner is reflexive enough to recognize the paradox: while he believes himself to be autonomous, he is nevertheless conforming to what his firm has socialized him to do, think, and believe. As Tourish[39] emphasizes in his study of leadership in cults, 'people in many organizations, including cults, are habitually assured that they are empowered and free, and encouraged to roam in any direction they wish...but they roam at the end of a leash, constrained to move within an orbit sharply defined by the governing cultural assumptions of the organization'.

Studies of corporate culturalism are normally conducted within conventional organizations, where power lies almost exclusively with the leaders, and workers are portrayed as essentially passive recipients of their leaders' acts of domination and subjectification.[40] But in professional organizations the workers are highly motivated and educated; in partnerships the professionals are themselves owners of the firm. In this context, the conventional juxtaposition of oppressed workers and exploitative bosses is far more nuanced. In effect, the bosses are themselves oppressed—by themselves.

The following section explores the phenomenon of social control in one particular firm (and the autonomy/control paradox associated with that) and outlines the mechanisms by which it is created.

A Cult(ure) of Social Control

The firm is the leader in its field, with several hundred senior professionals they call 'partners' operating in forty countries (the firm is not a partnership but mimics partnership in many key respects—see Chapter 4). The Chair describes himself as an insecure overachiever and recognizes that many of his best-performing colleagues are too. He believes that this causes his colleagues to provide a better service to their clients. A comment from the firm's founder, displayed in the firm's marketing material, states:

> We only have places in our ranks for zealous family members. (Founder)

39. Tourish 2011: 224.
40. P. Fleming and A. Spicer. 2014. Power in management and organization science. *Academy of Management Annals* 8(1): 237–98.

Numerous interviewees refer proudly to the distinctive and cohesive culture of the firm, and how they themselves are happy to be a part of it (i.e. to conform to and internalize the firm's identity as part of their own). As a selection of interviewees[41] explain:

> If you've ever watched *Star Trek* there is a group called the Borg.[42] The Borg is a collective. They are this mass of things that go forward. If bits drop off, like limbs and heads, it's completely replaced. And that's us.

> When I was going through the interview process I thought, 'this place seems like a cult'. But now I have been here a while, I think it is wonderful.

> The firm is like a very, very big organism that moves in a particular direction and there's no real brain.

The language used by interviewees to describe their firm ('the Borg', 'cult', 'organism', 'no real brain') might appear disconcerting, or even oppressive, to an outsider. Yet interviewees talk about having the freedom to live the life 'they have always wanted to live'.

> Every one of us will tell you: 'I didn't join the firm to be part of a machine. I came to this firm because it allows freedom of expression and it gives me empowerment.'

> Culturally people self-select into this firm.... It's a relatively unrestrained environment.... It's confined by certain rigid principles that are extended into accepted behaviours. But the space you can travel in is a large one, with very few road signs or limits.

Mechanisms of Social Control

This degree of conformity (combined with a belief in autonomy) is particularly remarkable because professionals in this elite firm have typically enjoyed successful careers in other sectors. Strong-culture professional organizations typically recruit staff straight from university and intensively

---

41. In the following analysis, interviewees' titles are not given in order to emphasize the fungibility of individual professionals within the firm.
42. The Borg are cybernetically enhanced humanoid drones of multiple species, organized as an interconnected collective, the decisions of which are made by a 'hive mind' or collective consciousness. The Borg use a process called assimilation to force other species into the Collective by injecting them with microscopic machines called nanoprobes. Individual Borg rarely speak. Instead, they send a collective audio message to their targets, stating that 'resistance is futile', generally followed by a declaration that the target in question will be assimilated and its 'biological and technological distinctiveness' will be added to their own. See Wikipedia. 'Borg (*Star Trek*)'. <https://en.wikipedia.org/wiki/Borg_(Star_Trek), accessed 27 August 2016.

'socialize' their young recruits to ensure conformity (see Chapter 4). In this elite firm, however, they do not have homogenous backgrounds and lack a collective organizational and professional socialization, though many will at least have an MBA qualification in common. They have internalized the norms from a wide variety of other sectors and firms, which must then be assimilated into the firm's dominant culture (again the Borg analogy applies). The potential heterogeneity is compounded by the geographically dispersed nature of the firm; there is no single dominant office.

In spite of these challenges, interviewees express a strong sense of cohesion and identification. The founder quoted earlier refers to 'zealous family members'. One particularly reflexive practice head, however, describes the firm as a cult and regrets that he is unable to commit wholeheartedly to it:

> I have very, very conflicting feelings about here. . . . I feel envious that I haven't bought into the Kool-Aid[43] because I truly believe that 90% of the people here have. . . . Why do I stay? Well one day, I might actually buy the Kool-Aid and I want to, I really do want to, and I'm envious of people who have.

My analysis suggests that this cohesion and strong sense of identification arises from four key social control mechanisms.

Socialization during recruitment process. Because the firm does not have the luxury of many years of socializing young recruits, its most explicit socialization happens during the recruitment process. Candidates may be given up to forty interviews by senior professionals in offices around the world. Interviewers focus on explaining the qualities that make the firm distinctive, ensuring that candidates appreciate these qualities, and deciding whether they are capable of embodying them. As one professional explains:

> I think that during this time you're kind of getting brainwashed. . . . What really impressed me was that I truly felt this was a firm whose values resonated with me, this was a firm where I could see myself for the next twenty-five years . . . I think in the process, I just got sucked in and then it all became an emotional decision rather than a rational decision.

Socialization through feedback. The socialization process continues after joining the firm. It is an 'incredibly feedback-intensive environment', as interviewees explain:

43. This term alludes to the 'Jonestown massacre' of 1978, the infamous death of almost 1000 members of the People's Temple cult who were told by their leader, Jim Jones, to engage in a mass act of 'revolutionary suicide' by drinking a Kool Aid flavoured drink laced with cyanide. It is often used ironically to refer to a person accepting an idea in response to peer pressure.

We tend to give each other feedback on a daily basis. There is a lot of walking around. There is a lot of listening—'Is everything OK here?'.... There is a lot of confirmation, mutual reconfirmation.... That happens in a very friendly and constructive way.

A colleague the other day walked into my office and he said, 'I can feel you are, at times, a little bit critical about me' ... because once, I actually spoke out of emotion.... I became a bit angry because he was criticizing the firm, which hurt me, and I said, 'It hurts me.' And we had a very good conversation and I gave him very honest feedback in a much broader sense about some behavioural things, how he should handle and approach people.

Collective remuneration. During the protracted recruitment process interviewers explain the remuneration system to potential recruits. The firm, operates a pure lockstep model. This is one of the ways in which it mimics a partnership. Lockstep is supposed to ensure that professionals collaborate without constraints—teamwork is something which they believe distinguishes them from their direct competitors, who operate 'eat what you kill' models of remuneration. Any interview candidate who expresses concern about lockstep is deemed to be too individualistic and is rejected. As an office head explains:

> Our model is a communistic kind of model. We're all in it together and we all succeed.

Leader as the avatar of social control. The senior professionals in this firm act autonomously, although their actions are influenced by strong social controls. They do what they want, but they have been carefully selected and 'groomed' to want only what is good for the collective. If the firm is like the Borg, the Chair performs the role of the Borg Queen. In Star Trek, the Borg Queen is an expression of the Borg Collective's overall intelligence, not a controller but the avatar of the collective.[44] The Chair's primary leadership role in this context is to embody the firm, and to ensure that all his colleagues are equally effective embodiments of the firm. As he explains:

> The vast majority of our offices I feel are so aligned, I am totally comfortable that they're not making any mistakes. I know the decisions they're making are the right decisions. This model is incredibly self-correcting, self-motivating, self-reinforcing.

44. Ibid.

The Chair's interactions play a dual role in enabling autonomous action but also in exerting subtle control.

> My life is spent on the phone or face-to-face with colleagues, often with clients—that's how I spend my life, getting here at eight in the morning, leaving at eight or nine, and I'm on the phone all day working time zones. It is about listening rather than pushing agendas—primarily listening, staying close to people, building trust so that, when problems do occur, I get the call and we can work it out.

As Chapter 5 explains, professional organizations typically need two leaders (a leadership dyad) to embody and reconcile the conflict between the individual and the collective. In this firm, however, only one senior leader is needed because the strong culture and social control mechanisms ensure there is no conflict between the individual and the collective.

Reconciling the Autonomy/Control Paradox

In this globally dispersed organization the Chair acts like a glue, 'working time zones', twelve hours a day. Most of his leadership activities are conducted on a one-to-one basis and are directed towards supporting and enabling his colleagues. This process of 'listening, staying close to people, building trust' makes it possible for him perpetually and subtly to reinforce social control. It is a much overused cliché to refer to the process of leading professionals as 'like herding cats'. In this firm the Chair is, in effect, helping the cats to construct their own cages. But the cats do not feel constrained because they are very attractive cages which provide just the right amount of room to roam around in.

Autonomous professionals in this elite firm not only conform to, but actively co-create and celebrate, strong social controls. In the process, they develop a powerful sense of identification which anchors their potentially insecure identities. Their espousal of the concept of 'cult' in effect enables them to resolve the autonomy/control paradox. They deploy the concept of cult with pride rather than irony.

Is this firm so extreme that it is irrelevant to other professional organizations? No. As Tourish[45] argues: 'Rather than organizations being cults or not

---

45. Tourish 2011: 224.

cults, elements of cultism are widely distributed in many organizations. . . . Cults merely manifest certain behaviours in a particularly extreme manner.'

Overwork: The Dark Side of Social Control

So far, this chapter has emphasized the symbiotic relationship that exists between insecure overachieving professionals and the elite professional organizations in which they work. In return for the psychic and financial rewards on offer, many professionals submit to a form of social control which leads them to work exceptionally long hours, whilst experiencing this as self-chosen (the autonomy/control paradox).[46]

While the nature of modern technology has exacerbated the situation,[47] it is not a new phenomenon, as Kunda's[48] study of engineers demonstrated twenty-five years ago. Also writing in the early 1990s, Pentland[49] identified the phenomenon of the 'audit machine', a term auditors use to praise colleagues who are capable of working enormously long hours at exceptional levels of intensity. As Pentland states, 'life as an audit machine can be a difficult and dehumanising experience'. Or as an accountant in one of my studies explains:

> I really became a robot. I thought it was normal. It shocked me when everyone around me, my husband, my parents, and friends asked me, 'Are you crazy?' I replied, 'No, it's normal.' It's like brainwashing. You are in a kind of mental system where you are under increasing demands, and you say to yourself that it doesn't matter, that you will rest afterwards, but that moment never comes. (Manager, Accounting Firm)

This kind of situation has led Haight[50] to argue that contemporary professional workers 'toil on the verge of depression, much as wage workers once toiled on the verge of starvation'. Of course, this is not universal. However,

---

46. For detailed data and analysis of the causes of consequences of overwork in the accounting sector, see Lupu and Empson 2015.
47. M. Mazmanian, W. J. Orlikowski, and J. Yates. 2013. The autonomy paradox: The implications of mobile email devices for knowledge professionals. *Organization Science* 27(5): 1337–57.
48. Kunda 1992.
49. B. T. Pentland. 1993. Getting comfortable with the numbers: Auditing and the micro-production of macro-order. *Accounting, Organizations and Society* 18(7): 605–20. See especially p. 614.
50. A. Haight. 2001. Burnout, chronic fatigue, and Prozac in the professions: The iron law of salaries. *Review of Radical Political Economics* 33: 189–202. See especially p. 189.

taken to excess, the symbiotic relationship between professional and professional organization becomes acutely unhealthy, not just for the individual
professional but for the organization itself, which must deal with valuable
individuals 'burning out' and the impact this has on their colleagues. Leaders
role-model the practices of overwork to their junior colleagues, who learn
that this is what it takes to 'get ahead'.

> The Head of Audit is in the office regularly from 5:30 a.m. until 10:00 p.m., at
> weekends too. So is our Managing Partner. This is not exceptional. The rest of
> the firm sees the senior people working these hours and emulates them.
> (Partner, Accounting Firm)

Ekman[51] suggests that professionals and their leaders engage in a kind of
'mutual seduction' whereby they act out a fantasy image of themselves as
'work warriors'. As Muhr's[52] study of 'cyborg leaders' in professional organizations emphasizes, these individuals are much admired by junior professionals for their 'mechanistic superiority'. Michel[53] describes investment
bankers pursuing work beyond the point of physical breakdown who
present this extreme overwork as self-chosen. For example, one Managing
Director, incapacitated by back pain, conducts client meetings by lying
stretched out on clients' meeting room tables. The investment bankers in
Michel's study compete intensely with each other and fear the consequences
of losing. Once they move into leadership positions, they ensure that those
below them are subjected to similar degrees of pressure. As one banker
explains: 'When you lose the feeling for your body, and compassion and
respect for yourself, you do the same to others.'

Ultimately, the costs of this overwork are paid for not just by the
professionals, but by their families. As a partner in one of my studies explains:

> It is true that I have sacrificed my family life but, ultimately, I sacrificed not
> only my family but also myself. I mean, I'm the first to suffer from having spent
> entire weekends alone at work. Forty to forty-five weekends alone at the
> office, including Sundays. (Partner, Accounting Firm)

51. S. Ekman. 2014. Is the high-involvement worker precarious or opportunistic? Hierarchical
    ambiguities in late capitalism. *Organization* 21(2): 141–58.
52. S. L. Muhr. 2010. The leader as cyborg: Norm-setting, intimidation and mechanistic super-
    iority. In *"Metaphors we lead by: Understanding leadership in the real world,"* ed. M. Alvesson and
    A. Spicer. London: Routledge, 138–61.
53. Michel 2011. See especially p. 347.

The following comment reflects the peculiar nature of the autonomy/ control paradox. In a single comment, an interviewee explains that she has chosen to overwork, and yet feels she had no choice but to do so.

> I was working a lot. I had several miscarriages. I was travelling too much, on airplanes, on trains; it's not good when a woman is pregnant. . . . I paid for it dearly. . . . *It was my choice* . . . . I wanted to have a baby. But it's such a great pressure, the unavoidable responsibility. It's just that, *you have no choice.* (Auditor, Accounting Firm)

What then are the responsibilities of the leaders of professional organizations in this context?

Conclusions: (Ir)responsible Leadership

I began this chapter with an observation about a Director of HR in an elite accounting firm who was seeking out insecure overachievers and getting them 'hooked' on the status and highly contingent security which her firm could offer. I conclude with some further examples from my own experience.

When I was a young member of faculty at Oxford University, I was responsible for undergraduates in my college. One sat sobbing in my office the day she was offered a job at McKinsey. She did not want the job but wanted reassurance from me that she was not a 'freak' since all her friends envied her the job offer. I noted that the peer pressure exerted by this elite professional organization was already working on her. Another student was found hanging in his room—a rejection letter from Goldman Sachs on his desk. I wondered how an elite professional organization could exert so much power over this vulnerable young man, that their rejection had rendered his life unendurable.

The issues of individual insecurity, the appeal of social control, and the tendency to overwork in professional organizations are bound together and inextricably linked to a set of complex individual, organizational, and societal issues. They are both good and bad, healthy and unhealthy, profitable and costly. The leaders of elite professional organizations need to understand the complex dynamics in which they are caught up. They have the ability to transform the lives of brilliant and potentially vulnerable young people, to help them achieve their most profound fantasies about the people they dream of becoming, and to devastate them by denying them that opportunity.

Greater awareness is a good place to start. Leaders of elite professional organizations should consider the extent to which they themselves may be caught up in the insecure overachiever/social control/overwork dynamic. They have been immensely successful within these environments, and unless they are able to step back and adopt a degree of objectivity and reflexivity, they will be driven to reproduce the more pathological aspects of the organizations in which they have been socialized. So, if you are the leader of a professional organization, or wish to become one, the first step in helping others is to think about yourself—to better understand what is still driving you after all these years, the extent to which it is healthy or unhealthy for yourself and the people you care about, the kind of role model you present to your colleagues, and whether you are willing to accept and respect colleagues whose attitudes and behaviours are demonstrably different from your own.

I attended a Board meeting of an elite professional organization at which one of the Board members dialled in by phone. He was on holiday on the other side of the world so it was the middle of the night for him. About three hours into the six-hour meeting, I noticed the sound of gentle snoring coming from the speakerphone. The other Board members, perhaps out of embarrassment, started talking more loudly to cover the sound. The absent Board member continued to snore gently on the other side of the world. Bemused, I drew attention to the snoring. The Chair's response was 'shall we put him on mute?' The Board agreed.

I reflected on the absurdity of this situation. The organization championed progressive work–life balance and well-being initiatives for their junior professionals, and had received positive press coverage for this. The leaders' commitment to their junior professionals' well-being appeared genuine. Yet they themselves simply talked louder to drown out the sound of an exhausted colleague who was supposed to be on vacation. When the Board could no longer talk loudly enough to cover the sound of his snoring, the solution was simply to put him on mute.

This chapter has focused on individuals, but the negative consequences of insecure overachievers, social control, and overwork can also be experienced at an organizational level and more broadly within society as a whole. To what extent were the accountants, consultants, lawyers, and investment bankers caught up in Enron and other more recent corporate scandals simply responding entirely rationally to the deep social conditioning of the elite organizations they had worked for?

The Chair quoted earlier believes that the best client relationship partners in his firm are insecure. Yet Chapter 2 explains how professionals need to be free to use their professional judgement about how to give the best possible advice, even if that advice is unwelcome and causes the firm to lose a valuable client. Do we really want our professionals to be 'hell-bent on making their clients feel good about them', as the Chair quoted earlier suggests?

Remuneration plays an important role in exacerbating this dynamic. When remuneration is transparent, and insecure overachievers can see what their peers are earning, they will know where they are in the 'pecking order'. Realizing they are earning less than a colleague may increase their insecurity and fuel their determination to do better next year. Conversely, realizing they are earning more than a colleague may also amplify their insecurity as they may worry they are not worth it (the irony of 'imposter syndrome' is that success is likely to amplify rather than diminish anxiety). But opaque remuneration systems also exacerbate insecurity—not knowing how one is doing relative to one's peers can be just as worrying for the insecure overachiever.

The issue therefore is not simply about transparency but rather about the performance metrics themselves and the nature of the rewards on offer. As long as professionals are measured on one thing (fees earned or hours billed) and rewarded in one way (more money), they will replicate the dynamic of overwork. If they are measured on multiple dimensions and offered a broader range of rewards, they have an opportunity for greater choice about how they want to succeed. This creates the possibility of multiple definitions of success within a firm, undermining the singularity of the insecure overachiever/social control/overwork dynamic.

Some might argue that this dynamic is a thing of the past. Elite professional organizations are acutely aware that they are losing high-performing professionals who are unable to reconcile their competing desires to be successful both as professionals and as parents. Regardless of changing societal expectations, however, the dynamic is likely to persist. Ultimately elite professional organizations only need to attract and retain a relatively small number of the 'brightest and best' of our university students. As long as there are 'pushy parents' ambitious to do the 'best' for their children, and elite schools eager to remain at the top of performance league tables, insecure overachievers will remain in plentiful supply.

The insecure overachiever/social control/overwork dynamic can be positive and productive. Elite professional organizations offer insecure professionals the opportunity to give themselves wholeheartedly to a job they find fascinating and believe to be worthwhile, to work closely with colleagues who share their values, to know they have done outstanding work for their clients, and to become very wealthy as a result. What's not to like? But taken to excess, this dynamic can lead to mental and physical breakdown, and result in unethical and commercially reckless behaviours. It is, therefore, the role of responsible leaders to help their insecure overachievers channel their insecurities in a way that is healthy and productive, for the individual, for the organization, and for society as a whole.

7

Leading Discreetly

Management Professionals as Consummate Politicians

Empson: So what's it like then, being Director of Marketing, doing
               your job without being a partner or a fee earner?
Interviewee: Bloody awful. Next question?
Empson: Can you expand upon that a bit?
Interviewee: It's frustrating because you want to perform to the best of
               your ability but you're prevented from doing so by partners
               who say, 'Yes, we want professional management, but we
               want the right to veto what you suggest.' So, a lot of the
               things I do are subtle, they're behind the scenes, they're
               about influencing people.

Introduction

The complex power dynamics inherent in professional organizations can
make it very difficult for individuals—even those at the heart of the leadership constellation—to effect change.[1] This chapter introduces some new
individuals to the leadership constellation: senior management professionals
(Figure 2.1). These individuals have overall responsibility for the business
services functions. They may include people such as the Chief Operating
Officer (COO), Chief Financial Officer (CFO), and the Directors of business

---

1. This chapter is based on an article I wrote with two co-researchers. The original article was a
   contribution to theories of institutional work. See L. Empson, I. Cleaver, and J. Allen. 2013. Managing
   partners and management professionals: Institutional work dyads in professional partnerships. *Journal
   of Management Studies* 50(5): 808–44. This chapter focuses more on the practical implications from a
   leadership perspective and incorporates new data as well as new interpretations of the analysis.

services such as Human Resources (HR), Marketing, Knowledge Management, and Strategy.

Two factors make management professionals different from other individuals within the leadership constellation. First, they possess a management expertise, distinct from the prevailing professional expertise within the organization. Second, they have no direct responsibility for income generation. Often they have been recruited from the corporate sector, in the expectation that they will contribute the supposed benefit of their corporate expertise.

This chapter explains how, just like Managing and Senior Partners, management professionals[2] need to engage in 'negotiating' and 'manoeuvring', as outlined in Chapter 3 (i.e. to assert control whilst enabling autonomy and to act politically whilst appearing apolitical). However, the dynamics with which they must contend are even more complex, as the quotation at the start of the chapter shows.

Management professionals may have been hired by the Managing or Senior Partner with the brief to 'professionalize' management, but have very little formal authority to do so. As one CFO explains:

> You've got an awful lot of partners who may not appear in a management structure but you can't just give instructions to them. You have to get them to do what you want through different means, compared to working in a corporation, and you have to spend a lot more time persuading them. (Management Professional)

Whereas the senior leadership dyad may have an electoral mandate from the partnership to bring about change, the management professionals have none and may be strongly resented when they attempt to do so. They are in an invidious position.

As this chapter explains, management professionals need to develop a very close working relationship with the senior leadership dyad and engage in a complex range of political activities to bring about the change they have been tasked with achieving. To be effective, they must become consummate politicians, displaying a range of political skills, from networking ability and interpersonal influence to social astuteness and apparent sincerity (see

---

2. In this chapter, the term 'management professional' appears in lower case throughout the main text whereas the term 'Managing Partner' appears in upper case. This is to emphasize the distinction between the outsider status of the management professional and the insider status of the Managing Partner, whose role is formally recognized within the organization's governance structure.

Chapter 3). They may not be identified as leaders within their organization, but by exercising influence to bring about change, they are nevertheless performing a leadership role.

This chapter explores management professionals' relationship with the senior leadership dyad and the Managing Partner in particular.[3] The Managing Partner and management professionals possess very different forms of power in terms of their formal authority, specialist expertise, and social capital.[4] The chapter demonstrates how, as the relationship develops over time, they are able to exploit these differences. Through a complex set of political activities, they can collaborate to shift the balance of power, away from the senior fee-earning professionals and towards the leadership of the organization, without the fee earners necessarily recognizing or accepting that there is a need for such a change. In other words, this chapter shows how it is possible for outsiders to lead discreetly.

The analysis focuses on one specific context and set of circumstances: the introduction of rigorous management systems and structures into international law firm partnerships. It represents an extreme case of what is meant by the term 'professionalization' of management. As will be demonstrated, law firm partnerships have traditionally been highly resistant to the introduction of management professionals and practices, yet the large UK-based law firms have pioneered the professionalization of management in this sector.

Institutional Change

Sociologists of the professions, such as Leicht and Fennel[5] and Adler et al.,[6] emphasize the profound changes these institutions are undergoing, which challenge long-standing assumptions about the nature of professional work

---

3. Throughout this chapter, the standardized term 'Managing Partner' is used when referring to the partner with overall executive responsibility for managing the organization, who works most closely with the management professionals (a variety of other terms are also used in the organizations studied).
4. The concept of social capital refers to the pattern and intensity of networks among people and the shared values which arise from those networks. It represents a form of power for individuals who are well placed within networks of people who control access to key resources.
5. K. Leicht and M. Fennel. 2001. *Professional work: A sociological approach.* Oxford: Blackwell. See especially p. 2.
6. P. S. Adler, S. W. Kwon, and C. Heckscher. 2008. Professional work: The emergence of collaborative community. *Organization Science* 19(2): 359–76.

and the role and status of professionals. According to Leicht and Fennel, this process of institutional change constitutes 'a melding of the professional and managerial work worlds'. Professionals themselves refer to this more colloquially as 'corporatization'.[7]

In 'corporatized' professional organizations, the traditional emphasis on diffuse authority and individual autonomy is replaced by more explicit and hierarchical governance structures and more stringent performance measurement and management systems for professionals in general and partners in particular.[8,9] How does this process of institutional change come about?

Scholars of institutional change, such as Greenwood and Suddaby[10] and Sherer and Lee,[11] focus on long-standing and deep-rooted beliefs and practices that govern organizations within an established social structure and explore how these change over time. The institutional actors (i.e. the organizations or, more specifically, the individuals within those organizations) tend to adopt similar beliefs and practices, either because they deliberately imitate each other or because they develop independently under similar constraints. This concept is known as institutional isomorphism. Once institutional norms are established, institutional inertia ensures that the status quo is likely to be maintained within the institutional field.[12]

There is an inherent paradox to overcoming institutional inertia. Dominant institutional actors may have the power to force change but typically lack the motivation to do so, as they occupy a position of privilege within the institution. By contrast, peripheral institutional actors may have the incentive to champion change, but often lack the power to

7. T. Angel. 2007. Sustaining partnership in the 21st century: The global law firm experience. In *Managing the modern law firm: New challenges, new perspectives*, ed. L. Empson. Oxford: Oxford University Press, 196–217.

8. R. Greenwood and L. Empson. 2003. The professional partnership: Relic or exemplary form of governance? *Organization Studies* 24: 909–33.

9. M. Galanter and W. Henderson. 2008. The elastic tournament: The second transformation of the Big Law firm. *Stanford Law Review* 60: 102–64.

10. R. Greenwood and R. Suddaby. 2006. Institutional entrepreneurship in mature fields: The Big Five accounting firms. *Academy of Management Journal* 49: 27–48.

11. P. Sherer and K. Lee. 2002. Institutional change in large law firms: A resource dependency and institutional perspective. *Academy of Management Journal* 45: 102–19.

12. P. DiMaggio and W. W. Powell. 1983. The iron cage revisited: Collective rationality and institutional isomorphism in organizational fields. *American Sociological Review* 48(2): 147–60.

achieve it.[13,14] In other words, institutional insiders with the most power to bring about change will also be most likely to resist it, whilst institutional outsiders with something to gain from change will struggle to achieve it. To bring about change in an institution's deeply embedded beliefs and practices, actors require strong political skills and the ability to navigate creatively within their institutional field, to work in original and potentially counter-cultural ways.[15]

In the context of this chapter, the institution is the professional partner-ship, the institutional field is large international law firms based in the City of London, the dominant actors (i.e. the insiders) are the partners, and the peripheral actors (i.e. the outsiders) are the management professionals.

Research Study

Inspired by established studies of institutional change, two questions guided my analysis: *how do 'outsiders' become 'insiders' within a professional organization? And how do they exert influence to bring about change?* The focus on influence and change relate directly to the overall theme of leadership.

The study is based on fifty-seven interviews, research I did with my colleagues Imogen Cleaver and Jeremy Allen. The majority of interviews were with Managing and Senior Partners and management professionals in twenty-one of the largest international law firms operating in the City of London. Fourteen Managing and Senior Partners and thirty-one manage-ment professionals were interviewed. Many management professionals had the title COO or CFO; the remainder were Directors of Marketing, Human Resource Management, and Knowledge Management. Interviews explored a broad range of themes, such as the nature of the interviewee's role, how their role had evolved over time, how they worked with their colleagues, specific challenges associated with their role and relationships, and personal background.

13. J. Battilana, B. Leca, and E. Boxenbaum. 2009. How actors change institutions: Towards a theory of institutional entrepreneurship. *Academy of Management Annals* 3: 65–107.
14. R. Garud, C. Hardy, and S. Maguire. 2007. Institutional entrepreneurship as embedded agency: An introduction to the special issue. *Organization Studies* 28: 957–69.
15. T. Lawrence and R. Suddaby. 2006. Institutions and institutional work. In *The SAGE handbook of organization studies*, ed. S. Clegg, C. Hardy, T. Lawrence, and W. Nord. London: SAGE Publications, 215–54.

Two further rounds of data collection were conducted, to examine change across the legal profession as a whole, and the rise of management professionals in particular. First, twelve additional external actors were interviewed, including executive search consultants specializing in recruiting management professionals to law firms. Second, archival analysis was conducted, encompassing 700 editions of leading trade journals and publications by professional bodies and government regulators, published between 1991 and 2011.

The analysis of the actions and interactions of the Managing Partners and management professionals drew upon the theoretical concept of 'institutional work' developed by Lawrence and Suddaby.[16] Lawrence and Suddaby have identified numerous forms of institutional work, such as policing, advocating, and mythologizing. As explained in detail below, these actions represent the micropolitics of leadership, by which change is effected within institutions.

Through a detailed analysis of interview and archival data, a model was developed (Figure 7.1). It explains how management professionals move from a position of outsider to insider, to become a part of the leadership constellation, and to work with the senior leadership dyad to change the practices, systems, and structures within a professional organization.

Management Professionals and the Micropolitics of Leadership

Figure 7.1 and the detailed analysis that follows outline a four-stage process by which management professionals move from a position of 'outsider' to 'insider' within their organizations. The management professionals and Managing Partners begin by establishing their relationship, then start to collaborate more closely. As the relationship strengthens and the management professionals become more firmly embedded, they can challenge the Managing Partner more directly. He in turn can exploit his[17] relationship

---

16. Lawrence and Suddaby 2006.
17. Almost all the leaders interviewed for this book were male, reflecting the gender imbalance in most professional organizations, but this book has been careful to avoid portraying these roles as inherently male. In this chapter, however, attempts to maintain gender-inclusive language break down because interviews repeatedly deploy male-gendered terms ('heroes', 'great men', 'right-hand man'). It is notable that female-gendered terms are entirely absent from

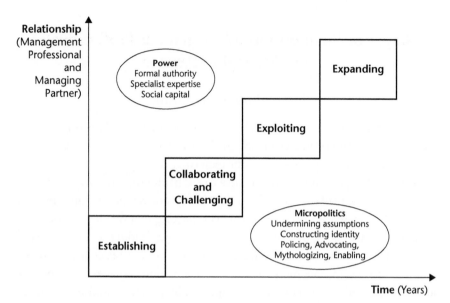

Figure 7.1 Management professionals and the micropolitics of leadership

with the management professionals more effectively. Over time, the management professionals expand their sphere of influence within the leadership constellation and the organization more generally.

Figure 7.1 also identifies three forms of power (formal authority, specialist expertise, and social capital), which the Managing Partner and management professionals possess to varying degrees. By working together, they can exploit these forms of power effectively.

The figure also identifies a series of interactions, or micropolitics, in which the Managing Partner and management professionals engage. These include undermining assumptions, constructing identity, policing, advocating, mythologizing, and enabling.

These stages, forms of power, and micropolitics collectively explain how management professionals move from the position of outsider to insider within a professional organization, and how they exert influence to bring about change.

interviewees' discourse; even female interviewees use exclusively male metaphors. The Managing Partners interviewed were exclusively male so this chapter uses the male pronoun when referring to the Managing Partner to distinguish them more easily from the management professionals, who are referred to as 'they'.

Stages of Relationship: Management Professionals and Managing Partner

Establishing Relationship

The first stage is to establish the relationship between the Managing Partner and the management professionals. In the early 1990s, very few law firms employed anyone with management expertise. Management tended to be undertaken by a committee of partners (see Chapter 9), typically chaired by the Managing Partner, with a few relatively junior people in support roles (e.g. book keepers and finance managers reporting to a finance partner, but without a Finance Director or CFO). As one leading trade journal[18] described it, 'the running of multi-million pound enterprises has been left in the hands of management novices', or 'amateur managers', as another journal[19] termed them. They were supported by relatively junior functional specialists. Looking back, interviewees from the research study report that these were 'pure operational managers, not thinking managers' who 'did the bidding' of the partners to whom they reported. As a management professional and Managing Partner explain:

> It was more a sort of master–servant type relationship. (Management Professional)

> If partners wanted to use a different phone to everybody else, or they wanted their PC configured in a different way, generally the support services ran around and tried to make that happen for them. (Managing Partner)

In the early 1990s, however, the large City of London law firms embarked on a sustained programme of international expansion[20] and needed to develop globally integrated business services, more standardized professional practices, and more rigorous performance management systems. This required more sophisticated management expertise than the partners of the firm possessed.[21] In other words, they needed experienced management

---

18. *Legal Business* 1994. 'Managing the managing partners'. January/February: 10–15.
19. *Legal Week* 2002. 'The end of the amateur'. 28 March: 19.
20. J. R. Faulconbridge, J. V. Beaverstock, D. Muzio, and P. J. Taylor. 2008. Global law firms: Globalization and organizational spaces of cross-border legal work. *Northwestern Journal of International Law and Business* 28(3): 455–88.
21. *Legal Business* 2003. 'Linklaters' bear market'. May: 49–55.

professionals. With its revealing title 'Bringing in the administrators', a *Law Society Gazette* article of April 1996[22] managed to convey the increasing need for non-lawyer managers, whilst simultaneously signifying the relatively lowly status that lawyers conferred upon them.

Typically, it was a relatively far-sighted Managing Partner or equivalent who sought out the management professional. As one Director of HR explains:

> Our Managing Partner was ahead of a lot of his competitors in seeing the importance of how we build recruiting strategies, develop our people and move them forward. The whole point of professionalization of management—he saw that. He wasn't seeing it happening within the legal industry and therefore went outside to recruit for it. (Management Professional)

The Managing Partner typically told the management professional that he wanted to bring about the 'professionalization' of management but did not go into much more detail than that. Many Managing Partners did not yet fully recognize or accept the implications of the scale of change they had envisaged when they sought to 'professionalize' management because they had no direct experience of the potential opportunities created by hiring 'thinking managers'.

Interviewees emphasize the iterative process by which hiring decisions about management professionals were made, involving abortive experiments with individuals who lacked the necessary specialist expertise or political skills, or who refused to work within the constrained environment of a partnership. In one firm, a Managing Partner hired a sequence of increasingly senior management professionals, with each one being given more authority than his predecessor. The relationship between Managing Partner and management professional therefore developed gradually over time.

Collaborating and Challenging

In the second stage, the Managing Partner becomes more comfortable delegating aspects of his own work to the management professionals and allowing them to operate with only limited oversight. As one management professional explains:

> I am left alone. . . . The limits are my own creativity and ability to come up with something that will deliver what they want. (Management Professional)

---

22. *Law Society Gazette* 1996. 'Bringing in the administrators'. 17 April: 14.

For other work, the Managing Partner collaborates closely with management professionals. Many management professionals stress the close relationships they have developed with their Managing Partners, so they see themselves in the role of 'right-hand man'. Some management professionals explain that the Managing Partner may spend more time with them than with any individual partner. As one COO states:

> We sit next door to each other. We spent all day yesterday out on a strategy session, just me and him. (Management Professional)

Sometimes the Managing Partner sends the management professional to represent him in an important meeting. As a COO says: 'I sit on all the committees. I deputize for the Managing Partner.' At other times, the Managing Partner takes the management professional with him for support—for example, the CFO may participate in difficult budget negotiations with a practice head.

As a reflection of management professionals' growing status within the partnership, they are able to challenge the Managing Partner directly, whilst recognizing the need to do so in private 'so that people's dignity is maintained' (Management Professional) and so that the conflict does not become apparent to the partnership. One COO recounts how, when the Managing Partner asked him to recruit another Director of Marketing, he refused to do so 'until you get your act together'; the previous three Directors of Marketing had resigned after being heavily criticized by the partnership and not supported by the Managing Partner.

Exploiting

In the third stage, the Managing Partner begins to exploit the management professional. Some management professionals emphasize that their Managing Partner deliberately uses them for protection in politically awkward situations with fellow partners. One CFO recalls:

> As we went into the meeting, [the Managing Partner] said to me, 'We are going to play this as a good cop, bad cop.' I was supposed to be the bad cop. (Management Professional)

As the management professionals become more established within the organization, the Managing Partner is able to shelter strategically behind them. A management professional describes this 'fall guy' phenomenon as he experienced it:

> We introduced partnership assessment centres four or five years ago but it was a little bit like *Alice in Wonderland*. . . . No one was actually failed. . . . So I said, 'This can't be right; you have got to fail a number of people on this.' The Senior Partner and Managing Partner said, 'Yes, we agree.' So we failed 10% . . . and all hell breaks loose, from the senior people whose candidates have failed . . . and this battle raged for two to three weeks until finally it died down a bit and the Senior Partner and Managing Partner put their heads back above the parapet and said, 'Yes, we agree with this, and have agreed all along.' (Management Professional)

When introducing controversial initiatives, a Managing Partner may require his management professionals to take the lead so that he can protect himself from the anticipated partner backlash. As will be explained, the Managing Partner is forcing the management professionals to 'spend' their own social capital rather than put his own social capital at risk. The management professionals accept this potentially exploitative relationship because they are still dependent on the patronage of the Managing Partner for their own position.

Expanding

In the last stage, the management professionals expand their relationships, becoming insiders within the organization, though not necessarily the partnership. While management professionals' most significant relationships are with their Managing Partner, they also need to develop strong relationships across the organization as whole. Referring to the partner group, one management professional says: 'I would like to think we regard each other as peers.' Another explains:

> I work closely with a dozen partners around the world who manage certain clients. I have a close professional relationship with them and they value what I do. (Management Professional)

The support of these partners is essential for management professionals to carry out their initiatives. According to a Director of HR:

> One thing I have noticed is the importance of identifying key influencers. If you want to bring in a new policy you don't have to get the approval of every single partner in the business, but if there are key people who have an interest in something, you need them on your side otherwise it will get blocked. (Management Professional)

As management professionals become established, they gradually come to be recognized as organizational insiders by the partners, as people in their own right, rather than as the embodiment of something 'other'. As a Director of Knowledge Management says:

> What happens is, as you grow into the organization, people treat you less as a functional 'something' and treat you more as who you are. They say, 'Oh, Andrew will do that,' and they start to believe that Andrew doesn't need to have this sort of shadow group of professionals making sure he's doing the right things because Andrew's been so embedded in the way that we do things, he knows how to keep people involved and consulted and so on. (Management Professional)

But the management professionals' position is always precarious. They must deal with prima donna professionals, and can fall foul of them if they overstep their authority. As a Director of Marketing explains:

> These people have an ownership in the business and therefore, when you upset them, they are very wrathful. (Management Professional)

To survive and thrive, management professionals need to come to terms with the fact that some prima donna partners will never be convinced of their value. According to two partners:

> The Heads of Business Services are functionaries. . . . They have a function to fulfil—they do it very well on the whole. Their views are interesting, but only interesting. I wouldn't say that they are influential. . . . That's not to denigrate the individuals because they are very talented . . . but culturally we have a snobbery about lawyers being superior. (Partner)

> The last time I went to a Management Committee meeting I thought there were too many non-lawyers on it. . . . This is a law firm. Everybody has a part to play but the most important people, unashamedly so, are the lawyers. . . . The major challenges for us are our clients, and the people who know the clients best are the lawyers. Fees? The people who know best are, guess what, the lawyers. Recruitment; why are we losing our lawyers? Well, the people who should know are the lawyers. So, for every essential business decision, the people I believe who know best, or have the most information in this area, are the lawyers. (Partner)

Power

Previous studies of institutional work[23] have identified two 'enabling conditions': formal authority and social capital. Formal authority describes an

---

23. Battilana et al. 2009.

Table 7.1 Relative power of managing partner and management professionals

	Managing Partner (Insider)	Management Professionals (Outsiders)
Formal authority	Extensive (at least notionally). But entirely contingent on ongoing support of partnership.	*Amongst partners:* Limited. Contingent on ongoing support of Managing Partner. *Within business services:* Potentially extensive.
Specialist expertise in management	Limited.	Extensive (relative to Managing Partner).
Social capital	Extensive. Built up over many years within partnership. Evidenced by election to partnership and subsequently to Managing Partner.	*Amongst partners:* Develops gradually and partially. Result of relationship building and successful track record. Also through association with social capital of Managing Partner and other influential partners. *Within business services:* Develops over time.

individual's legitimately recognized right to engage directly in creating change. Social capital is about an individual's connections and informal position in a network. Both represent forms of power. For the Managing Partner and management professionals there is a third form of power which influences their ability to make change happen: specialist expertise in management.

As Table 7.1 shows, all three of these forms of power are possessed to varying degrees by the Managing Partner and management professionals. By harnessing their collective power, they can work together to bring about far-reaching change in their organizations.

Formal Authority

Notionally, Managing Partners have the formal authority to bring about change in their firms. But, as repeatedly emphasized throughout this book, their authority is highly contingent. As Chapter 3 explains, any Managing Partner who asserts control too forcefully at the expense of individual partner autonomy is likely to be resisted. In order to maintain a stable equilibrium whilst bringing about controversial changes, the Managing Partner and management professionals need to find more discreet ways of developing and asserting their formal authority within the partnership.

The formal authority of management professionals is initially restricted to the business services functions and is therefore limited by the relatively weak position of business services within the organization. According to a Director of Marketing:

> When you are called a support department it's like the business is over there and you are here supporting the business. I still can't get my head round this because I always thought I was *in* the business—I was in the trenches. . . . This notion that I am supporting the business creates this dynamic of being servant to the business . . . as if I'm a highly paid butler. (Management Professional)

Management professionals can gradually increase the strength of their position by initiating specific changes within their direct remit, such as dismissing low-grade business services staff and 'raising the level of professionalism within the individual functions' (Management Professional). At the same time, management professionals can introduce structural changes which enable them to gain greater control over the business services areas. Business services staff traditionally tend to report to the Managing Partners of their local offices, thus ensuring that formal authority is consolidated among the fee-earning staff at a local level (and minimizing the formal authority of both the Managing Partner and the management professionals). By introducing a matrix structure, management professionals ensure that business services staff around the world report directly to them at a global level. As one COO explains:

> The supporting functions are now effectively run as a business as opposed to six different functions that just happen to get together on occasions. (Management Professional)

In the process, management professionals substantially strengthen their own formal authority since they can now control access to key resources, i.e. support services.

Eventually, management professionals can 'earn the right' to serve on the major committees of governance, and thus extend their formal authority beyond the business services functions. Some long-established management professionals report that they regularly attend Board meetings without formally being a Board member, while others have secured significant formal positions in the governance structure. Referring to the position of these non-lawyers on the Management Committee, a Managing Partner notes:

> This does give them a certain degree of authority in the organization. . . . They are privy to decision making, to information that is not available to all of the partners. (Managing Partner)

Specialist Expertise in Management

Most of the Managing Partners in the law firms studied have only limited expertise in finance and accounting; only one has an MBA. They also have very limited experience of performing management roles and of working outside the legal sector. Apart from perhaps a brief secondment to the legal department of a client organization, the Managing Partners have usually worked in law firms (and often just one law firm) for their entire careers. By contrast, the management professionals have experience of other sectors, such as accounting, investment banking, management consulting, and the corporate sector. Management professionals therefore possess a specialist expertise in management which gives them power relative to the Managing Partner. As two Managing Partners explain:

> My attitude is that *these* are the people that actually know how to run things. (Managing Partner)

> We are in a world now where we need a fusion of skills—of course the lawyer's skill is one of the fundamentals in being a successful law firm, but it is not the only skill and, in some senses, it is not even the predominant skill any more. . . . Effective management is just as important. (Managing Partner)

The Managing Partner (the insider) therefore supplements his limited specialist management expertise by recruiting and working closely with high-calibre management professionals (the outsiders). In so doing, the insider develops an advantage over fellow partners, who also lack specialist management expertise, and thus further increases his power. As the saying goes: 'In the country of the blind, the one-eyed man is king.'

Social Capital

The Managing Partner possesses considerable social capital within the organization, as evidenced by his election by the partnership. They have generally established close professional (and sometimes personal) relationships with their peers and are deeply embedded in the informal networks of the firm. As one management professional explains:

> It took me years to work out but actually it's vital that you do have a sense of the mood of the partnership.... The loyalties ... I've never had a sense about them. (Management Professional)

Management professionals must display considerable networking ability (a core political skill—see Chapter 3) to become established within these networks and accepted by the partnership.

> The partners have grown up sort of man and boy at this firm and many go back to university together. As Head of Business Services, you have to be able to come in and work out where the flows are, the very make-up of the partnership, before you can start to really get traction, and start to influence the outcome of the discussions ... to bring to bear the full effect of your leadership skills. (Management Professional)

In time, a long-serving management professional may develop social capital within the partnership, to behave as though they are an insider within the firm whilst remaining an outsider to the partnership. One CFO has been with the firm for twenty years. He has worked with a series of Managing Partners and serves on the Board. His continuity of tenure has enabled him to develop a high degree of trust among the partnership. Incoming Managing Partners look to him for advice. Another management professional has worked with the firm's previous five Managing Partners. He attributes his longevity to the fact that he has never appeared to be too closely aligned to an individual Managing Partner. 'I have always been apolitical which is why I think I have survived so long.' A third management professional emphasizes: 'You must never be seen as the Managing Partner's poodle.'

Like the other individuals within the leadership constellation described in Chapter 2, management professionals need to be able to act politically whilst being perceived by the partners as having integrity.

Micropolitics of Leadership

As explained, the Managing Partner and management professionals work together to effect change by combining their differential forms of power to enhance their collective power. How exactly do they get things done? Exerting influence to achieve change is the essence of leadership, so what are the micropolitics, the specific interactions, that lie behind it?

Undermining Assumptions

The process of change begins with the Managing Partner's frame-breaking act of recruiting the management professionals. This undermining of assumptions is continued and strengthened by the management professionals themselves. Partner performance measurement and management represent a particularly sensitive area of change, and management professionals can help their Managing Partner address this shibboleth of partner autonomy.

One example of undermining assumptions is the way in which the previously cited management professional challenges the findings of the partner assessment centre, by telling his Managing Partner: 'This can't be right. You have got to fail a number of people.' According to another management professional:

> I demanded that they have really got to understand where you make money and where you don't. And that was very controversial originally. (Management Professional)

Looking back on how underlying assumptions have changed in recent years, a Managing Partner explains:

> There has been quite a significant shift in firm culture from a position where management is there to run the partnership for the benefit of existing partners, where a lot of people were fifteen years ago, to a situation where management is running the business . . . as a business. (Managing Partner)

Advocating

In order to effect change outside their immediate remit, management professionals need to actively support and promote change amongst the partner group (i.e. to engage in advocacy). One COO explains how he does this:

> Take the offshoring project. That was quite a radical change for us. . . . How did I go about that? Well, first of all, I worked out that it really was a good idea and there was a proper business case for doing it. I then went to the management group and put the proposal there and got reactions and adjusted things

that I thought were necessary to get it approved. . . . I then went and talked to [the practice areas]. (Management Professional)

Even when changes fall directly within management professionals' remit, they may need to engage in intense advocacy among the partnership. For example:

We had to go through an organizational restructuring to get the marketing team sorted out. . . . That came across a lot of resistance because the partners felt they understood how marketing should be run . . . but I did succeed in getting them to accept the change. (Management Professional)

Meanwhile the Managing Partner is engaged in advocacy among the partnership group on behalf of the management professionals. One explains he has been 'working very hard' on the partners to persuade them to 'respect the skills of the very highly trained non-lawyers that we have in the building'. More generally:

There are a number of people who are opinion formers, people whom, when the Managing Partner wants to introduce something, he will consult. . . . Once he has got them on side, then he knows he can move and there is somebody there other than him to counter disagreements . . . the Managing Partner hasn't taken the decision on his own. (Management Professional)

Constructing Identity

Management professionals are engaged in constructing multiple identities, on three different fronts, ensuring that different people see them in different ways. First, they are negotiating a relationship with the Managing Partner, to become accepted as a 'right-hand man' who can deputize for him, rather than being a 'servant' carrying out orders. Second, they are defining a new identity among the business services staff, helping them to develop a sense of themselves as a coherent group in their own right, rather than simply a fragmented group of 'partner pleasers'. Third, they are negotiating a relationship with the wider partner group, to establish their legitimacy to become viewed as a peer.

As an earlier quote from a Director of Knowledge Management explains, this identity construction is successful when partners no longer conceive of him as 'other', a non-lawyer, a management professional, but just think of him as 'Andrew', who can be trusted to do right by them and their firm.

Meanwhile, the Managing Partner is also engaging in identity work, to construct a new relationship with his fellow partners as he develops a stronger managerial identity. The management professional plays an important role in this:

> When they went into the recession I remember taking a list to the Managing Partner showing how much partners had billed and him asking whether he ought to have that information. (Management Professional)

This Managing Partner needs an outsider to explain to him that, now he is responsible for running the firm, he has the right to see the billing figures of his fellow partners. In the above comment, the management professional says 'they' rather than 'we' went into a recession, even though he was responsible for the finances of the firm. This phraseology emphasizes how he understands his identity as an outsider. As an employee, he is internal to the organization but remains external to the partnership.

Policing

Policing is necessary to establish and maintain the new order within the more 'corporatized' partnership, i.e. to curb the more unreasonable examples of partner autonomy and prima donna behaviour. When it comes to policing, it is important that the Managing Partner and management professionals go on patrol together. Management professionals may play a central role in developing metrics and collecting data to monitor partner performance but they have no authority to act in an enforcement capacity, so they must encourage the Managing Partner to make difficult decisions (for example, the partner assessment centre which was 'a bit like *Alice in Wonderland*'). At the same time, as previously explained, the Managing Partner may protect his own social capital by using management professionals as a shield: for example, taking his CFO with him to difficult partner meetings and deciding when to play 'good cop, bad cop'.

Successful management professionals are careful not to allow themselves to be positioned exclusively in a policing capacity because they need to build a support base among professionals more generally. As one Managing Partner explains, management professionals will fail 'if they are just basically seen as management's Rottweiler'. Management professionals must aspire to be seen as professionals in their own right, neither 'Rottweilers' nor 'poodles'.

Mythologizing

Telling stories and repeating organizational 'myths' are important ways in which people create and reinforce individual and organizational identities. Myths can be developed to demonize the past as well as to valorize the present, thus subtly creating a case for change. For example, management professionals sometimes use hyperbole to emphasize how bad things used to be before they rose to prominence in their firm. One management professional explains how law firm management was essentially no more than 'arguing over the choice of toilet paper'. Some partners also use hyperbole when describing attitudes to management:

> We'd all like to be able to say that we can influence the choice of pencil type that goes in the stationery cupboard, but in fact we really don't want to spend time on those kinds of issues. (Partner)

Previous studies of institutional work[24] refer to the legends of 'great men' which form part of the history of institutions. The process of corporatizing throws up two potential kinds of 'hero': the Managing Partner and the management professional. Management professionals enhance their own image by mythologizing their Managing Partner. They refer to him as 'far-sighted', 'visionary', and 'ahead of his competitors' for choosing to hire them. Some engage more directly in self-mythologizing. The management professional who explains how he is used as a shield by his Managing Partners is, in effect, presenting himself as the self-sacrificing hero who protects the 'great man' Managing Partner.

Some interviewees combine self-mythologizing with hyperbolic descriptions which demonize the past. One management professional explains how he 'threw' himself at a law firm having seen an opportunity to bring external management expertise into a sector which appeared to be '100 years back in time'.

Enabling

To enable change it is often necessary to create new rules. One management professional describes how, when he joined the firm, there were no formal processes in place for approving investment in new office space. 'Any

24. Lawrence and Suddaby 2006.

regional partner who had a good idea was basically allowed to go out and do it.' The management professional created a new global committee to examine and approve regional Managing Partners' investment plans.

The corporatization of the partnership therefore involves the creation of rules which increase the authority of the Managing Partner and management professional, whilst undermining the autonomy of individual partners by taking rights away from them. The subtle political skills required to engage in this process are expressed by a Director of Knowledge Management.

> Each time you give a presentation to partners it's like you're burning something of theirs, you're taking something away from them. You need to know how much to say and when to say it and who to say it to—you have to realize you've got no God-given right to be able to keep banging on about something—as opposed to a corporate where you would be given a remit to go and deliver. (Management Professional)

One COO explains how recent changes in reporting structures have increased his authority over the partners, alongside the Managing Partner.

> In the last couple of years, we've appointed a new head of compliance and he formally reports to the pair of us. (Management Professional)

Note his use of the term 'we', implying the strength of his relationship with the Managing Partner and his desire to emphasize his insider status. In terms of the disruptive changes experienced in recent years, as one management professional summarizes it: 'lawyers have let go.'

Some management professionals in international law firms now serve on major committees of governance, have access to information not available to the general partners, take a leading role in strategy development, and initiate actions that have a direct impact on how partners work. Some also have the right to vote as partners and share in the profits of the partnership (without actually being partners). In two of the firms studied, some long-serving senior management professionals receive the same levels of remuneration as the most highly paid partners in the firm. According to one survey,[25] following the UK's Legal Services Act, 54 per cent of the UK's 150 largest law firms say they are 'likely' to invite non-lawyer management professionals to join the partnership.

---

25. *Legal Business* 2010. 'Burning platforms'. March: 49–53.

Conclusions: Leading Discreetly

This chapter has focused on an extreme context, law firms, to highlight the difficulties and successes of management professionals in helping to bring about institutional change. In different kinds of professional organizations, the specific challenges may take different forms, but they are fundamentally the same.

For example, management professionals in healthcare organizations may be formally mandated by the government or HMO to fulfil their role, but they will struggle to be effective until they have won the respect and cooperation of the medical professionals. By contrast, CFOs in accounting firms and General Counsel in law firms appear to be in a better position because they have the same specialist expertise as the partners within their firms and may have previously been fee-earning partners. However, as a result, they lack a relative power advantage in terms of expertise and will likely encounter partners who believe they could do the job better themselves (though they prefer to focus on the 'more important' client work).

Regardless of the professional context, in order to bring about change management professionals need to develop relationships with individuals within the leadership constellation, identify and combine differential power bases, and engage in the micropolitics of leadership. The work of the management professionals may not look like leadership in the conventional sense, but very little about leadership in professional organizations does. The Managing Partner and management professionals may know that that they are leading the organization together, but they must be careful not to make their client-facing colleagues feel that they are being forced to follow them.

Individuals with specialist management expertise garnered in the corporate sector may be drawn to professional organizations, attracted by the high salaries, opportunities to add value, and the challenges they offer. However, it takes a special kind of person to succeed as a management professional within such organizations. They need to be exceptionally good at the job but also willing to stay out of the limelight. They need to be happy to allow the Managing Partner to shine, to let him take credit for their initiatives. In the interests of building a strong relationship, they may need sometimes to take the blame for his failures. And they need to be able to withstand the arrogance of prima donna professionals. Many of the most successful management professionals I have studied take as much pride in their ability to persuade and manoeuvre their way around client-facing professionals as they take in the more explicit aspects of the job.

This chapter has focused on the relationship between the Managing Partner and management professionals, because the Managing Partner is likely to be the individual most engaged in the day-to-day management of the organization. But what about the other member of the senior leadership dyad—the Senior Partner? When the Managing Partner becomes very close to the COO, for example, what happens to the relationship between the Managing and Senior Partner?

As Chapter 5 explains, relational systems theory[26] emphasizes that triads are inherently unstable. In any group of three, there will always be two insiders and one outsider. The outsider will always try to become an insider, but in the process, one of the original dyad may be forced to become an outsider. The management professional who gets too close to the Managing Partner may potentially disturb the delicate balance of the senior leadership dyad. Chapter 8 explores the potentially dangerous consequences of this, when the Managing Partner of a 'corporatized' law firm becomes so absorbed in working with his team of senior management professionals that he becomes disconnected from his fellow partners.

26. M. Kerr and M. Bowen. 1988. *Family evaluation.* New York: W. W. Norton & Company.

PART III

Leadership and Organizations

8

Leadership Evolution
Growing Up and Growing Older

Looking back, there was an unworldly feel about the place. . . . It had a lot to do with the nature of the relationships between partners, in the sense of the concepts of trust, concepts of generational legacy, and that lack of individualized competition—a whole stream of things which in theory you ought to find in a partnership, but in practice are increasingly rare, certainly in a partnership of this size. (Partner, Consulting Firm)

Introduction

I teach an MBA elective at Cass Business School called 'Succeeding in Professional Services'.[1] For my lecture on organizational growth, I begin with two pictures and ask my students, 'What do you see?'

In the first picture, they see four white male professionals from the 1960s, leaning over a desk, with their attention focused on a single object. The MBAs reckon the well-dressed, smooth-looking man is probably the sales guy. The man with the loosened tie and sleeves rolled up could be the technical specialist. The serious-looking man in glasses might be the finance guy. The fourth man is much younger and stands slightly in the background.

My MBA students like the image of this organization and want to be a part of it, though they recognize that, back in the 1960s, this opportunity would probably only have been available to the white men in the class. The MBAs like the sense of colleagues totally focused on trying to solve a problem, united by their physical and mental propinquity. None of the men is smiling but they seem to be enjoying their work.

---

1. Some of the material contained in this chapter first appeared in L. Empson. 2012. Beyond dichotomies: A multi-stage model of governance in professional organizations, in *Handbook of research on entrepreneurship*, ed. M. Reihlen and A. Werr. Cheltenham: Edward Elgar, 274–95.

The second picture is of a very large open-plan office, full of identically dressed, bored-looking men stuck inside little cubicles. No one is talking and no one looks happy. None of my students wants to work there.

Then I suggest that the three older men in the first picture founded a professional organization in the 1960s that went on to become phenomenally successful—so successful that the organization now has offices all over the world that look much like that in the second picture. Maybe the young man standing behind one of the founders in the first picture is now running the organization in the second picture. I then ask my MBA students to consider: as a professional organization grows, what is lost and what is gained?

It does not matter where these pictures come from: the point is that they represent archetypes[2] and can therefore be used as the basis for interpretation. In management theory, the concept of archetype has been particularly influential among scholars of professional organizations. These scholars typically focus on two distinct types of professional organization—broadly categorized as the traditional partnership[3] and the more 'corporate' form[4] (where management has been 'professionalized', as described in Chapter 7).

Professional organizations do not spring into existence fully formed, nor do they remain static. They grow and develop over time, introducing different structures and ways of organizing in response to increasing scale and complexity.

So how does this growth happen? How are ownership and power transferred from an organization's founders to a wider group of professionals? And when the organization becomes too unwieldy to manage collectively, how does a large group of professionals delegate authority to an emerging group of leaders? In other words, how does the locus of power

2. According to psychologist Carl Jung, archetypes are collectively inherited unconscious ideas and patterns of thought which are universally present in individual psyches and which form the substrate from which the basic themes of human understanding emerge. A. Stevens. 2006. The archetypes. In *The handbook of Jungian psychology: Theory, practice and applications*, ed. R. Papadopoulos. Hove: Routledge, 74–93.

3. R. Greenwood, C. R. Hinings, and J. Brown. 1990. 'P²-form' strategic management: Corporate practices in professional partnerships. *Academy of Management Journal* 33: 725–55.

4. D. J. Cooper, C. R. Hinings, R. Greenwood, and J. Brown. 1996. Sedimentation and transformation in organizational change: The case of Canadian law firms. *Organization Studies* 17(4): 623–47.

shift around a professional organization as it grows, and what are the implications for leadership?

This chapter presents a multi-stage model of evolutionary and revolutionary growth in professional organizations—adapting a classic but generic model of the stages of organizational growth first developed by Greiner[5] to reflect the distinctive context of professional organizations. It shows how, as a professional organization increases in size and complexity over time, unresolved governance problems may precipitate organizational crises which can in turn lead to dramatic shifts in the locus of power. It identifies five key stages of growth (Founder-Focused, Collegial, Committee, Delegated, and 'Corporate') and four crises (Exclusion, Disorganization, Frustration, and Disconnection) through which professional organizations may pass. It goes further to illustrate the complex and messy reality of leadership in a professional organization, through two case studies—a small, young consulting company and a large, long-established law partnership—emphasizing the crises and reversals that can occur during aborted attempts at governance change. It highlights the need for leaders to be sensitive to the consequences of these changes as the locus of power shifts around their organization, and to adapt their approach to leadership accordingly.

Organizational Archetypes

Studies of organizational archetypes identify alternative idealized forms, and the management systems, structures, and cultures through which they are manifested.[6] Particularly influential among scholars of professional organizations have been studies by Greenwood et al.[7] and Cooper et al.,[8] which identify and define two distinct archetypes: the Professional Partnership (P^2) and the Managerial Professional Business (MPB). These two archetypes represent the picures I show to my students. The P^2 is the relatively small and informal organization characterized by the first picture; the MPB is the relatively large and bureaucratic organization characterized by the second

5. L. E. Greiner. 1972. Evolution and revolution as organizations grow. *Harvard Business Review* 50(4): 37–46.
6. H. Mintzberg. 1993. *Structure in fives: Designing effective organizations.* Englewood Cliffs, NJ: Prentice-Hall.
7. Greenwood et al. 1990.
8. Cooper et al. 1996.

picture. The concepts of P^2 and MPB have in effect become an intellectual shorthand among academics for distinguishing between the traditional partnerships and the larger and more commercialized 'corporate' style of professional organization.[9]

Unfortunately, this approach promulgates a somewhat simplistic distinction between two dichotomous types of organization and does not consider how organizations make transitions between these archetypes. This limitation of archetype theory in the study of professional organizations is perhaps surprising since two of the core studies on which it is based explicitly examine transitions between archetypes. For example, Miller and Friesen[10] highlight the forces of inertia that can prohibit organizational development and argue that extreme changes or even crises in organizational conditions are required to bring about archetype change. Similarly, Greenwood and Hinings[11] suggest that aborted organizational change is particularly likely when established power relationships (e.g. a group of powerful partners) mobilize to protect the status quo.

To understand fully how organizations change and grow, we need to look outside the literature on professional organizations and turn to studies of organizational life cycles.

Stages of Organizational Growth

Life cycle models of organizations identify various key stages in an organization's development and emphasize the periodic 'crises' which precipitate a move to the subsequent stage.[12] The specific stages vary according to the focus and scope of the study (e.g. industry sector, aspect of management practice, etc.) but tend to emphasize the earliest,

9. M. Smets, A. von Nordenflycht, T. Morris, and D. Brock. Forthcoming. *25 years since 'P²': Taking stock and charting the future of the professional organization.* Special issue of *Journal of Professionals and Organizations.*

10. D. Miller and P. Friesen. 1980. Archetypes of organizational transition. *Administrative Science Quarterly* 25(2): 268–99.

11. R. Greenwood and C. R. Hinings. 1988. Organizational design types, tracks and the dynamics of strategic change. *Organization Studies* 9(3): 293–316.

12. For a detailed summary, see S. H. Hanks, C. J. Watson, E. Jansen, and G. N. Chandler. 1993. Tightening the life-cycle construct: A taxonomic study of growth stage configurations in high-technology organizations. *Entrepreneurship: Theory and Practice* 18: 5–29.

'entrepreneurial' stages of development. While life cycle models have been criticized on several counts[13] they nevertheless represent a useful way of developing a more nuanced understanding of how professional organizations grow.

Greiner's[14] model of the stages of organizational growth is the most influential. It is based on five key assertions:

- An organization will pass through several stages as it grows and matures.

- Organizational solutions which are appropriate at a certain stage in an organization's growth will cease to be appropriate as it grows and matures.

- Management may be slow to recognize the need for change until the underlying problems become acute.

- These problems may precipitate dramatic upheavals or 'crises'.

- At any stage, failure to deal with these underlying problems may lead to the reversal or even death of the organization (the ultimate failure to mature).

Greiner asserts that an organization passes through specified stages of growth via alternating periods of evolution and revolution. In other words, an organization will experience periods of gradual development punctuated by periods of dramatic change.

Greiner's model was developed without reference to professional organizations. He acknowledged this limitation in his 1998 revision[15] to his 1972 article, and subsequently presented a model of the stages of growth in consulting organizations which differed substantially from his original study.[16] Unfortunately, in his revised model the stages are still primarily associated with the entrepreneurial start-up stage of growth and say little explicitly about governance or leadership.

13. A review of the life cycle literature identified thirty-three distinct models, which share many fundamental premises but present variations on established typologies. See R. Phelps, R. Adams, and J. Bessant. 2007. Life cycles of growing organizations: A review with implications for knowledge and learning. *International Journal of Management Reviews* 9(1): 1–30.
14. Greiner 1972.
15. L. E. Greiner. 1998. Evolution and revolution as organizations grow. *Harvard Business Review* 76(3): 55–68.
16. L. E. Greiner and J. K. Malernee. 2005. 'Managing growth stages in consulting firms'. In *The Contemporary Consultant*, ed. L. E. Greiner and F. Poulfelt. Mason, OH: Thomson South-Western, 3–22.

Research Study

Two questions guided my analysis: *How does governance change over time as a professional organization increases in size and complexity?* And *what are the implications for leadership?*

My research focused on thirteen in-depth case studies: six management consulting firms, four law firms, and three accounting firms. The organizations ranged in size from thirty to 190,000 staff and £4 million to £15 billion fee income. The youngest firm had been in existence for ten years and the oldest 117 years.

As part of these studies I conducted over 500 hours of interviews, alongside archival analysis and detailed observation of meetings. Since the studies were processual in nature and concerned with change, substantial amounts of historical and contextual data were gathered as interviewees offered narratives of organizational development going back over many decades. Where firms had published their organizational histories, I studied these also.

The analysis identified consistent narratives across interviewees' historical accounts. Inspired by Greiner's framework, I applied these narratives to his basic concepts of organizational life cycles and 'evolution and revolution'. I realized that my analysis supported his core assertion that organizations pass through a series of identifiable stages as they grow and mature. This allowed me to develop a multi-stage model of growth specific to the context of professional organizations (see Figure 8.1) and which applies equally to partnerships and corporations alike.

A Multi-Stage Model of Growth in Professional Organizations

As Figure 8.1 demonstrates, growth in a professional organization is a process of evolution and revolution. The model focuses on the two key contingencies of age and size and identifies the stages a professional organization may pass through as it grows and matures, as described in the next five sections.

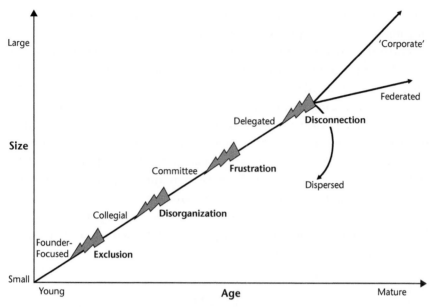

Figure 8.1 Multi-stage model of growth in professional organizations

Founder-Focused Stage

During the initial Founder-Focused stage, governance and leadership are fairly simple. There are no external shareholders, so power, benefit, and accountability (the key dimensions of governance—see Chapter 4) rest unambiguously with the founder(s). Management structures and processes are limited and informal. One Vice President of an operations consulting firm owned and led by its founder describes decision making as follows:

> The ten Senior Vice Presidents were the only guys who confronted Bob (the founder) and got away with it.... We were at a senior management conference. Bob handed out badges to us which said 'No whining' and told us to put them on. Then he said, 'I've sold the company.' (Vice President, Consulting Firm)

As the organization succeeds and grows, the founders hire more senior professionals to sell and run projects. In time, these senior professionals seek greater involvement in decision making and a share of profits. Their desire for autonomy means that they want enough power to control their own destiny; they also want to be rewarded appropriately to reflect their role in winning and developing substantial amounts of business.

This is the Exclusion crisis. Letting go of power and profit share may be a struggle for the founders. In terms of power, Chapter 5 refers to a professional organization where the founder invited a colleague to become the firm's first Managing Partner, to take over the day-to-day running of the business, yet regularly undermined his initiatives in front of the other partners. In terms of profits, the founders may be prepared to sell some of their equity to senior colleagues but may ask a higher price than their colleagues are prepared to pay. See later in this chapter for a detailed discussion of the 'Exclusion' crisis in one particular company.

A common solution is to sell a controlling stake to another organization. However, as discussed in detail in Chapter 9, mergers and acquisitions create a whole new set of problems.

Collegial Stage

If the founders are able to sell or transfer some of their equity to their senior colleagues and involve them in decision making, the organization moves on to the Collegial stage. As long as the founders remain with the organization, they will retain informal influence. Gradually, however, the power of the collective partner or director group (depending on whether it is legally a partnership or a corporation) will become more fully established. Talking about the founder of a strategy consulting firm, a partner explains:

> Philip attracted enormous personal loyalty from the other partners. He was the Daddy of the group. He had huge personal credibility. . . . But he couldn't get things done unless the rest of the partnership were on board. (Partner, Consulting Firm)

Decision making becomes consensus-based amongst the expanded group of professionals, typically focused on a weekly meeting of all partners or directors. As the organization continues to grow, and more professionals are brought into the equity, more people expect to be consulted about management issues. Consensus becomes harder to achieve. According to an interviewee in a human resource consulting firm:

> Recently there has been a lot of pressure from people, including me, to acknowledge that we are too big to carry on with this lack of structure. In the old days, we were about ten people who could meet around the coffee

machine and talk through the day-to-day issues. But now we need strong management systems to underpin our expansion. (Manager, Consulting Firm)

In time, senior professionals may become concerned about the slow pace of decision making and inadequacy of the management systems and structures (the Disorganization crisis). A typical response is to establish committees.

Committee Stage

When senior professionals recognize that they can no longer be involved in all aspects of management, but are not yet ready to devolve authority fully to a senior leadership group, their typical solution is to create a series of committees to undertake hiring, promotion, budgeting, marketing, strategy, and other core management tasks. They take it in turn to serve on these committees. A partner in an actuarial consulting firm recalls:

We had a Central Committee that appointed membership to all the other committees—the Operations Committee, the Finance Committee, the Marketing Committee, etc.... The committees met monthly. There was no decision making between meetings and decision making was only by the consensus of those committees. (Partner, Consulting Firm)

While these committees may initially resolve the Disorganization crisis, new problems arise as the organization continues to grow. Committees proliferate, and increasing numbers of senior professionals gradually become involved in management. Frustration builds among professionals as hoped-for efficiency gains fail to materialize, and management activities consume increasing amounts of time to limited effect. Or, as one lawyer puts it:

We were spending all our time in bloody meetings when we should have been out there with our clients. (Partner, Law Firm)

The Frustration crisis looms. Up until this stage in a professional organization's growth, the core themes of governance—power, benefit, and accountability—have remained essentially bound together, albeit embedded within an increasingly large partner or director group. For a professional organization to progress to the next stage, its members must be willing to allow the power, benefit, and accountability, which have been densely interwoven, to be unpicked. A professional organization progresses to the Delegated stage only if senior professionals are willing to relinquish authority to one or more of their peers.

Delegated Stage

In the Delegated stage, senior professionals delegate a limited amount of power to one or two individuals (variously called a Senior Partner, Managing Partner, Chair, Managing Director, or CEO) on the understanding that benefit still lies with the senior professionals as a whole. In other words, the organization is being run by the senior leaders for the benefit of the professionals, so the professionals still define what benefits they seek. The desired benefits could, for example, be about the organization becoming larger or more profitable, about winning more interesting or high-status work, or about preserving professional autonomy. The senior leaders do not get to decide for themselves, though they may influence the decision. One accountant explains this contingent delegation as follows:

> The decisions of the Senior Partner are absolute, as long as he has the confidence of the partnership. As very few decisions are actually voted on, it is very important for the Managing Partner to ensure that he keeps in tune with his colleagues. (Partner, Accounting Firm)

Authority remains contingent and inextricably bound up with accountability—senior professionals can rescind the delegation of authority at any stage, either through formal governance procedures or through a more informal, collective loss of confidence in the senior leadership. During the Delegated stage, authority is delegated from fee-earning professionals to specific individuals at a point in time, but the professionals have not yet accepted the principle of the separation of power, benefit, and accountability.

Chapter 7 explains how a Managing Partner can work closely with a group of management professionals whom he or she has hired to 'professionalize' management. Having gathered together a team with experience of the corporate sector, committed to increasing the efficiency and effectiveness of the organization, the Managing Partner may become disconnected from the partnership as a whole (Disconnection crisis). At times like this, the leadership dyad may come into play (see Chapter 5) as the Senior Partner can play an important role in maintaining the connection with the professional staff, and rein in the Managing Partner and his or her team of management professionals. See later in this chapter for a detailed discussion of the 'Disconnection' crisis in one particular partnership.

'Corporate', Federated, or Dispersed Stages

As a professional organization becomes very large, more centralized systems and structures are necessary, with the organization becoming more 'Corporate' (even if it remains legally a partnership). Professionals often talk suspiciously or disparagingly about large firms in their sector that have 'gone over to the dark side' and become 'corporate'. In other words, they have abandoned the partnership ethos (see Chapter 4) of consensus-based decision making and mutual monitoring and control in favour of bureaucratic systems, professional management, and centralized direction (Chapter 7).

Professional organizations working in heavily regulated sectors such as accounting may reach the 'Corporate' stage more quickly because of the need to ensure regulatory compliance. In this context, the regulator is effectively enhancing the power of the senior leadership. Partners may still expect to be consulted about key aspects of running their businesses, but they must ultimately accept the power of the regulator, or rather the way in which the senior leadership has chosen to interpret that power.

Shying away from the full-on 'Corporate' stage, professionals may prefer to adopt a Federated approach to governance, by operating as a group of smaller, relatively loosely connected units. Each of these units can potentially revert to the Collegial stage, which often remains as a folk memory in the minds of the organization's most senior professionals.

If a substantial subgroup of senior professionals is unwilling to accept a move to the 'Corporate' or Federated stage, they may create a series of spin-off organizations and become Dispersed. Dissatisfied entrepreneurial individuals will leave to set up their own firms and thus revert to the Founder Focused stage.

In reality, of course, change does not happen in the neat and sequential manner outlined in the model. Not all organizations progress through these stages and certainly not all reach the large and bureaucratic 'Corporate' endpoint. Some may experiment and then retreat; others stall at a certain stage and find they are unable to grow further; still more are challenged by sudden growth due to a merger or acquisition and may lose their identity altogether.

These difficult transitions and aborted excursions are examined through two case studies: a small, young consulting company struggling to resolve an Exclusion crisis, and a large, long-established law partnership experiencing a crisis of Disconnection.

Exclusion Crisis: From Founder-Focused to Collegial

It was an astonishing and emotional off-site. Feelings ran very high. People cried. People stormed out. A lot of stuff was processed that needed to be got through.... But we recognized that the firm could no longer be founder-managed. (Associate, Consulting Firm)

Three consultants grew frustrated within a very large 'Corporate' professional organization and decided to set up their own consulting company. Within three years, they had recruited twenty-seven staff to cope with rapidly growing client demand.

From the beginning, the founders (Margaret, Stephen, and David) acknowledged that they would want to realize their investment at some point. They therefore established the firm as a company rather than as a partnership, believing this would make it easier for them to sell equity at a later stage. They also believed strongly in encouraging staff to have a sense of ownership in the business—literally, in terms of shares, and figuratively, in terms of involvement in decision making.

So, the founders held regular office meetings at which all employees (including support staff) discussed and agreed key management issues. Within five years of establishing the company, the founders had sold 1 per cent of their shares to each of their ten most senior employees. Each founder retained a 30 per cent stake. In this way, the founders were attempting to mimic aspects of the Collegial stage whilst also retaining control of the organization.

As the founders began to reduce their shareholdings, they also began to formalize staff involvement in the leadership of the company by creating a management structure termed 'the Executive'. This included five staff members, with founder Margaret as CEO and Chair. Founders Stephen and David had no formal role in the Executive, though David continued to be responsible for financial management.

In time, members of the Executive became frustrated by the lack of formal authority and the considerable amount of time involved in carrying out these roles. As one explains:

The Executive was a sort of information-sharing shop. When it came to really key issues it was clear that the founders still made the decisions. (Executive Member, Consulting Firm)

Within two years, the Executive was replaced by the Management Board. Founder Margaret remained Chair and Chief Executive and a senior consultant who had joined the company two years previously took over David's responsibility for finance. Yet founders David and Stephen continued to wield considerable informal power. Whilst this was an attempt to formalize a more Collegial form of governance, the company remained resolutely Founder-Focused. As a Board member explains:

> Where the founders disagreed with the way that the Board were doing things, you could feel decision making drifting back to them. They often used to meet in one of the upstairs rooms. Everyone knew they were talking about the business—the door was shut and decisions were being taken, even though the Board was supposed to be managing the business. (Board Member, Consulting Firm)

A small group of senior consultants was particularly frustrated by the founders' power. They wanted greater involvement in decision making and a larger share in the profits of the company. As fee income and profitability increased, the value of the company increased dramatically. Because the founders were not willing to sell their shares at a substantial discount, their employees could not afford to buy them. The company was stuck in the Founder-Focused stage (now with forty employees) and unable to move to the Collegial stage. As the senior professionals became increasingly frustrated, a crisis of Exclusion loomed.

This crisis became manifest when the founders were approached by a potential acquirer. The founders recognized it was an opportune time for them to realize their investment but their initial reactions were mixed.

> The approach came at about the time we had recognized that we needed a firm as a senior partner of some kind. We had been concerned about how we could realize our asset. We could see a synergy between the two businesses, and financially the number they talked about was really high. (Founder Stephen, Consulting Firm)

> There was a good strategic argument for working with this company. We had already done some work with them. There was quite a lot of money on the table. We had always known we would sell one day. (Founder David, Consulting Firm)

> I felt very sad about the bid because I felt that the dream had gone. We were going to become part of a big group. But I did feel excitement about the money too. (Founder Margaret, Consulting Firm)

The founders negotiated in private with the bidder and did not involve the Board in their discussions. Once they had reached an agreement with the bidding firm, they held a meeting to announce their decision to all employees. Board members and secretaries were equally surprised:

> The atmosphere was electric. People were absolutely stunned. (Board Member, Consulting Firm)

> It was rather a shock. It was the first time we had been *told* that something was going to happen rather than consulted. (Secretary, Consulting Firm)

> There was a sense of betrayal. I think people thought, 'Ha! They are just going to get a pile of money out of this. They have dumped us.' (Founder Stephen, Consulting Firm)

Over the next nine months, three senior staff resigned, fee income plummeted, the acquiring firm withdrew its offer, and four staff were made redundant. At an off-site meeting, the 'astonishing and emotional' event referred to at the start of this section, the remaining staff gathered to consider the future of the company.

> We had a really cathartic day. A lot of harsh things were said. The firm demanded to know if the founders' hearts were still in it.... There was a huge sense of mourning but also a demand that the founders show some real emotional and physical commitment to rebuilding the firm. And the founders did display that emotional commitment, very visibly so. (Associate, Consulting Firm)

The Board was partially restructured, and founders David and Stephen once again became a part of the formal Management Committee. More rigorous systems for sales and cost management were introduced.

> Within three months we had successfully turned the firm around. But where to, next? (Board Member, Consulting Firm)

> We stated clearly that we must break the parent–child relationship between the founders and the rest of the staff. We concluded that we had to break the capital structure. (Board Member, Consulting Firm)

As the existing staff could not afford to buy the founders' shares at market value, the only available option was a sale to a third party. The move to the Collegial stage could not occur, in spite of the founders' rhetoric of inclusion, because they were not willing to sell at a discount.

Within fifteen months, the company was sold and ceased to exist as an independent entity. The now thirty-person firm was acquired by a privately owned corporation of 5300 staff which operated a strong and centralized management structure (i.e. a 'Corporate' professional organization). Seeking to end the problematic 'parent–child relationship' between the founders and the employees, they accepted a new parent for all of them. The company therefore failed to make the transition from the Founder-Focused stage through the Exclusion crisis to the Collegial stage, and in effect suffered an 'organizational death'.

Disconnection Crisis: From Delegated to 'Corporate'

> At the partner conference my table said: we think this [the leadership's proposal] is unacceptable, this is something that we should be rejecting straight away.... The next table stood up and said the same thing. There were then about seven hours of discussions.... There was genuine hostility in tone against the entire leadership.... There was absolutely not a single partner who spoke in favour of any of the proposals. (Practice Head, Law Firm)

The 500 partners of the global law firm had gathered for their annual meeting. The firm had been established more than 100 years earlier and had grown very rapidly recently following a series of international mergers. It now comprised 5000 staff, about 50 per cent of whom were based in the London office, with the remainder scattered across the much smaller offices of the global network.

The mergers had prompted the Management Committee to introduce more formalized budgeting and reporting procedures and more globally standardized approaches to recruiting and business development (in other words, the professionalization of management—see Chapter 7). Taken individually, none of these changes was substantive. Looked at collectively, they represented a consolidated attempt to introduce centralized controls over a disparate global network of offices. The partners grew increasingly concerned. They were happy to delegate responsibility to the senior leadership of the firm, but they were not willing become fully 'Corporate'.

> There was a perception that we'd become an incredibly bureaucratic organization—that virtually anything that we wanted to do had lots of pieces of paper attached to it.... Some poor guy in Spain, who happened to be looking after several different product groups and practice areas, now had to

write something like fourteen different business plans. (Head of Business Development, Law Firm)

Resentment of this so-called 'creeping corporatization' was shared by the partners in the largest as well as the smallest offices. Although the London office had over 250 partners, the individual practices emulated the Collegial stage. As much as possible, the partners preferred to rely upon traditional methods of mutual monitoring and control, electing their own practice leaders, for example, as well as the firm's Managing Partner and Senior Partner.

The senior leadership dyad had assumed increasing authority for the day-to-day management of the global firm and were behaving as if the firm had moved into the 'Corporate' stage of governance. Partners' concern that the firm was becoming 'Corporate' was reinforced by symbolic changes, such as the Managing and Senior Partners' decision to change their respective titles to CEO and Chairman. Partners meanwhile perceived that the senior leadership dyad was becoming more remote and disconnected from the partnership.

According to two members of the Management Committee:

> The leadership was struggling with a whole load of quite difficult issues post-merger, and became more and more closed in on themselves. . . . They took decisions themselves, didn't talk to other people. I think, to the average partner, that appeared very arrogant. (Management Committee Partner, Law Firm)

> I think we were just getting on with trying to mould the new firm but, in doing that, we sort of became more authoritarian automatically. The old partners really noticed the difference. I think there was probably a note of overconfidence as well. I think we thought we were really clever to have pulled off the mergers. (Management Committee Partner, Law Firm)

The 500 partners were in a fractious mood when they gathered at the annual partner conference. From the start, partners objected to the overall design and format of the meeting, which they deemed to be too highly structured and 'infantilizing'. Seated in a large conference hall in an unglamorous hotel in an uninteresting location, they were asked to sit together at small tables and given set periods of time to work together on allocated tasks. They were asked by an external facilitator to record their thoughts with coloured pens on flip charts. One partner recalls the sentiment in the room:

> Who is this woman, treating us like nursery school children, making us sit at little tables and write with coloured pens on flip charts! We're lawyers for God's sake! (Partner, Law Firm)

As owners of the firm, the partners saw the partner conference as an opportunity to reward themselves by spending time together in a desirable location.
They also expected an opportunity for meaningful debate.

The first task they were given by the external facilitator was to consider a
proposal from the senior leadership of the firm to introduce a partner
appraisal system. The Chairman and CEO believed that a standardized and
transparent system would ensure fairness and consistency across the global
network. The reactions of the partner group were intense, 'there was
genuine hostility . . . against the entire leadership', as the quote at the start
of this section describes. The proposal was unanimously rejected.

Part of the day had been set aside for the election of a new CEO. The
current CEO had already identified his preferred successor (Michael).
Responding to strong encouragement from many partners, a second candidate
decided to put himself forward (Alistair). As two partners explain:

> Alistair was obviously seen as an anti-management candidate, even though he
> was on the Management Committee, whereas Michael—because he was the
> preferred candidate of the CEO—was viewed as the management candidate
> and therefore had lost before he started. (Practice Head, Law Firm)

> Alistair gave a speech which, while light on specific details, contained the
> promise to 'give the partnership back to the partners'. It was a brilliant speech.
> In about thirty minutes Alistair touched every single point of insecurity among
> the partners and said, basically, 'Don't worry, everything is going to be all
> right.' (Partnership Secretary, Law Firm)

Alistair was elected CEO by a substantial majority. Shortly thereafter, he
changed the titles back to Managing and Senior Partner.

During his first year in office, Alistair resolved the crisis of Disconnection
between partners and the senior leadership dyad. He engaged in a relentless
international travel programme to speak to all the partners, to understand their
concerns and allay their fears. In retreating from the 'Corporate' stage, Alistair
relinquished the ability to exercise delegated authority and, in effect, attempted to
revert to a more Collegial stage of governance—among a global partnership of 500.

The partners became increasingly concerned as many merger-related
issues remained unresolved and profitability declined steadily. Both the
Senior and Managing Partner seemed to be performing the same role,
focusing on rebuilding trust among the partnership rather than building
profitability (a harmonious but dysfunctional example of the Intuitive Collaboration dyad—see Chapter 5).

The response was to replace the COO, a management professional from outside the legal sector, with a partner (Lloyd) who had previously been a very successful leader of a core practice area within the firm. Lloyd was well known in the firm and somewhat feared by his colleagues for his confrontational and uncompromising personal style. He used the deterioration in profits as an opportunity to introduce wide-ranging budget cuts and tougher performance management systems, and thus consolidate his power within the partnership. The slide in profitability was reversed.

After serving a four-year term, Alistair did not put himself forward for re-election. Instead, Lloyd stood for election as Managing Partner, promising tougher management controls and even higher profits. As no other partners were prepared to stand against him, he was elected unopposed. He introduced a rigorous partner appraisal system shortly afterwards. Over the next few years, numerous changes were introduced which the partners might previously have decried as 'Corporate'. However, the symbolically significant titles of Managing Partner and Senior Partner were retained.

In retrospect, partners recognized that their concerns about the apparent 'corporatization' of the partnership had been bound up with their more personal concerns about the previous leadership dyad who were trying to bring about the changes. Presented with a different rhetoric, at a different time, by different leaders, these moves towards a more 'Corporate' style of governance were accepted as the inevitable price of becoming one of the world's largest and most successful law firms.

Conclusions: Leadership Evolution

This chapter has examined how a professional organization grows up and grows older. Life cycle models have been criticized for blurring the distinction between description and prescription.[17] Some models suggest that all organizations should, and indeed must, pass through the specific stages identified if they are to grow and mature.[18] Greiner's assertions are more

---

17. J. A. Andersen. 2008. An organization called Harry. *Journal of Organizational Change Management* 21(2): 174–87.
18. Phelps et al. 2007.

modest, arguing that life cycle models provide a road map of possible futures.[19]

Each professional organization is unique. How quickly it passes through each of the stages will vary, as will the intensity of the crises it encounters, reflecting the distinctive complexities and contingencies with which it must contend. The model presented in this chapter is therefore intended to sensitize professionals and scholars to the issues that may lie ahead, and to help make sense of the past. Like a map from the Age of Exploration, where the phrase 'Here be dragons' denoted *terra incognita*, it will not be precise. It will, nevertheless, be considerably more useful than setting out on a voyage without a map at all.

The model expresses how the locus of power shifts around an organization. In the initial, Founder-Focused stage, power resides with the founders, who typically possess all the bases of power, including legitimate, coercive, reward, expert, and information power (see Chapter 2). In addition to these bases of power, the founders are also likely to possess considerable referent power, because they are often admired as role models by the professionals who have chosen to join the organization they created.

During the Collegial and Committee stages, power becomes dispersed amongst a wider group as an increasing number of professionals control access to key resources, such as client relationships. Beyond a certain point, however, power becomes too diffused among too many professionals and the organization can no longer function effectively. The Delegation stage ensures that power is once again concentrated on a smaller group of professionals—not the founders this time, but formally elected leaders.

Leaders need to understand clearly what power has been delegated to them and what power is safe for them to assume for themselves. The mistake of the law firm CEO in the Disconnection crisis earlier in this chapter was to move too quickly and too blatantly to strengthen his position, at a time when the partners were feeling confident in their own. This suggested he lacked the necessary political skills (see Chapter 3). However, when partner confidence was undermined a few years later by deteriorating profits, the Managing Partner was able to wield power over them in a way that would previously have been unacceptable. So the extent to which leaders can assume and exert power will be highly context-specific, as Chapter 10 demonstrates in detail.

19. Greiner and Malernee 2005.

This raises the question: do different stages of a professional organization's life cycle require different kinds of leaders? To some extent, the answer lies in the leadership dyad (see Chapter 5). At each stage in a professional organization's growth there is an advantage in having one leader who focuses on people (i.e. the professional workforce) and one who focuses on production (i.e. profitability). As the organization moves through the various stages, however, the locus of power within the dyad may shift, with the leader who is more focused on professionals coming to the fore during the Collegial stage, and the leader who is more focused on profits taking a more dominant role during the 'Corporate' stage. In general, the most effective leadership derives from the productive tension between the two.

The chapter has highlighted the importance of carefully managing transitions. From a leadership perspective, the key is to recognize when you are at an inflexion point, and whether to provoke a crisis or avert it. The challenge for leaders is to harness, and potentially amplify, the momentum for change that is building up within the professional workforce. As Chapter 9 demonstrates, it is when colleagues start complaining about a 'leadership vacuum' that they are ready to delegate the authority to their leaders to lead their organization to the next stage of development.

9
Leading Mergers
The Ultimate Change Challenge

I think the work they do is awful and their people are awful. We have an extremely classy, sexy reputation. . . . In theory, there are lots of synergies from knowledge sharing, but in practice I am ashamed to work with them.

(Manager, Consulting Firm)

On one occasion, I had to physically restrain one of my team from hitting one of their consultants at the client's offices. Throughout the project their Associate and one of their Analysts had systematically denigrated everything that my guys were doing. My guys were slogging their guts out and their consultants were insulting them at every possible opportunity.

(Manager, Consulting Firm)

Introduction

Mergers and acquisitions[1] can bring out the worst in professionals, as the above quotations suggest. While the reactions of these professionals may appear extreme, their prima-donna-like behaviour is grounded in quite rational concerns. Mergers provoke anxiety in the most prosaic of individuals, as they represent a change which potentially threatens established work norms. Carefully laid plans are thrown into question, and there is always the underlying threat of job losses.[2] Professionals, with their desire for autonomy

1. In the research literature, the terms 'merger' and 'acquisition' are often used interchangeably. In this chapter, the single term 'merger' is used, partly for the sake of linguistic simplicity, but also to reflect widespread practice in professional organizations. Professionals typically prefer to use 'merger', regardless of the actual legal and financial basis of the deal, in order to de-emphasize the potential imbalance of power relations between the combining organizations.
2. D. N. Angwin. 2004. Speed in M&A integration: The first 100 days. *European Management Journal* 22(4): 418–30.

and inherently insecure working environments (see Chapter 6) are likely to experience particularly acute merger-induced anxiety.[3] They have a clear incentive not to cooperate with attempts to make the merger a success and the leaders who instigated the merger cannot compel them to do so,[4] whether their organizations are partnerships or publicly quoted corporations.[5] This is why mergers represent the extreme change challenge for leaders of professional organizations. When so many mergers fail,[6,7] why are they so common among professional organizations?

Chapter 8 explains how professional organizations experience a series of crises as they grow. What works well for younger, smaller organizations can inhibit growth past a certain point. Leaders of professional organizations may choose instead to pursue a merger, avoiding the need to work through the crises associated with organic growth.

A merger presents professional organizations with the opportunity for accelerated growth. By sharing knowledge, merging organizations can fill in gaps in their service provision, by responding to clients' demands for increasing coverage and developing new services. By sharing each other's clients, they can expand their footprint in different sectors and countries, or entrench their power in existing markets. By integrating their brands, they can develop a reputation in new markets or become better known in existing markets. While potentially resolving one kind of crisis, however, mergers can provoke another—as the opening quotations suggest.

The problem with the above paragraph is the word 'they'. We talk about organizations as though they are capable of acting, thinking, or even feeling ('they share knowledge'; 'they experience a crisis'). In other words, we reify them. This is a dangerous mistake to make when thinking about mergers in the context of professional organizations. While professional organizations exist in a legal sense as objective entities, capable of owning assets, they are also made up of individuals. It is the individuals who are sharing and experiencing; who are acting, thinking, and feeling; who know the clients,

3. L. Empson. 2001. Fear of exploitation and fear of contamination: Impediments to knowledge transfer in mergers between professional services firms. *Human Relations* 54(7): 839–62.
4. L. Empson. 2000. Mergers between professional service firms: Exploring an undirected process of integration. *Advances in Mergers and Acquisitions (JAI Series)* 1: 205–37.
5. M. E. Pickering. 2017. Post-acquisition integration processes in publicly owned professional service companies: Senior professional behaviour and company performance. *Journal of Organizational Behavior*.
6. C. Tuch and N. O'Sullivan. 2007. The impact of acquisitions on firm performance: A review of the evidence. *International Journal of Management Reviews* 9(2): 141–70.
7. D. R. King et al. 2004. Meta-analyses of post-acquisition performance: Indications of unidentified moderators. *Strategic Management Journal* 25(2): 187–200.

possess the knowledge, and embody the reputation of the organization. Their cooperation is essential to the success of the merger—and their resistance can be responsible for its failure.

This chapter focuses on the potentially sudden and dramatic change represented by a merger. It explains why the leaders of professional organizations who initiate a merger have very limited power to ensure its success. It identifies two reasons why professionals may be reluctant to cooperate with merger objectives: fear of exploitation and fear of contamination. It presents a model developed from my research—the 'School Dance' model of post-merger integration. It argues that leaders of merging professional organizations require a subtle understanding of what drives professionals, the nerve to hold back from direct action, and the perceptiveness to judge the right time to intervene.

Challenge of Mergers between Professional Organizations

Until the 1990s, management writers emphasized three main reasons for undertaking mergers: to turn around poorly performing organizations through the introduction of superior management; to increase potential markets through diversification; and to secure competitive advantage through increasing monopoly power. It was only in the early 1990s, with the development of the resource-based view of the firm and the increased emphasis on knowledge as a core resource,[8] that mergers and acquisitions came to be widely recognized as an opportunity to create value through gaining access to new knowledge.[9,10]

Resource-Based View and the Merger Process

According to the resource-based view, an organization's competitive advantage derives from its ability to assemble and exploit an appropriate

---

8. R. M. Grant and J. C. Spender. 1996. Knowledge and the firm. *Strategic Management Journal* 17 (Winter): 5–11.
9. D. Greenberg and P. J. Guinan. 2004. Mergers and acquisitions in technology-intensive industries: The emergent process of knowledge transfer. In *Mergers and acquisitions: Creating integrative knowledge*, ed. A. L. Pablo and M. Javidan. Oxford: Blackwell, 135–55.
10. A. L. Ranft and M. D. Lord. 2002. Acquiring new technologies and capabilities: A grounded model of acquisition implementation. *Organization Science* 13(4): 420–42.

combination of resources, and to continuously develop existing (and create new) resources in response to changing market conditions. From this perspective, knowledge represents an important value-creating asset.[11] A key function of a firm, therefore, is to establish conditions under which individuals can integrate specialist knowledge and create value through the production of goods and services.

As a direct result of the increased focus on integrating resources for value creation, process-based perspective on mergers and acquisitions have become increasingly influential within the management literature.[12] This strand of research emphasizes that leaders devote considerable effort to negotiating the right price for a merger, yet fail to recognize that all value is created post-merger.[13,14] A process-based perspective emphasizes that this lack of attention to the merger integration process is one of the main reasons why so many mergers fail.

Mergers and acquisitions are notoriously problematic, regardless of the sector in which they take place. When knowledge is involved, mergers are more likely to destroy rather than create value.[15] A study has shown that, when the value of the target organization is based primarily on intangible assets such as knowledge, buyers on average experience an economic loss of 12 per cent over a five-year period post-acquisition.[16]

There are many possible explanations for this poor performance, but probably the most convincing explanation is the simplest. A merger creates uncertainty, fear, and distrust among professional staff,[17] even when there are no plans for redundancies and the express purpose is to create value through sharing resources. Individuals in both the acquired and the acquiring organizations may fear loss of status and changes to their established

11. Grant and Spender 1996.
12. P. Haspeslagh and D. Jemison. 1991. *Managing acquisitions: Creating value through corporate renewal*. New York: The Free Press.
13. M. Sirower. 1997. *The synergy trap: How companies lose the acquisition game*. New York: The Free Press.
14. D. N. Angwin and M. Meadows. 2015. New integration strategies for post-acquisition management. *Long-Range Planning* 48(4) August: 235–51.
15. R. Schoenberg. 2001. Knowledge transfer and resource sharing as value creation mechanisms in inbound continental European acquisitions. *Journal of Euromarketing* 10(1): 99–114.
16. A. M. Arikan. 2004. Does it pay to capture intangible assets through mergers and acquisitions? In *Mergers and acquisitions: Creating integrative knowledge*, ed. A. L. Pablo and M. Javidan. Oxford: Blackwell, 156–80.
17. S. Cartwright and C. L. Cooper. 1992. *Mergers and acquisitions: The human factor*. Oxford: Butterworth Heinemann.

work norms.[18] When seeking to create value through integrating knowledge, clients, and reputation, leaders are wrestling with the intangible. They are often beaten.

Sharing Resources in Professional Organizations

In conventional organizations, mergers are often driven by the opportunity to exploit economies of scale. Senior executives, therefore, have plenty of 'easy wins' from rationalizing and disposing of resources (e.g. selling off fixed assets and sacking staff). Mergers between professional organizations, however, are typically motivated by different objectives because professional organizations rely upon three kinds of resources: technical knowledge, client relationships, and reputation.

Technical knowledge is proprietary to each professional and is derived from their previous work experience, education, and unique mix of client assignments.[19] In time, elements of this tacit individual knowledge become codified and collective, as professionals disseminate their knowledge both formally and informally.[20,21] However, professionals constantly develop their tacit knowledge through their ongoing client engagements so the most innovative and valuable knowledge remains proprietary to individuals.

Strong relationships between individual professionals and their clients are essential to the successful sale and delivery of professional services.[22] Professional services cannot be inspected in advance; they are purchased and consumed on the basis of trust. Over a protracted client engagement, more and more professionals may develop relationships of trust with more and more clients, but there is still typically one individual in the professional

18. D. M. Schweiger and A. S. Denisi. 1991. Communication with employees following a merger: A longitudinal field experiment. *Academy of Management Journal* 34(1): 110–35.

19. L. Empson. 2001. Introduction: Knowledge management in professional service firms. *Human Relations* 54(7): 811–17.

20. J. Faulconbridge. 2015. Knowledge and learning in professional service firms. In *The Oxford handbook of professional service firms*, ed. L. Empson, D. Muzio, J. Broschak, and B. Hinings. Oxford: Oxford University Press, 425–51.

21. T. Morris and L. Empson. 1998. Organization and expertise: An exploration of knowledge bases and the management of accounting and consulting firms. *Accounting, Organizations and Society* 23(5–6): 609–24.

22. J. Broschak. 2015. Client relationships in professional service firms. In *The Oxford handbook of professional service firms*, ed. L. Empson, D. Muzio, J. Broschak, and B. Hinings. Oxford: Oxford University Press, 304–26.

organization who is responsible for (i.e. controls) the relationship with the key decision maker in the client organization.

Similarly, the reputation of a professional organization is an integral component of a client's purchase decision.[23] It is created through a complex interaction of an individual's image and an organization's brand.[24,25] As Chapter 2 argues, high-profile professionals with significant reputations are likely to command significant power within their organizations; their personal success is intimately associated with the success of the organization as a whole.

Valuable tacit knowledge can only be communicated in person and close client relationships are similarly difficult to 'transfer'—the sharing of both requires deep-seated trust between colleagues and between professionals and their clients. In the post-merger environment, professionals have not developed relationships with their counterparts in the merger partner organization, and potentially have much to lose from sharing their knowledge and clients. As explained in Chapter 2, these resources represent the bases of a professional's power within an organization. Given the insecure post-merger environment, professionals therefore have a clear incentive to avoid cooperating with their merger partner colleagues.

Research Study

The ideas in this chapter originated in a longitudinal study I conducted into the post-merger integration process as it unfolded within six firms over a three-year period. During this time, I interviewed 200 professionals, including repeated interviews with the senior leadership teams. The questions guiding my analysis were: *why exactly do professionals resist post-merger integration?* And *how is it possible to create, rather than destroy, value in mergers between professional organizations?*

23. W. Harvey and V. Mitchell. 2015. Marketing and reputation within professional service firms. In *The Oxford handbook of professional service firms*, ed. L. Empson, D. Muzio, J. Broschak, and B. Hinings. Oxford: Oxford University Press, 279–303.

24. M. Alvesson. 2001. Knowledge work: Ambiguity, image, and identity. *Human Relations* 54(7): 863–86.

25. M. Alvesson and L. Empson. 2008. The construction of organizational identity: Comparative case studies of consulting firms. *Scandinavian Journal of Management* 24(1): 1–16.

The six organizations (i.e. three cases) comprised two accounting firms and four consulting firms. Three were partnerships and three were incorporated companies. One case was legally a merger and two were acquisitions but these were always officially referred to by the leadership as mergers.

Case A is a merger between a strategy consulting partnership (Sea) and an operations consulting company (Land). At the start of the merger, Sea employed 500 professional and support staff in its twelve offices worldwide, including eighty staff in the UK. Total fee income was $100 million. Land employed 600 professional and support staff worldwide, including ninety staff in the UK. Total fee income was $140 million.

Case B is an acquisition of a small London-based change management consulting company (Valley[26]) by a large international consulting company (Hill), which advises clients on a range of people management issues. At the time of the acquisition, Valley employed fewer than thirty people and earned income of £4 million. Hill was one of the largest consulting firms in the world, with fee income of $750 million.

Case C is an acquisition of a UK-based accounting partnership (Moon) by a large global accounting partnership (Sun). Sun and Moon were engaged in very similar activities, offering a wide range of audit and tax and advisory services. Their client bases, however, were fundamentally different. At the time of the acquisition, Sun had over 4000 partners and professional staff in the UK. UK fee income was over £400 million. Moon had 1300 partners and professional staff, earning fee income of £60 million.

Based on detailed analysis, I developed two concepts which explain why professionals resist post-merger integration: 'fear of exploitation' and 'fear of contamination'. I also developed the School Dance model of the post-merger integration process (see Figure 9.1).

Twin Fears: Exploitation and Contamination

The antagonism among professionals highlighted at the start of this chapter originates from a fear of exploitation. This arises when professionals do not value the expertise of their merger partner colleagues and believe they have

---

26. Valley was the small consulting firm featured in Chapter 8. The founders turned to a merger as a means of resolving the crisis of Exclusion, but, as this chapter will demonstrate, created new problems for themselves and their organization.

nothing to gain, and much to lose, from cooperating with them. It is exacerbated by a fear of contamination, where professionals believe that their carefully cultivated client relationships and reputation will be undermined by association with their merger partner colleagues.[27]

Fear of Exploitation

Knowledge is difficult to value. Professionals engage in a complex and subtle set of behaviours to convince clients that they know something that is worth paying for. The process is bound up with issues such as image, identity, and reputation.[28] In the context of a merger, professionals need to convince their merger partner colleagues as well as their clients that their knowledge has value. This may be particularly difficult when professionals are engaging in very different kinds of work, as the following comments from merger partner colleagues explain:

> Case A: Some Sea people were saying, 'The Land people can't understand what I do but anyone can do what they do.' (Manager, Sea)

> Case A: We viewed the Sea consultants as intellectual butterflies. What exactly was it that they were doing with their clients? (Manager, Land)

> Case B: I come back from integrated project meetings swearing. There are serious questions about who is giving the intellectual lead and the intellectual capacity of the Hill people. (Consultant, Valley)

> Case B: People at Hill say it is like the emperor's new clothes. Valley's change management offering is just a hologram. It is all smoke and mirrors. (Consultant, Hill)

While interviewees in Sea and Valley emphasize the inherently tacit nature of their knowledge, interviewees in Land and Hill emphasize the more codified aspects. The consultants in Sea and Valley assume that the codified knowledge of their new colleagues in Land and Hill is simplistic and unsophisticated. Or as one Valley consultant puts it: 'We look upon ourselves as strategic architects. The Hill guys are more like plumbers.' At the same time, the consultants from Land and Hill do not recognize the legitimacy of the tacit knowledge of their new colleagues in Sea and Valley, dismissing it as insubstantial or unreal.

---

27. The ideas contained in this section are developed in considerably more depth in Empson 2001.
28. Alvesson 2001.

In other words, consultants from each of the firms perceive their own knowledge to be more valuable than that of their merger partner colleagues. The professionals in these cases are not simply arrogant prima donnas, as they might first appear. They are experiencing real and well-grounded anxiety because they perceive that they are being asked to give away valuable knowledge whilst being offered little of value in return. This phenomenon is the fear of exploitation.

It is worth noting that this fear of exploitation does not arise in Case C, the two accounting firms, because accountants share a formally codified and accredited knowledge base. They have all passed the same professional examinations, so there is less scope for disagreement over the validity of what they know. They may dispute the quality of each other's work but do not dispute the legitimacy of each other's knowledge.

Fear of Contamination

Resistance to sharing knowledge focuses on different understandings of what constitutes valuable knowledge. By contrast, resistance to sharing clients focuses on different perceptions of the reputations of the combining organizations. In each of the three cases, professionals in one organization perceive their own organization's image to be considerably superior to their merger partner's.

The strategy consultants at Sea perceive themselves as more 'upmarket' than the operations consultants at Land. Meanwhile, the change management consultants at Valley describe their organization's external image as 'innovative' and 'classy'. They complain that the human resources consultants at Hill are 'dreary' and 'lacking in polish'. As a result, when their leaders call upon them to collaborate with their merger partner colleagues, professionals in the supposedly more upmarket firms express considerable resistance. Talking about his merger partner colleagues, a Sea consultant says: 'Land is the McDonalds of consulting.... What are my clients going to make of them?' Or, as another of his colleagues explains:

Case A: Some Sea people are saying, 'Who are these hairy-arsed guys? Is my reputation as an elite strategy consultant going to be sullied by contact with these labourers?' (Manager, Sea)

The change management consultant from Valley quoted at the start of this chapter refers to his organization's 'extremely classy, sexy reputation'.

Speaking of his merger partner colleagues in Hill, he goes on to say, 'I just feel tainted by having anything to do with them.' Another colleague of his expresses this fear of contamination from association with Hill as follows:

> Case B: We've had to convert our logo to conform with Hill's. Our previous logo was classy. The new one is naff, brassy, it lacks style, it's unimaginative and uncreative. . . . It makes us look like a firm that manufactures recycled lavatory paper. (Consultant, Valley)

Association with a 'downmarket' colleague may have a direct impact on the fees a professional can charge. At an individual level, a professional's personal image is integral to how clients perceive the value of the service they are receiving.[29] At an organizational level, there can be considerable costs associated with 'image contamination' in the context of credence-based services.[30] Professionals therefore risk diminishing the perceived value of their reputation if they allow their image to be called into question. There is, therefore, a commercial logic behind the somewhat emotional reactions of the consultants quoted above.

However, it is also more complicated than that. Various writers[31] have highlighted the close relationship that can exist between organizational identity and an individual's self-concept. Changes to organizational identity can prove highly threatening at an individual level.[32] The problem is particularly acute in professional organizations because the identity of the organization and the individual professional are so closely associated with the client's perception of the quality of the service.[33] Consequently, while professionals may articulate their fear of contamination in terms of the negative impact on clients' perceptions, their concerns may also derive from a more fundamental anxiety about their sense of self-worth. For insecure overachievers, who derive particular pride and a sense of well-being from association with an elite professional organization (see Chapter 6), this can provoke a particularly intense reaction.

For these reasons, conventional leadership injunctions to embrace change, and look forward with optimism to the opportunities presented by a merger,

29. Alvesson 2001.
30. Harvey and Mitchell 2015.
31. M. J. Hatch and M. Schultz. 2002. The dynamics of organizational identity. *Human Relations* 55(8): 989–1018.
32. J. E. Dutton, J. M. Dukerich, and C. V. Harquail. 1994. Organizational images and member identification. *Administrative Science Quarterly* 39: 239–63.
33. L. Empson. 2004. Organizational identity change: Managerial regulation and member identification in an accounting firm acquisition. *Accounting, Organizations and Society* 29(9): 759–81.

will likely fall on deaf ears. Professionals resent their leaders telling them what to do: they respond even less positively to being told what to feel. The deep-seated and emotional attitudes demonstrated by the individual professionals described above encapsulate the leadership challenge. How then is it possible for leaders of merging professional organizations to create, rather than destroy, value?

'School Dance' Model: An Undirected Integration Process

Within the social sciences, the vocabulary of metaphor is used to express, conceptualize, and understand complex and abstract phenomena.[34] I have therefore adopted a metaphorical approach to better understand how post-merger integration comes about in professional organizations, and have developed the School Dance model of post-merger integration.[35]

At traditional school dances, boys and girls line up on either side of the school gymnasium. Unwilling to make the first approach, they may conceal their anxiety by making disparaging comments to their friends about the girls or boys across the dance floor. Eventually, the boldest individuals cross the floor to find a partner. Encouraged by their success, more and more boys and girls seek out partners on the other side of the gymnasium. Those who fail to do so leave the dance. By the end of the evening, 'integration' has been successfully achieved.

From a leadership perspective, the key point is the role that authority plays in this integration process. While the teachers may have organized the dance committee, set the date for the dance, and helped with complex issues such as budgeting or health and safety, it is the students themselves who actually organize the dance. Once the dance begins, the teachers remain on the sidelines, keeping a watchful eye on proceedings to make sure nothing goes wrong, but trying not to spoil the fun. Crucially, they do not decide who dances with whom and they cannot ensure that everyone has a good time. The teachers provide the context for a successful dance, but the impetus to dance must come from the students themselves.

---

34. H. Tsoukas. 1991. The missing link: A transformational view of metaphors in organizational science. *Academy of Management Review* 16(3): 566–85.
35. The ideas contained in this section are developed in considerably more depth in Empson 2000.

In professional organizations, integration follows a similar process (as illustrated in Figure 9.1). The process and timings outlined here are derived from my analysis of six organizations I studied over a three-year period, as summarized here and described in detail in the sections that follow.

At the point of Closure (Figure 9.1a) the only people in the merger partner organizations who have established contact are the leaders who negotiated the merger. During the Acclimatization phase (Figure 9.1b), one to two years post-merger, most professionals avoid contact with their merger partner colleagues and leaders adopt an essentially passive role. However, 'integration entrepreneurs' advance the integration process, by seeking out like-minded and potentially useful colleagues in the merger partner organization, to explore opportunities for cooperation. The second and third years post-closure are periods of Transition (Figure 9.1c), as the more recalcitrant professionals recognize the benefits of greater cooperation, and the most adamant change-resisters resign. From the third year onwards Integration begins to occur (Figure 9.1d), as the perceived boundaries of the organizations become blurred and individual affiliations start to change.

Years One to Two: Acclimatization

In all three cases, very little integration occurs for the first two years following Closure. Separate brand names, management structures, and administrative systems are retained, and all merger partner organizations continue to occupy separate offices. Interviewees describe this period as 'stalemate', 'ring fencing', and 'phoney war'. Leaders in all cases adopt an essentially passive role, focusing primarily on day-to-day operational issues. They do not develop detailed implementation plans and do not seek to advance the integration process. Instead, they allow professional staff and clients to determine the pace of change.

> Case A: There was no apparent architecting at the top. It was a case of, 'Thou shalt go out and work together.' (Manager, Sea)

> Case B: We have not formally guided change from the top. We have just said, 'Go to it.' (Managing Director, Valley)

> Case C: We said to the Moon people, 'Your future is in your hands. We are empowering you.' (Partner, Sun)

This approach reflects the difficulty of evaluating intangible assets prior to a merger. After the deal is concluded, professionals in each organization need

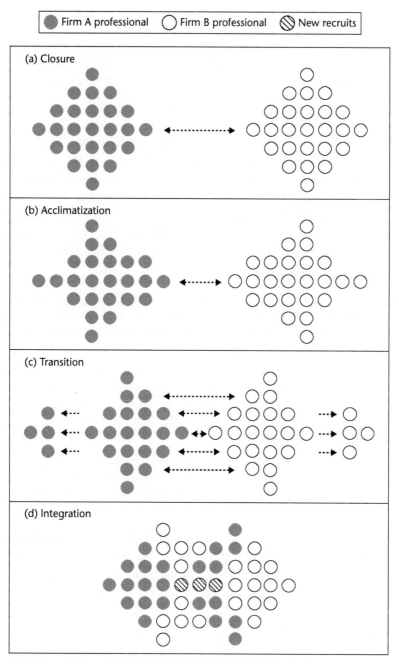

Figure 9.1 'School Dance' model of merger integration

time to familiarize themselves with their merger partner colleagues. As a Sea partner says:

> Case A: We thought a lot about integration issues prior to the merger but it was difficult because we did not have access to so much crucial information. There were a whole set of issues that were not strictly analysable: the culture, the values, how we did business. (Partner, Sea)

At the same time, the leaders of the merging organizations are acutely aware that they run the risk of alienating key professionals if they push ahead too rapidly with integration. There is no 'burning platform' in any of the organizations. The lack of an immediate crisis means that the leaders do not have the benefit of derived authority to force through unpopular change (see Chapter 10). On the contrary, in the partnerships, where a full vote of the partners was required to approve the merger, the senior leadership won approval by emphasizing continuity rather than change:

> Case A: We would expect over time that each firm would begin to understand and participate in the opportunities created by the other distinctive channel, but they would remain reasonably separate firms for a period of time. (Memo from Senior Leadership to Partners, Sea)

> Case B: Our approach to integrating Valley has been like re-potting a plant which has outgrown its previous pot. You take the plant out of the pot and loosen the earth around the roots a bit, but not too much. Then you put it in a slightly larger pot, but not too large or the plant becomes too straggly. (Managing Director, Hill)

> Case C: We approached integration as follows: stay loose; take time to learn about them; don't impose your initial vision on them. Don't move faster than the market demands. Be prepared to operate with a degree of chaos. (Director of HR, Sun)

The leaders' cautious approach is not just about keeping the professionals happy. Clients also need to be reassured. Leaders try to convey a complex message of stability and opportunity to both clients and staff (i.e. 'Your job/ the service you receive will not change unless you want it to' and 'The merger enables us to serve clients even better than we did before'). As the Managing Partner of Sun explains:

> Case C: I knew one thing about the merger. As the deal was entirely driven by our desire to gain access to Moon's FTSE100 audit clients, it was vital that clients would not be lost as a result of the merger. Sun people were coming to

me with suggestions about what we should do with Moon and I would say, 'Will this help us to keep their clients?' If the answer was 'no' I was fairly brutal about stopping their flights of fancy. (Managing Partner, Sun)

At the same time, while assuring professionals that change will not be forced upon them, senior leaders encourage staff to pursue opportunities for cooperation with their merger partner colleagues. Not all professionals resist integration: some recognize the opportunity it presents. These individuals, the integration entrepreneurs, play a vital role in advancing the integration process by seeking out like minded colleagues in the merger partner organization to explore opportunities for cooperation.

> Case A: During the first year there was very little communication going on between the two firms. I started talking to Joe at Sea about how to sell work jointly. We decided I should move my desk into his office and just get on with it. (Vice President, Land)

> Case B: You find people you like and just start working with them. I like Jane at Hill because she's smart and quick and laughs a lot. It's stuff like that which drives integration, not grand thought. (Consultant, Valley)

> Case C: I have formed a good relationship with one of the Sun partners, David. I approached him initially and he tested me out with a few bits of work. When I passed the test, he gave me more. . . . David and I have similar interests. It's a personal thing. We are the same kind of people. (Manager, Moon)

In the process of establishing inter-organizational relationships, the integration entrepreneurs also build personal relationships. One interviewee describes these friendships as 'bridges for transferring skills between firms'.

Years Two to Three: Transition

Previous studies have shown that following a merger or acquisition, staff may start to idealize their own organization as they become acutely aware of what they risk losing.[36] At the same time, they may start to demonize the merger partner organization. For example:

> Case C: We were frightened that Sun would behave like an aggressive animal and tear everything apart. (Manager, Moon)

---

36. A. Nahavandi and A. R. Malekzadeh. 1988. Acculturation in mergers and acquisitions. *Academy of Management Review* 13(1): 79–90.

Those who have only limited contact with individuals in the merger partner organization may seize upon any negative evidence to confirm their
concerns about the merger (in decision-making theory, this is known as
'confirmation bias'). In all three cases, integration entrepreneurs helped to
forestall the demonization of the merger partner organization by establishing
personal relationships with their merger partner colleagues. These new
relationships between integration entrepreneurs translate into new projects
and increased fees, which prompt some recalcitrant colleagues to consider
how they too can get involved.

In terms of the School Dance model, the more confident individuals who
have crossed the dance floor first return to their friends standing against the
wall and encourage them to take a risk and try to dance with someone. As
the initially recalcitrant professionals have more contact with their new
colleagues, they cease to demonize the merger partner organization and
begin to identify individuals with whom to cooperate.

> Case A: Gradually we worked out who were the good guys and who were the
> bad guys in Land. We started to realize that, behind the gung-ho facade, they
> were just as fragmented and political as we were. (Partner, Sea)

> Case B: In the last year I have had contact with a lot of individuals from Hill
> and have worked with a few people I like very much. A whole set of small
> personal experiences has helped to change the way I feel about Hill. (Con-
> sultant, Valley)

> Case C: We had this idea when Sun joined us that they would be superhuman
> and we would be lost . . . . But we have built some strong links at an individual
> level. Some Moon people now feel that they have more in common with Sun
> people than with other Moon people. (Junior, Sun)

In other words, these professionals have overcome the innate tendency to reify
organizations. They no longer look upon the merger partner organization as a
single and unappealing entity and they no longer look upon their merger
partner colleagues as a cohesive group of 'them', potentially threatening 'us'.
Instead the merger partner organization becomes 'Tom, Dick, and Harry',
'Jane, Mary, and Kate'—made up of some people they like and respect, and
others they do their best to avoid, just as in their own organization.

In all three cases, during the second year following closure, the pressure for change increases as a growing number of professionals begin to
engage with the integration process. Professionals who are keen to work
more closely with their merger partner colleagues become frustrated by the

remaining structural impediments to integration, such as the maintenance of separate locations, brand names, reward structures and accounting systems. Professionals who are less receptive to merger-related change find it difficult to tolerate prolonged uncertainty about their future.

Professionals begin to complain that their senior leaders are failing to provide effective leadership and put pressure on them to accelerate the pace of integration—the term 'leadership vacuum' starts to be heard. The following comments represent a widespread frustration with the leadership in all three cases.

> Case A: One evening, after I'd had a few drinks, I told our Managing Director that the firm needed more leadership. I told him, 'We are fed up with all this involving of everyone in the integration decisions. We just want someone to stand up and say, "This is what is going to happen."' (Manager, Land)

> Case B: I would love our Managing Director to take people by the balls and push change through. (Consultant, Hill)

> Case C: There is no leadership or overt direction. We have become a festering mass of uncertainty. (Partner, Sun)

As the majority of staff come to advocate greater integration, the most recalcitrant professionals recognize that change is inevitable and that passive resistance is no longer sustainable. Some of these resisters respond by resigning, but not all. During the second year following the merger, some professionals undergo a conversion and come to recognize the benefits of integration. The change management consultant quoted earlier in this chapter, who felt 'tainted' by contact with his merger partner colleagues, describes why he overcame his demonization to develop a new attitude to them:

> A year ago my counterpart at Hill seemed like the devil incarnate. But in the last year he has sold some big projects, which I have not been able to do in this tough market. I respect him for that and I realize that his work may provide me with a route back into certain clients. (Consultant, Valley)

This change in attitude helps prepare the way for full-scale integration.

Year Four: Integration

In all three cases, substantial progress towards integration occurs during the third year following closure, with new brand names, organizational structures, and new offices.

Professionals' perceptions of the boundaries of the organizations begin to blur and their organizational affiliations start to change.

> Case A: The new office proved once and for all that Sea and Land were dead and that there was no point in looking back any more. In a way, I feel as though I joined a new firm the day I moved to the new building. (Manager, Sea)

> Case B: I would love to move to Valley. My colleague who has moved over has said, 'It is wonderful. How soon can you come?' (Consultant, Hill)

> Case C: I don't mind whether I am called Sun or Moon. I have two sets of business cards and I use whichever is most likely to work in each situation. I would say that I was a Sun person if I wanted to impress someone, though I still don't feel like a Sun person. (Manager, Moon)

Conclusions: Creating and Exploiting the Leadership Vacuum

The reactions of some of the professionals quoted in the preceding analysis may seem extreme and leaders of professional organizations may struggle to imagine their colleagues saying such things. In fact, there is a good chance leaders will never hear colleagues express their fears of exploitation and contamination in such frank terms. These are deeply rooted and highly personal concerns, which professionals have articulated to me in the context of confidential research interviews, but which they may be reluctant to discuss more widely. In public, and when speaking to the senior leaders who have instigated the merger, professionals are more likely to talk in positive terms—whilst, nevertheless, passively resisting attempts at post-merger integration. At times of heightened insecurity, therefore, leaders of professional organizations need to be particularly alert to the possibility that many of their colleagues will not be telling them the truth.

There may be another reason why leaders of merging professional organizations do not hear this kind of negative talk. Their colleagues may simply not care sufficiently about the organization to be concerned about the merger.[37,38] They do not identify with their organization particularly strongly, and know they can easily move as soon as a better opportunity

37. Nahavandi and Malekzadeh 1988.
38. Empson 2004.

comes along so they do not actively resist integration. But they may not do much to assist it either.

The School Dance model of post-merger integration is a metaphor for undirected organizational change. Leaders who instigate the merger can help to create the context for integration, but they cannot control the process by which it evolves—at least not directly. There are some things, however, that leaders can do.

In the pre-merger planning phase, when seeking to learn about the culture of the potential merger partner organization, leaders need to understand not just what the culture is, but how closely professionals in the merger partner organization identify with that culture. The more closely they identify with their culture, the more likely they are to resist attempts at post-merger integration.

In the early weeks following a merger, leaders can focus on identifying the key resources within both organizations—working out exactly where the value resides in terms of knowledge, clients, and reputation, and more particularly within whom it resides. The knowledge, clients, and reputation of these individuals represent the 'crown jewels' of the merger, whose value must be preserved.

Leaders can also challenge colleagues' tendency to demonize the merger partner organization and idealize their own. They can create opportunities for merger partner colleagues to learn more about each other, to understand and minimize potential fears of exploitation and contamination.

Leaders can also be on the lookout for integration entrepreneurs and try to facilitate their initiatives. These professionals are likely to stand out as being particularly optimistic and confident, experienced at change and comfortable with ambiguity. They may also be highly critical of the leaders and the merger. They will have their own ideas about the rights and wrongs of the merger and be keen to put them into effect. For the School Dance model to play out effectively, the integration entrepreneurs also need to be well regarded by their colleagues, to ensure they are listened to with interest when they return with their tales from the dance floor.

As integration entrepreneurs begin to build bridges between the merging organizations, leaders can facilitate the process by gradually reducing obstacles to integration—focusing initially on changes which deliver immediate tangible benefits through increased profitability or reduced complexity. Thereafter, leaders can focus on eliminating systemic and structural distinctions which may be highly important to professionals in the early stages of post-merger integration but which gradually come to be seen as anachronistic and frustratingly bureaucratic as the merger progresses. Significant structural changes, such as standardization of job titles and redesign of roles and responsibilities, are best left until professionals start to demand accelerated change.

When professionals start complaining about a leadership vacuum, this is the time for leaders to take decisive action and press ahead to remove remaining impediments to integration. Some of the remaining impediments may be the highly valued 'crown jewels' identified at the start of the merger, i.e. those individuals who control access to key resources. There comes a stage in the integration process when key influencers who remain resistant to integration can cause more harm than good by remaining within the organization. Their ongoing resistance becomes a focus of discontent—instead of the crown jewels, they become potential saboteurs.

Above all, leaders of merging professional organizations need to make finely tuned judgements about the velocity of change, in what direction to lead change, and how much force to apply to achieve change. In other words, leadership in this context is about knowing how to create, and when to exploit, the leadership vacuum.

10

Leadership and Ambiguity

Acting Decisively without Authority

After everything we had done to sort of pull this leadership group together . . . it was kind of the moment of truth that we arrived at. . . . 'Can it work effectively in a crisis, in a very dangerous crisis?' And I think the answer to that was, 'Yes.'

(Senior Partner)

Introduction

This book has approached the theme of leadership from multiple directions. It has explained why plural leadership is the prevailing model in professional organizations and introduced the concept of the leadership constellation to express the informal power dynamics that coexist alongside the formal authority structure (Chapter 2). It has explored the microdynamics through which plural leadership dynamics are constructed and the inherent instability that results (Chapter 3). It has analysed the roles and relationships of senior leadership dyads (Chapter 5) and identified the micropolitics they engage in alongside their management professionals when seeking to bring about change (Chapter 7). And it has explained how sometimes, for leaders of professional organizations who want to bring about change, the best thing they can do is nothing (Chapter 9).

The analysis has been conducted across a wide range of professional organizations. While this is necessary to develop generalizable insights, it inevitably makes it harder to identify precisely what is going on. So this chapter delves deep inside a single professional organization, to examine in intricate detail the leadership dynamics within the leadership constellation: who is involved, who has the power to decide who is involved, how do they work together under normal circumstances, and how do they respond to a crisis?

In Chapter 9, the leaders have the luxury of time—they instigate the change and control the timetable. In this chapter, the leaders have change forced upon them—they must respond quickly but do not have the authority to act decisively. The conventional view is that organizational crises demand clear and decisive responses from strong leaders. Yet this is hard to reconcile with the extensive autonomy and contingent authority which determine the distinctive power dynamics of professional organizations.

At the heart of the analysis that follows, therefore, is the question: how, when authority is ambiguous, are leaders able to respond effectively in a crisis? The answer is that under the cloak of ambiguity, leaders may be able to exercise considerable informal power by mobilizing and exploiting the organization's hidden hierarchy. This chapter explains exactly how it is done.

Ambiguity and Authority

As explained in Chapter 2, under plural leadership, leadership roles are shared amongst multiple actors and authority is ambiguous and potentially contested.[1] Leadership is a collective process, unfolding over time and arising from the actions and interactions of an extended group of individuals.[2] As a result, it is more temporary, more insecure, and more subject to negotiation than conventional individualized notions of leadership.[3]

The concept of the leadership constellation (Figure 2.1) expresses the informal power structure that overlaps with, and sits alongside, the formal authority structure. Individuals within the leadership constellation do not form a leadership team in any explicit sense, because the constellation as a whole has no formally defined boundaries or overt identity. The hierarchy within the constellation is opaque to outsiders, as roles and relationships are negotiated between individuals on an ad hoc basis.

1. J.-L. Denis, A. Langley, and V. Sergi. 2012. Leadership in the plural. *Academy of Management Annals* 6: 211–83.
2. J.-L. Denis, L. Lamothe, and A. Langley. 2001. The dynamics of collective leadership and strategic change in pluralistic organizations. *Academy of Management Journal* 44: 809–37.
3. D. S. DeRue and S. J. Ashford. 2010. Who will lead and who will follow? A social process of leadership identity construction in organizations. *Academy of Management Review* 354: 627–47.

This all sounds very ambiguous, and it is—at least to people who are not at the heart of the leadership constellation. The management literature teaches us that ambiguity is a bad thing—a complex problem for leaders to overcome when attempting to pursue collective action.[4] When professionals are sent to business schools they are taught that values must be explicit, strategies clearly defined, budgets specified, and targets set, at an organizational, departmental, and individual level.

Various studies of leadership and change in professional organizations emphasize the 'ugliness' of ambiguity,[5] and the difficulties it represents to professionals who seek to lead them.[6] For example, two studies[7,8] of organizational change in accounting and law firms find that the lack of organizationally prescribed hierarchies makes it difficult to bring about effective change. Similarly studies of leadership in hospitals[9,10] find that ambiguous authority makes it difficult to maintain cohesion within the leadership constellation and to create alignment between the leadership constellation and professionals more generally.

Two other key studies, however, have suggested that ambiguous authority *can* be effective in a professional context. Robertson and Swan[11] examine a consulting firm where demarcations of power are 'extremely fuzzy'. High levels of ambiguity surround roles and power relations, which sustain fluid forms of working and mediate tensions between autonomy and control. Similarly, Cohen and March[12] explore the dysfunctionality of decision making under conditions of 'leadership and ambiguity' in a university setting, but argue that leaders may use this ambiguity to their advantage.

4. P. Jarzabkowski, J. Sillince, and D. Shaw. 2010. Strategic ambiguity as a rhetorical resource for enabling multiple interests. *Human Relations* 63(2): 219–48.
5. M. Alvesson and S. Sveningsson. 2003. Good visions, bad micro-management and ugly ambiguity: Contradictions of non-leadership in a knowledge-intensive organization. *Organization Studies* 24: 961–88.
6. T. Morris, R. Greenwood, and S. Fairclough. 2010. Decision making in professional service firms. In *Handbook of decision making*, ed. P. Nutt and D. Wilson. Chichester: John Wiley & Sons, 275–306.
7. C. R. Hinings, J. Brown, and R. Greenwood. 1991. Change in an autonomous professional organization. *Journal of Management Studies* 28: 376–93.
8. T. Lawrence, N. Malhotra, and T. Morris. 2012. Episodic and systemic power in the transformation of professional service firms. *Journal of Management Studies* 49(1): 102–43.
9. J.-L. Denis, A. Langley, and L. Cazale. 1996. Leadership and strategic change under ambiguity. *Organization Studies* 17: 673–99.
10. Denis, Lamothe, and Langley 2001.
11. M. Robertson and J. Swan. 2003. 'Control—what control?' Culture and ambiguity within a knowledge intensive firm. *Journal of Management Studies* 40(4): 831–58.
12. M. Cohen and J. March. 1974. *Leadership and ambiguity: The American college president*. Boston: Harvard Business Review Press.

Sillince et al.[13] go further, suggesting that ambiguity can be intentionally constructed and continually interpreted by powerful individuals to enable them to achieve their own goals. In other words, they suggest, 'powerful actors can exploit ambiguity'. But who decides who has the power to construct this ambiguity?

Some scholars have stressed that within the leadership constellation, ambiguity can result in rivalry, competition, and conflict, particularly when leaders have similar expertise, power, and roles. To avoid these difficulties individuals should have clearly differentiated, specialized, and complementary roles and responsibilities. This has been most clearly articulated by Hodgson et al.[14] and Denis et al.[15] in their studies of hospital leadership, which present these as necessary preconditions for bringing about change within professional organizations. Other scholars have suggested that even when roles and responsibilities are clearly differentiated, specialized, and complementary, individuals within the leadership constellation may still need to engage in emotional labour in order to create and sustain a productive leadership collaboration.[16] In other words, they have to work very hard to deal with the negative emotions that arise.

Other researchers into plural leadership present a more positive perspective. They articulate a much looser leadership dynamic, based on 'intuitive mutual adjustment'.[17] According to Gronn and Hamilton, who have conducted detailed and wide-ranging research into leadership in educational environments, these kinds of intuitive working relationships reflect the 'unspoken and implicit understandings'[18] that emerge over time as individuals negotiate their leadership roles and power relationships as they gradually evolve into a 'joint working unit'.[19]

13. J. Sillince, P. Jarzabkowski, and D. Shaw. 2012. Shaping strategic action through the rhetorical construction and exploitation of ambiguity. *Organization Science* 23(3): 630–50. See especially p. 647.

14. R. Hodgson, D. Levinson, and A. Zaleznik. 1965. *The executive role constellation*. Boston, MA: Harvard University Press.

15. Denis, Lamothe, and Langley 2001.

16. W. Reid and R. Karambayya. 2009. Impact of dual executive leadership dynamics in creative organizations. *Human Relations* 62(7): 1073–112.

17. Denis, Langley, and Sergi 2012.

18. P. Gronn and A. Hamilton. 2004. 'A bit more life in the leadership': Co-principalship as distributed leadership practice. *Leadership and Policy in Schools* 3(1): 3–35. See especially p. 6.

19. P. Gronn. 2002. Distributed leadership as a unit of analysis. *The Leadership Quarterly* 13: 423–52. See especially p. 430.

Partnerships may be particularly fertile environments for the development of intuitive mutual adjustment. In many partnerships, professionals remain with the same firm for many years and become enmeshed in a network of social relationships, supported by a cohesive set of behavioural norms and values. This phenomenon, of partner relationships deeply enmeshed within a network, is what scholars mean by the term 'social embeddedness'.[20]

Research Study

The research is based on an in-depth case study of an elite professional service organization. The question initially guiding my analysis was: *what are the dynamics and composition of the leadership constellation?* However, as the study was conducted in the immediate aftermath of the global financial crisis of 2008/9, a second question became equally important: *how can a leadership constellation act decisively in response to a crisis?*

The firm is one of the global leaders in its sector, ranking among the largest in terms of revenue and regularly winning industry awards for its outstanding work. In 2009, at the time of the study, it generated approximately US$1500 million in revenue, had approximately 500 partners, and employed approximately 5000 staff, with offices in twenty-five countries.

My initial objective was to identify and analyse the dynamics of the leadership constellation, to understand the leadership constellation in terms of both its formal composition and its informal power structure. I therefore used a 'snowball' method of sampling where I asked interviewees to identify individuals they recognized as part of the leadership constellation. In total I conducted thirty-four formal interviews.

Initially I struggled to achieve clarity, as interviewees found it difficult to articulate the nature of their leadership roles, the authority they had to carry out these roles, and how they interacted with colleagues in similar and overlapping roles. Gradually I recognized that this lack of clarity was in itself a finding and reflected the highly ambiguous composition and authority of the leadership constellation.

In order to map the leadership constellation, I analysed interviewees' statements to identify where they placed themselves within the informal power structure. I focused initially on the nineteen individuals who were consistently

20. M. Granovetter. 1985. Economic action and social structure: the problem of embeddedness. *The American Journal of Sociology* 91(3): 487.

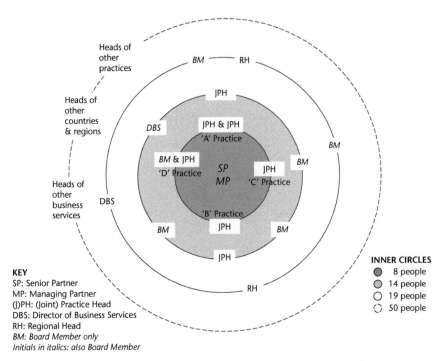

Figure 10.1 Composition of leadership constellation in a professional organization

identified as part of the leadership constellation. I then cross-referenced these statements against other interviewees' comments about their relative position. In seeking to answer my questions, interviewees repeatedly referred back to their recent experience of responding to the global financial crisis. Gradually I was able to identify an informal 'inner circle' of eight leaders who recognized each other as of equivalent significance within the firm (see Figure 10.1).

Once the theme of ambiguity was established, my analysis focused on the interactions of the leadership constellation in that context. Returning to the literature, it became clear that under normal conditions, 'intuitive mutual adjustment' (rather than specialization, differentiation, and complementarity) was the prevailing dynamic, facilitated by social embeddedness within the leadership constellation and the partnership as a whole. However, when confronted with the global financial crisis, a new leadership dynamic emerged as a hierarchy was mobilized within the leadership constellation. I termed this 'deliberate mutual adjustment'. At the final stage of the analysis I developed the model of plural leadership dynamics (see Figure 10.2) which represents how the dynamics of plural leadership change in response to a crisis.

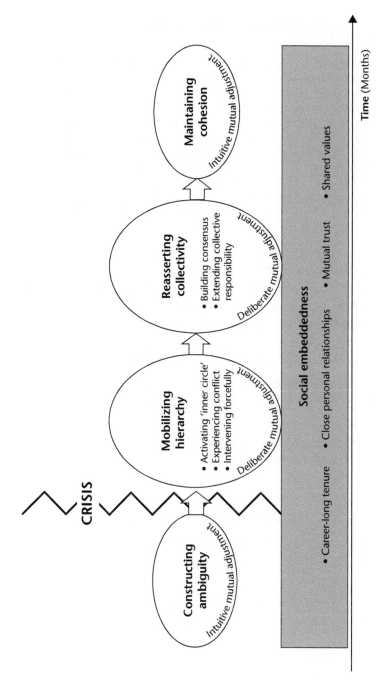

Figure 10.2 Plural leadership dynamics in response to crisis

Constructing Ambiguity

I do think that ambiguity . . . can perform a very, very useful role because it allows for gaps into which pressure can dissipate. If you make everything too rigid, too bureaucratized—'Did you have a mandate for this, did you get the right number of votes for that, is that your responsibility or my responsibility?'—you have to create so many hard lines that it becomes unworkable and also quite destructive as people are always saying: 'I'm worried, am I supposed to be doing that or is somebody else supposed to be doing that?'. . . . And the other advantage of ambiguity is I don't have to decide, and nor does anybody else, who is the real leader. Some people might consider this to be slightly dishonest. It's not meant that way. . . . It's just, you're not forced to make decisions. As soon as you're forced to decisions—'Who's the leader? Tom or Harry? Make your mind up'—you're having to sort of stake something which doesn't need to be staked. (Joint Practice Head)

As described above, in this organization ambiguity characterizes both the composition and interaction of the leadership constellation. This group encompasses the senior executive dyad of Senior and Managing Partners, as well as some of the joint heads of major practices, some members of the Board, and some members of an unofficial 'management team'. They deliberately create overlapping roles and responsibilities and do not attempt to clarify or resolve ambiguities about whether they have the authority to perform these roles. As the lengthy quotation above makes clear, they recognize this ambiguity and are comfortable with it. As a practice head explains:

We have a written constitution, but the way we operate is not what is reflected in the constitution. . . . I don't know why we are like this but I do think it's one of our strengths. (Joint Practice Head)

Senior Executive Dyad

The Global Senior and Managing Partners are elected by the partnership for a five-year term. As a draft governance document[21] explains, their roles are not defined or distinguished:

In practice, there is no strict demarcation between the roles as currently carried out—in fact there is considerable overlap. This reflects the consensual nature of

---

21. This has never been formally adopted as part of the Partnership Agreement but remains the clearest statement of roles and responsibilities for the senior executive dyad.

our partnership decision-making processes, the need for each to be available for decision making when the other is away, the interlocking nature of many of the issues, and the close personal working relationships. (Draft Note on Senior Partner and Managing Partner Roles)

This ambiguity is amplified by the fact that, however they define their roles, neither the Senior nor Managing Partner has formal constitutional authority to perform them.

As a Senior Partner or Managing Partner, we have absolutely no constitutional power whatsoever.... there is nothing in the Partnership Agreement which says 'you can do this' or 'you have powers to do that'. (Senior Partner)

In responding to the question, 'Who's in charge?' (see the opening of Chapter 5), the Managing Partner states: 'I think it's the two of us actually. We rarely disagree. It's instinctive.' The Senior and Managing Partners acknowledge the ambiguity inherent in their leadership dyad but find it easy to deal with.

Other individuals within the leadership constellation see the Senior Partner as 'clearly the leader' but recognize that the Senior and Managing Partners 'merge very happily across the boundaries'. As a practice head describes it:

I sort of suspect [the Senior Partner] is the overall boss but it's difficult to say what issues you'd go to [the Managing Partner] with and what issues you'd go to [the Senior Partner] with.... I think they cross over all the time. (Joint Practice Head)

Joint Heads of Major Practices

In interviews, the heads of the four major practices[22] often struggle to remember their official titles; there are multiple permutations of Chairs and Managing and Senior Partners. As the Senior Partner explains: 'We always end up fudging these things because nobody wants any grand titles.' Each of the four major practices has at least two joint practice heads. These dyads arise on an ad hoc basis for various reasons and are configured in various ways. According to a joint practice head:

---

22. There are twenty-two practices in total but interviewees state that only four are considered major, though they are never formally designated as such.

> We shape the roles around the individuals available. It's our tradition. . . . Each
> practice has a different tradition. . . . It's a fascinating process because there is no
> process. (Joint Practice Head)

Again, as with the Senior and Managing Partners, the construction of this
shared role space is characterized by ambiguity. When asked how these
dyads have arisen, interviewees explain: sometimes 'well it emerges, frankly',
sometimes the Senior and Managing Partners take soundings among the
partnership to establish a consensus, and sometimes a formal election is held.
Sometimes two rival candidates decide to share the role.

At the time of the study one of the major practices had three leaders. This
was because, following the election of a new leadership dyad, the incumbent
was unwilling to step down so the newly elected leaders created a new role
of Chair for him. Once again interviewees emphasize the ambiguity and
their tendency to 'muddy the waters'.

Board

The Board consists of nine people. Most are elected by the partnership and
a few are co-opted by the Senior and Managing Partners to ensure that a
fair cross-section of partners is represented. The Senior and Managing
Partners also serve on the Board, together with the Finance and Human
Resources Directors. The Board has defined its formal role to include
acting as a 'check and balance on the executive team',[23] but its oversight
function is ambiguous since the executive team is not defined and many
elected Board members also perform significant executive roles. As one
practice head explains:

> We have people who are on the Board who are also sort of heads of the
> practices or otherwise heavily involved in managing their practices. Now
> I don't think that matters, I don't see that matters at all, because it's all a
> question of influencers and informal structures. (Joint Practice Head)

Very little is recorded in terms of formal governance arrangements, and
anyway 'none of it operates the way it's written down'. Once again interviewees see this blurring of roles and responsibilities as unproblematic.

---

23. Annual Report of the Board to Partners (2008/9).

'management team'

The final element of the leadership constellation is the 'management team' (a lower case 'm' and 't' are used deliberately within the organization to reflect the unofficial nature of this body).[24] As the Senior Partner explains:

> There was a concern among Board members that setting up an Executive Committee formally would usurp the perceived power of the Board. . . . So we had to call it a 'management team', which is basically the same thing but without the Executive Committee tag, so that everyone could get comfortable with the idea. (Senior Partner)

The management team is selected by the Managing Partner and convened on an ad hoc basis at his discretion. Its composition is fluid and ambiguous. Up to fifty people (see Figure 10.1), including partners in management roles and business services staff, are invited to attend meetings if the agenda is deemed appropriate. One interviewee recalls an occasion when the full management team was accidentally invited to a meeting of a subset of the management team:

> I think why we have this confusion around the management team, who's in it and who's really important, is because we can't quite bring ourselves to say, 'Actually you're small fry in the general scheme of things,' because 'He's my partner, he is my equal.' So that's where we fudge things and we have lots of distribution lists and then things go wrong and there's an embarrassment and everybody gets a bit cross. (Partnership Secretary)

Intuitive Mutual Adjustment

The prevailing behavioural dynamic within the leadership constellation is 'intuitive mutual adjustment'. As the Managing Partner says of his relationship with the Senior Partner: 'it's instinctive'. Another interviewee states: 'They instinctively feel broadly the same about important decisions.' A joint practice head echoes this dynamic when talking about his interactions with his co-leader:

> It's a very easy relationship. We're on a very similar wavelength. We seem to be able to anticipate what each other will think on things. . . . It feels quite easy. (Joint Practice Head)

---

24. The Partnership Agreement includes provision for an Executive Committee but this has never been established formally.

What exactly then does 'intuitive mutual adjustment' mean in practice?[25] In this firm it takes the form of two distinct sets of behaviours: *building consensus / creating collective responsibility* and *avoiding conflict / maintaining harmony*.

Even though intuitive mutual adjustment may 'feel quite easy', it still requires considerable effort. It takes time to build consensus. Once consensus has been reached among the leadership constellation, the leaders commit to supporting each other when interacting with other partners. According to the COO, the understanding is: 'Back me up in public even when I'm wrong and then we can chat about it privately afterwards.' As a practice head says:

> I think it's part of our DNA, that you can have your say in the privacy of the meeting room. . . . But once the decision is made, the implicit bargain is that you don't undermine a decision. (Joint Practice Head)

While building consensus and creating collective responsibility, the leaders also strive to avoid conflict and maintain harmony. As the Senior Partner explains:

> I'm the sort of person who tends to try and find a consensus and build a sort of sense of harmony because I find it such a waste of time for people to be knocking great chunks out of each other all the time. (Senior Partner)

When conflicts do arise, colleagues try to resolve them peaceably, or avoid discussions altogether in order to maintain harmony.

> There is a sort of gentlemanly approach to resolving conflict, there's a bit of 'Let's not go there, we'll gradually sort it out and it will gradually get better.' (HR Director)

Interviewees repeatedly cite the advantages of ambiguity as a means of maintaining harmony and avoiding conflict, as exemplified by the lengthy quotation at the start of this section.

Social Embeddedness

The desire to avoid conflict and maintain harmony reflects the fact that most partners remain at the firm for their entire careers. As one interviewee explains:

---

25. Chapter 5 identified the phenomenon of 'intuitive collaboration' within a leadership dyad. The term 'intuitive mutual adjustment' reflects the additional complexity and effort involved in working within a larger leadership group.

People are conscious, 'Well, you know I'm going to be your partner for thirty
years and if I have a row with you now it's going to damage our relationship
for the next five years when we should be working together.' (Finance
Director)

This last quote provides a clue to why this intuitive mutual adjustment
works. The leadership constellation embodies high levels of social embeddedness which derives from four characteristics of the partnership. These
are: *career-long tenure, close personal relationships, shared values*, and *mutual trust*.
Some of the partners attended the same university together and have
worked their way up through the ranks of the firm over the past twenty-
five years.

As a result, 'people have very close friendships within this firm'. The
Senior Partner and Managing Partner are 'good mates', or 'great friends',
even choosing to take a week's sporting holiday together every year,
together with fellow partners. Similarly, two joint practice heads describe
colleagues with whom they share responsibility for running their practices in
the following terms:

He and I are very good friends. We both see the world in many of the same
ways. (Joint Practice Head)

The reason it works for me and him is that we've worked with each other for
years and years and years. We like each other. We share the same values and we
find the same things amusing by and large. (Joint Practice Head)

The close personal relationships and the years of working together have
helped create shared values among the leadership constellation. As an
interviewee explains:

You can say, 'That's a [Firm] thing to do and that's not a [Firm] thing to do'
and everybody that's been elected to the Board is very much in the [Firm]
mould. (Partnership Secretary)

These shared values, close personal relationships, and career-long tenure
within the leadership constellation bring with them high levels of interpersonal trust. Interviewees talk in terms of their 'incredibly trusting relationships'. They most frequently refer to trust in the context of the Senior
Partner, who was elected by the partnership as a whole and is therefore an
important embodiment of the firm and its values.

This high level of social embeddedness among the partners in general, and
the leadership constellation in particular, creates the conditions in which

intuitive mutual adjustment can operate highly effectively in the context of high levels of ambiguity. As one interviewee states: 'Partners like to carry the idea of a partnership as a kind of band of happy brothers.' However, this ideal of 'brotherhood', of close personal friendships and mutual trust, of intuitive mutual adjustment and ambiguity, means that it is particularly difficult for the leadership constellation to act decisively when faced with an existential threat to the organization.

Mobilizing Hierarchy

[The Senior Partner] managed to bring a tricky group of people to unity. . . .
The way he executed the delivery was exemplary. It was his finest hour.
(Board Member)

In the autumn of 2008 the collapse of Lehman Brothers and the ensuing global financial crisis created a significant and sustained threat to one of the firm's core areas of business so that income and profits were likely to deteriorate dramatically. Partner drawings (i.e. salary plus profit share) represented a substantial component of the cost base. However, the Board had no authority to compel an unprofitable partner to leave without a full vote of the partnership; there was no facility within the Partnership Agreement to reduce an underperforming partner's share of the profits. The firm had never before undertaken a large-scale restructuring of the partnership.

A large-scale reduction in the number of partners threatened the social cohesion of the partnership as a whole. Partners would either be asked to prematurely curtail their career-long tenure or vote to expel individuals with whom they had long-standing and close personal friendships. In such an environment, it was difficult to see how the shared values and mutual trust could be sustained.

In spite of these restrictions, within five months the Senior and Managing Partners had announced that 10 per cent of partners would be asked to leave and a further 7 per cent would be asked to accept a reduction in their profit share. The following analysis shows how the leaders used the cloak of ambiguity to exercise considerable informal authority, and mobilized a hidden hierarchy which enabled them to take decisive action.

Activating Inner Circle

At the start of November 2008, the Senior Partner called an informal and highly confidential meeting of eight people to discuss the firm's response to the global financial crisis. This group (the inner circle of Figure 10.1) included some, but not all, of the joint heads of the four major practices and some, but not all, of the Board. As the Senior Partner explains:

> Neither [the Managing Partner] nor I believed we had all the answers. . . . We wanted to get the best minds round the table giving it their best shot. . . . It was a collective process of sharing thoughts and ideas. (Senior Partner)

Already, by seeking the views of those they perceived to be the 'best minds', and by not informing others of this meeting, the Managing and Senior Partner were revealing a hidden hierarchy within the leadership constellation. They recognized that ambiguous authority, which had previously worked 'fine', now represented a major difficulty in dealing with the crisis. In terms of a potential restructuring of the partnership, a practice head recalls:

> The big concern was how you actually get this done, because there's no constitutional power to do this unless you go out for a partnership vote. There was a strong view that we needed to avoid a vote because that would be divisive. (Joint Practice Head)

The Board meeting at the beginning of December agreed that the Managing Partner and Finance Director should commence formal contingency planning. Already a shift in the pattern of interaction was beginning to emerge—intuitive mutual adjustment within the extended leadership constellation was giving way to a more deliberate dynamic of mutual adjustment amongst a subset of individuals within the leadership constellation.

The Managing Partner and Finance Director worked throughout the Christmas and New Year holidays, analysing performance data and developing a list of partners for 'restructuring'.

Experiencing Conflict

At the January Board meeting the proposal was rejected. Board members objected strongly to the process by which partners from their own practices had been selected. They argued forcefully for a comprehensive review of *all* partners by *all* the major practice heads, using a formally defined set of criteria to ensure fairness, consistent with the partnership's values. The Board's forthright rejection of the Managing Partner and Finance Director's proposal denoted an increased willingness to experience conflict within the leadership constellation.

Selected practice heads worked together over several weeks to develop and revise the list of partners for restructuring. They repeatedly challenged and rejected each other's lists of partners and justified and revised their own. They came into direct conflict with each other.

> We had some open fights about people. We disagreed with each other but there was very little game-playing. (Joint Practice Head)

This lengthy process of consensus building, during a time of rapidly deteriorating financial performance, was deemed necessary to establish collective responsibility for a decision that would present a fundamental threat to the social embeddedness of the partnership.

The Senior and Managing Partners did not attend these meetings, believing that they should allow the practice heads to lead the process and resolve conflicts among themselves. However, consistent with the emerging pattern of deliberate mutual adjustment, the Senior and Managing Partners worked behind the scenes, speaking to each practice head privately and 'putting pressure on us individually as to whether we had gone far enough' (Practice Head). They never specified a target number for the restructuring but, according to the Senior Partner:

> My gut feel was around about 10 per cent was kind of the minimum you had to deliver for people to say, 'That's probably enough.' . . . If we'd done 5 per cent I think a lot of people would have said, 'Bloody hell, I'm probably next.' (Senior Partner)

Intervening Forcefully

The major practice heads proposed that only 5 per cent of partners be asked to leave. The Managing Partner describes one of the later meetings that he attended with the Senior Partner:

> Within the meeting room we really had to push—'Well, this is not enough, this is not enough.' But as soon as we had an agreement, the list got shorter— and within two days the list was down to 5 per cent again. . . . We had to go back to them several times and say, 'This is not enough.' (Managing Partner)

Towards the end of January, the Senior and Managing Partners became progressively more directive in their interventions, recognizing that the practice heads were unwilling to remove partners they had worked closely with for many years. As a Board member recalls:

> [The Managing Partner] got extremely forceful about this. At one famous meeting, he threatened to resign. (Board Member)

Reasserting Collectivity

> It was quite important to me to feel like someone was challenging the decisions we were coming up with.... You always wonder whether you're doing the right thing. (Joint Practice Head)

During the early stages of the crisis, the Senior and Managing Partners revealed and mobilized hierarchy by activating the inner circle. Once this inner circle had reached an agreement about the scale and scope of the restructuring, the Senior and Managing Partners sought to reassert collectivity by expanding the number of people involved in the decision.

Building Consensus

At the February Board the Senior and Managing Partners presented a proposed list of eighty-five partners (17 per cent of the partnership); approximately 10 per cent would be asked to leave and 7 per cent would be asked to accept a reduction in equity. Those Board members who had not been involved in drawing up the list challenged the eighty-five names, one by one. In the process, they were building consensus. According to a practice head:

> The core group didn't make any formal decisions; the Board made the decisions. Our group was merely making the proposal. (Joint Practice Head)

Once the decision was taken, it was important to build consensus more widely so that the partnership would accept their decision. As the Senior Partner explains:

> The most difficult thing in asking a partner to leave is not the conversation you have with that partner. It's the conversation you have with all the other partners who may not understand that decision, or worse, may violently object to it. (Senior Partner)

Extending Collective Responsibility

The Senior and Managing Partner worked systematically to extend collective responsibility. In the week preceding the announcement, they held private meetings with selected partners whom they had identified as having sufficient influence among the partnership to be capable of mobilizing opposition. By the end of this process, fifty partners (i.e. 10 per cent of the partnership) had been co-opted into the restructuring decision. The rest of the partners remained unaware; complete confidentiality had been maintained throughout the four months of deliberations.

A partner conference call was scheduled for 1:00 p.m. on 15 February 2009. In the hours leading up to the call, the major practice heads (working in pairs) spoke to each of the fifty partners who were to be asked to leave, offering them a substantial compensation package. The 500 partners around the world dialled into a conference call to hear the Senior and Managing Partners announce the restructuring and explain the process by which individual partners had been selected and informed. They emailed questions throughout the announcement.

The call lasted an hour (the notes provided afterwards, including the questions and responses, came to 5000 words). Between 2:00 p.m. and 4:00 p.m., the major practice heads contacted thirty-five further partners and asked them to accept a reduction in their partnership equity. At 4:00 p.m. the Senior and Managing Partners sent a personal email to all remaining partners notifying them that they were not directly affected by the restructuring. Ultimately all 'restructured' partners accepted the packages they had been offered.

Maintaining Cohesion

People recognized that something had to be done . . . and that it had to be done by a tight group and rolled out very quickly. Because as soon as you start talking to one person in a partnership all of a sudden all the partners know about it. (Board Member)

The leadership constellation had acted decisively to take an unprecedented action, without the authority to do so. According to interviewees, the partners accepted the decision for two main reasons: they could see no other way to stem the decline in profits and, as a result of the meticulous process of analysis, the 'right' partners had been selected (i.e. not them).

> At the end of the day most people did not disagree with the names of the people we had chosen. That was the acid test. People weren't really that surprised. (Senior Partner)

In spite of losing 10 per cent of the 'brotherhood', cohesion was maintained within the partnership and the partners remained supportive of the leadership constellation. But what about cohesion within the leadership constellation, now that the hidden hierarchy had been revealed?

Interviewees explain that, following the restructuring, they are now aware that an 'inner circle' exists within the leadership constellation. This inner circle is also referred to by interviewees as the 'inner core', 'inner group', 'core group', 'group of barons', 'group of cardinals', and the 'shadow leadership' who 'wield an enormous amount of power'. Reflecting the ambiguity that still prevails within the leadership constellation, the inner circle's existence is unofficial and its composition is contested, even among individuals within the leadership constellation. According to the Senior Partner:

> There's probably an inner core of leaders which is about fifteen, yes, something like that, and then there's an outer core which is probably around another ten or twelve people, something like that. (Senior Partner)

Other interviewees see the inner circle as no more than eight people, based on their observations of who is invited by the Senior and Managing Partners to key meetings (and who is excluded) and whose opinion the Senior and Managing Partners seek at the earliest stage about the most sensitive issues (and who they consult at a later stage). As one practice head describes it:

> I would say there's sort of the inner group. There's one or two from [A] practice, me from [B] practice, one from [C] practice. This is quite sensitive; I wouldn't pass this on to anybody. I don't know whether this is accidental or on purpose but I think it's on purpose. There's [the Senior Partner], there's [the Managing Partner], then probably two from [D] practice. The other head of [B] practice is not included. . . . The group doesn't include the other head of [A] practice, and didn't include my predecessor in [B] practice. (Joint Practice Head)

Certain individuals see themselves as part of the inner circle but are not recognized as such by others in this group (i.e. they are part of the group of 'about fifteen' that the Senior Partner refers to who are not aware of the smaller group of eight). As a result, all involved in the plural leadership dynamics of the firm are able to maintain the illusion that 'He's my partner, he is my equal'. This ambiguity is integral to maintaining cohesion within the larger group.

Conclusions: Power and Ambiguity

This chapter has explained how leaders of a professional organization can act decisively when they have no authority to do so. Unlike the mergers in Chapter 9, the leaders in this case were dealing with an externally induced crisis. The crisis, in effect, confers authority on the leaders—the 'burning platform' gives them power they would otherwise lack. Faced with a steady, organization-specific decline in profitability rather than a precipitous, industry-wide collapse, they would have had to adopt a much more consultative approach to partner restructuring.

A contingency-based perspective on leadership emphasizes that different conditions require different kinds of leaders. Individuals rarely have the flexibility to change their leadership styles, and will certainly struggle to change them quickly. So, when conditions change dramatically, the composition of the leadership team will likely need to change also. This case is particularly notable, therefore, for the speed with which the prevailing dynamic of the leadership constellation changes—from intuitive mutual adjustment to deliberate mutual adjustment, and back again—and the fact that the same individuals are involved throughout.

This is a potential advantage of the leadership dyad and leadership constellation. Professional organizations are not dependent on a single leader, with his or her inherent limitations, but can utilize a portfolio of leaders, each with their own distinct capabilities and perspectives. This can be a recipe for conflict and chaos but, when plurality is harnessed effectively, it can provide the flexibility and resilience needed to steer a professional organization through tumultuous times.

This flexibility is all the more notable in view of the high levels of social embeddedness within the leadership constellation. Most of the protagonists in this case have spent their entire careers in the firm. They have 'grown up' within a highly ambiguous authority structure, and operated highly successfully within it. They have no incentive to change it—quite the contrary. However, this raises questions about the ability of 'outsiders' within the organization to exercise power. They will probably struggle to make sense of all that is not written down but intuitively understood by those who are at the centre of the organization's informal power dynamics.

Whereas scholars have written about 'ugly ambiguity' in professional organizations, this case can be seen as an example of 'beautiful ambiguity'. It is that ambiguity which ultimately enables the Managing and Senior Partners to address and resolve the crisis facing the firm. Lacking formal authority, the senior executive dyad is nevertheless able to mobilize and utilize informal power under the cloak of ambiguity.

One thing is particularly ambiguous—the composition of the leadership constellation—unsurprising, since the leadership constellation is by definition informal and opaque. Returning to the depiction of power relations among the leadership constellation in Figure 10.1, where exactly is the leadership constellation? Power clearly lies at the centre with the Senior and Managing Partners, and radiates out from them. But what is to be made of the fact that the Senior Partner believes the firm is run by a group of 'about fifteen' (i.e. the two concentric circles at the centre of Figure 10.1), whereas several interviewees perceive there to be an inner circle of eight? To return to a question posed at the start of this chapter: who gets to decide who is, and who is not, part of the leadership constellation?

The most likely explanation for these differing perceptions is that the leadership constellation is fluid—it takes different forms in response to different issues, expanding, contracting, and shape-shifting according to the issue at hand. A politically skilled leader will understand this, and understand how to manoeuvre around these shifting patterns of power to maximize the contribution of a range of professionals within the leadership constellation.

The concept of the leadership constellation can be useful also to professionals who are outside the inner circle of power. Outsider status is not always obvious to those who possess it, since insiders are sometimes reluctant to draw attention to their privileged position. The concept can, therefore, help outsiders recognize their position, sensitize them to shifting patterns of power, help them predict and interpret these shifts, and work out how to interpose themselves into the power dynamics of the leadership constellation.

One final important reflection remains. In a book about plural leadership and a chapter about the leadership constellation, the importance of the individual in the plural comes through clearly. Though all professionals within the leadership constellation play their part in the process, it is the Senior Partner ultimately who constructs and directs it, unobtrusively working one-to-one with other individuals, judging when to delegate authority, when to exercise autonomy, and when to assert control. This ability to understand how to shift the leadership constellation from intuitive to directive mutual adjustment and back again, to know when to contract and when to expand the leadership constellation, displays highly sophisticated political skills. And, as Chapter 3 has emphasized, the greatest political skill is being able to do all this whilst appearing apolitical.

PART IV

Conclusions

I I

Paradoxes of Leading Professionals

From Unstable to Dynamic Equilibrium

Introduction

At one point I was thinking of calling this book *Leading Professionals: Power, Politics, Prima Donnas, and Paradoxes*, but I decided that was one 'P' too many. Nevertheless, the theme of paradox has run throughout the book, albeit implicitly. This concluding chapter makes the theme of paradox explicit by drawing together multiple strands of argument contained in each of the chapters.

Paradox in Organizations

Conventional studies of leadership emphasize the importance of choosing between competing demands, pursuing a singular vision, communicating with precision, and providing followers with clear and measurable goals. Paradox theory represents a very different approach, focusing instead on how leaders can, and indeed should, help their colleagues to recognize and respond to simultaneously contradictory demands.

In recent years, paradox theory has developed into a particularly intriguing and influential body of management research.[1] Within this strand of literature,

---

1. J. Schad, M. W. Lewis, S. Raisch, and W. K. Smith. 2016. Paradox research in management science: Looking back to move forward. *The Academy of Management Annals* 10(1): 5–64.

the concept of paradox has a precise definition.[2] A paradox comprises two or more elements that are inherently contradictory, interrelated, simultaneous, and persistent. The concept of paradox is therefore similar to, but a more challenging form of, concepts such as tensions, dualities, and dialectics.

Paradox theory emphasizes that because paradoxes are inherently irresolvable, leaders should not waste time and resources seeking to eliminate them. Instead leaders should learn to distinguish between tensions and paradoxes, to consider how to resolve the tensions and how to accommodate the paradoxes. Leaders should disentangle the paradoxical elements to enable them to be separately understood. They should examine how the elements are interconnected and seek to exploit their synergies. And leaders should encourage their colleagues to do the same, helping them to live with the confusion and insecurity which paradoxes can engender and recognize the opportunities which they potentially represent.[3]

In doing this, paradox theory argues, leaders are constructing a dynamic equilibrium. They are recognizing that their organizations will contain many opposing forces which are in constant flux, and that the resulting tensions can be constructive rather than destructive. In a simple equilibrium, the prevailing condition is stasis. In an unstable equilibrium, a small change in one element can destabilize the rest. By contrast, in a dynamic equilibrium, the 'steady state' is constant flux and continuous adaptation is required to accommodate the opposing forces which are constantly at work within it.

Ten Paradoxes in Professional Organizations

So this is why leading a professional organization is sometimes bewildering and frequently exhausting. Leaders sit at the fulcrum of a dynamic equilibrium which incorporates ten distinct paradoxes.

1. Autonomy and Control

Chapter 2 argued that the peculiar challenges of leading professionals derive from two interrelated organizational characteristics which coexist in constant

2. W. K. Smith and M. W. Lewis. 2011. Toward a theory of paradox: A dynamic equilibrium model of organizing. *Academy of Management Review* 36(2): 381–403.
3. W. K. Smith, M. W. Lewis, and M. Tushman. 2016. 'Both/and' leadership: Don't worry so much about being consistent. *Harvard Business Review* 94 (May): 63–70.

dynamic tension. These are: extensive autonomy and contingent authority. To some extent, leaders in any organization lead only by the consent of their colleagues—authority is always somewhat contingent. What makes professional organizations different is professionals' expectations of autonomy. Within some professional organizations, professional autonomy may be no more than a mythical relic of a bygone era, yet leaders still need to be seen to honour that relic. They must seek always to accommodate the paradox of autonomy and control. Social controls, where professionals experience control as self-chosen, make it possible to address and partially resolve the autonomy–control paradox. However, social control comes at the expense of potentially cult-like conformity, which creates a different set of challenges (see Chapter 6).

2. Reluctance and Ambition

As Chapter 3 explained, leaders who have reached the very top of a professional organization generally need to have displayed a degree of reluctance to take on a leadership role because their colleagues will hesitate to elect someone who seems overly eager to exercise power over them. This reluctance is entirely logical. Leaders are obliged to move away from their first love of fee-earning work to take on a role which confers considerable responsibility and relatively little authority. But the question remains: how can someone who is not personally ambitious for leadership end up leading a professional organization? Leaders need to persuade their colleagues that they are not personally ambitious for the role but are ambitious for the organization—that they have a vision of how much greater the organization can become (under their leadership). In so doing they are also encouraging colleagues to become more ambitious, both for themselves and for their organization.

3. Political and Apolitical Leadership

Chapter 3 presented another paradox. A professional organization can be highly politicized, while its politics are denied and obscured under an apolitical veneer. Professional organizations are infused with day-to-day political practices. Leaders, therefore, need to be highly politically skilled, able to engage routinely in complex political behaviours whilst never being seen to do so. This collective denial of politics may appear naive or disingenuous but is in fact highly functional. If politics becomes too visible, if everyone starts doing politics deliberately and systematically, a professional organization will collapse under the byzantine complexities of instrumental deal-making and double-dealing. Ultimately the ability to wear their politics lightly separates the most effective leaders of professional organizations from those who merely occupy leadership roles.

4. Individual and Collective Interests

Chapter 4 explained how professional organizations embody two sets of potentially contradictory interests: the interests of professionals as individuals and the interests of professionals as a collective. Leaders of professional organizations can address these paradoxical interests to some extent by identifying and articulating a set of collective interests around which professionals can coalesce. In the process, leaders can exert power indirectly. The ultimate power of leaders is the construction of organizational narratives and 'the management of meaning'.[4] One of the key roles of leaders is to embody the narrative of their organizations and, in the process, to control that narrative. However, if leaders of professional organizations wish to remain legitimate, their attempts to define the interests of the collective can never stray too far from organizational reality.

5. Harmony and Conflict

Chapter 5 emphasized the conflict inherent in professional organizations. Leaders need to embody and express this conflict, and seek to resolve it. In so doing they strive to create and preserve harmony. Yet the inherent and persistent nature of conflict within professional organizations means that harmony is inherently fleeting. Conflict will return as new challenges arise and old resentments resurface. Effective leaders need to enter into organizational conflict again and again, without being worn down by it, and without becoming consumed and distracted by interpersonal conflict.

---

4. L. Smircich and G. Morgan. 1982. Leadership: The management of meaning. *Journal of Applied Behavioral Science* 18(3): 257–73.

6. Insecurity and Confidence

Clients want their professionals to be confident—to offer clear and convincing advice with authority that is grounded in deep expertise and extensive experience. The more elite the professional organization, the higher the fees charged and the greater the clients' expectations of being served by self-confident professionals. Yet, as Chapter 6 explained, elite professional organizations deliberately recruit insecure individuals, and amplify and exploit their insecurities as they develop into high-functioning professionals. Taken to extremes this can have troubling consequences, not just for the individuals and organizations, but for clients and society, as it can result in untrammelled competitiveness and unethical behaviour. Leaders are responsible for ensuring this does not happen.

7. Commercial and Professional Priorities

Chapter 7 explained how leaders of professional organizations turn to outsiders to help them professionalize management. In the process, management professionals gain considerable power and help to ensure that their organization develops a stronger focus on commercial priorities. But if a professional organization is to survive and thrive, this cannot be done at the expense of professional priorities. Management professionals typically come from outside the profession and are not infused with the same professional priorities as their fee-earning colleagues—'professional' may mean something slightly different to them. Professional priorities are not simply about delighting the client but about challenging the client, not simply about creating a consistent quality of service but about enabling professionals to think for themselves. Leaders, therefore, need to ensure that commercial priorities do not override professional priorities.

8. Centralized Power and Distributed Leadership

Chapter 8 emphasized how, as professional organizations grow and mature, power shifts around them. It is initially highly centralized with the original founders, then more widely distributed among senior professionals, then delegated to a smaller group of individuals in leadership roles. But this does not mean that leadership itself must become centralized—quite the contrary.

As a professional organization grows, more professionals need to come to see themselves as leaders. The emphasis on individual autonomy privileges the rights of those who own or at least control access to key resources. The risk is that, as senior professionals delegate authority to a small number of colleagues in leadership roles, they become focused on their rights at the expense of their responsibilities. Ultimately, the responsibility for leadership resides with the senior professionals as whole.

9. Active and Passive Leadership

Chapter 9 presented a challenge to conventional views of leadership as action-oriented and initiative-taking. Instead it emphasized the importance, sometimes, of doing nothing. Leaders may instigate and encourage, but should allow space for other professionals to pursue, adopt, and implement. This more passive approach may prevent a backlash against unpopular initiatives. When professionals start to complain about a leadership vacuum, this is a sign that they are granting their leaders the authority to act. Knowing how to create and when to exploit the leadership vacuum is a matter of fine judgement, as one organization's leadership vacuum represents another organization's opportunity.

10. Ambiguity and Clarity

This brings us back full circle to paradox theory. Whereas conventional models of leadership emphasize the role of leaders in creating clarity, paradox theory emphasizes how leaders should help colleagues to cope more effectively with ambiguity. Chapter 10 emphasized the functional role that ambiguity can play in professional organizations. Ambiguity may be all-pervasive—entrenched in the systems and structures of governance, and the practices and processes of leadership. Ambiguity can become the cloak under which leaders exercise authority. Leaders, therefore, need to recognize when to create clarity and when to amplify ambiguity.

And Finally . . .

I often give speeches to audiences of professionals. Afterwards, professionals like to approach the conference platform and ask me for advice. They present a brief summary of their problem and ask me to tell them the answer. The academic in me is unsettled when someone asks me a question that I cannot answer and I am always conscious of the other professionals waiting to speak to me. I am tempted to offer each professional a superficial answer, to make myself look good, and to send them away satisfied. I try to discipline myself not to do this.

This book has not attempted to provide *the* answer to questions of leadership in professional organizations because there is no simple answer. Instead my aim has been to help readers (practitioners and academics alike) to ask better questions, to see familiar phenomena with greater clarity, and to think more rigorously about how to discover the answers for themselves.

In studying professional organizations, I seek always to discover and uncover that which is unknown, obscured, and repressed. I believe that, too often, these hidden things create confusion, inhibit communication, and provoke conflict. By revealing and explaining these phenomena I aim to shine a light on the darker recesses of organizational life, so that professionals and academics alike can recognize and cherish that which is good, and challenge and change that which is bad.

I hope this book has challenged some of your assumptions, inspired you to develop insights of your own, and encouraged you to bring these insights to fruition. Whether you are an academic or a practitioner, this is where leadership begins.

Bibliography

Adler, P. S., Kwon, S. W., and Heckscher, C. 2008. Professional work: The emergence of collaborative community. *Organization Science* 19(2): 359–76.

Aguilera, R. and Jackson, G. 2010. Comparative and international corporate governance. *Academy of Management Annals* 4(1): 485–556.

Alvarez, J. and Svejenova, S. 2005. *Sharing executive power: Roles and relationships at the top.* Cambridge: Cambridge University Press.

Alvesson, M. 2001. Knowledge work: Ambiguity, image, and identity. *Human Relations* 54(7): 863–86.

Alvesson, M. and Empson, L. 2008. The construction of organizational identity: Comparative case studies of consulting firms. *Scandinavian Journal of Management* 24(1): 1–16.

Alvesson, M. and Sveningsson, S. 2003. Good visions, bad micro-management and ugly ambiguity: Contradictions of non-leadership in a knowledge-intensive organization. *Organization Studies* 24: 961–88.

Ammeter, A. P., Douglas, C., Gardner, W. L., Hochwarter, W. A., and Ferris, G. R. 2002. Toward a political theory of leadership. *The Leadership Quarterly* 13: 751–96.

Andersen, J. A. 2008. An organization called Harry. *Journal of Organizational Change Management* 21(2): 174–87.

Anderson-Gough, F., Grey, C., and Robson, K. 1998. *Making up accountants: The organizational and professional socialization of trainee chartered accountants.* Aldershot: Ashgate Publishing.

Anderson-Gough, F., Grey, C., and Robson, K. 2000. In the name of the client: The service ethic in two professional services firms. *Human Relations* 53: 1151–74.

Angel, T. 2007. Sustaining partnership in the 21st century: The global law firm experience. In *Managing the modern law firm: New challenges, new perspectives*, ed. L. Empson. Oxford: Oxford University Press, 196–217.

Angwin, D. N. 2004. Speed in M&A integration: The first 100 days. *European Management Journal* 22(4): 418–30.

Angwin, D. N. and Meadows, M. 2015. New integration strategies for post-acquisition management. *Long-Range Planning* 48(4) August: 235–51.

Arikan, A. M. 2004. Does it pay to capture intangible assets through mergers and acquisitions? In *Mergers and acquisitions: Creating integrative knowledge*, ed. A. L. Pablo and M. Javidan. Oxford: Blackwell, 156–80.

Augur, P. 2000. *The death of gentlemanly capitalism*. London: Penguin.

Battilana, J., Leca, B., and Boxenbaum, E. 2009. How actors change institutions: Towards a theory of institutional entrepreneurship. *Academy of Management Annals* 3: 65–107.

Berglas, S. 2006. How to keep 'A' players productive. *Harvard Business Review* 84(9) September: 1–9.

Blake, R. and Mouton, J. 1964. *The managerial grid: The key to leadership excellence*. Houston: Gulf Publishing Co.

Bligh, M. C., Kohles, J. C., and Pillai, R. 2011. Romancing leadership: Past, present, and future. *The Leadership Quarterly* 22: 1058–77.

Bower, M. 1997. *Will to lead: Running a business with a network of leaders*. Boston, MA: Harvard Business School Press.

Broschak, J. 2015. Client relationships in professional service firms. In *The Oxford handbook of professional service firms*, ed. L. Empson, D. Muzio, J. Broschak, and B. Hinings. Oxford: Oxford University Press, 304–26.

Carsten, M. K., Uhl-Bien, M., West, B. J., Patera, J. L., and McGregor, R. 2010. Exploring social constructions of followership: A qualitative study. *The Leadership Quarterly* 21: 543–62.

Cartwright, S. and Cooper, C. L. 1992. *Mergers and acquisitions: The human factor*. Oxford: Butterworth Heinemann.

Chreim, S. 2015. The (non)distribution of leadership roles: Considering leadership practices and configurations. *Human Relations* 68: 517–43.

Clance, P. and Imes, S. 1978. The imposter phenomenon in high-achieving women: Dynamics and therapeutic intervention. *Psychotherapy: Theory, Research and Practice* 15(3): 241–7.

Clarke, C., Knights, D., and Jarvis, C. 2012. A labour of love? Academics in business schools. *Scandinavian Journal of Management* 28(1): 5–15.

Cohen, M. and March, J. 1974. *Leadership and ambiguity: The American college president*. Boston: Harvard Business Review Press.

Collinson, D. 2005. Dialectics of leadership. *Human Relations* 58: 1419–42.

Collinson, D. 2006. Rethinking followership: A post-structuralist analysis of follower identities. *The Leadership Quarterly* 17: 179–89.

Cooper, D. J., Hinings, C. R., Greenwood, R., and Brown, J. 1996. Sedimentation and transformation in organizational change: The case of Canadian law firms. *Organization Studies* 17(4): 623–47.

Covaleski, M. A., Dirsmith, M. W., Heian, J. B., and Samuel, S. 1998. The calculated and the avowed: Techniques of discipline and struggles over identity in Big Six public accounting firms. *Administrative Science Quarterly* 43: 293–327.

Daicoff, S. 2004. *Lawyer, know thyself: A psychological analysis of personality strengths and weaknesses*. Washington, DC: American Psychological Association Books.

Denis, J.-L., Lamothe, L., and Langley A. 2001. The dynamics of collective leadership and strategic change in pluralistic organizations. *Academy of Management Journal* 44: 809–37.

Denis, J.-L., Langley, A., and Cazale, L. 1996. Leadership and strategic change under ambiguity. *Organization Studies* 17(4): 673–700.

Denis, J.-L., Langley, A., and Sergi, V. 2012. Leadership in the plural. *Academy of Management Annals* 6: 211–83.

DeRue, D. S. and Ashford, S. J. 2010. Who will lead and who will follow? A social process of leadership identity construction in organizations. *Academy of Management Review* 354: 627–47.

DiMaggio, P. and Powell, W. W. 1983. The iron cage revisited: Collective rationality and institutional isomorphism in organizational fields. *American Sociological Review* 48(2): 147–60.

Dinovitzer, R., Gunz, H., and Gunz, S. 2015. Professional ethics: Origins, applications and developments. In *The Oxford handbook of professional service firms*, ed. L. Empson, D. Muzio, J. Broschak, and B. Hinings. Oxford: Oxford University Press, 113–34.

Dirsmith, M., Heian, J., and Covaleski, M. 1997. Structure and agency in an institutionalised setting: The application and social transformation of control in the Big 6. *Accounting, Organizations and Society* 22(1): 1–27.

Dutton, J. E., Dukerich, J. M., and Harquail, C. V. 1994. Organizational images and member identification. *Administrative Science Quarterly* 39: 239–63.

Ekman, S. 2014. Is the high-involvement worker precarious or opportunistic? Hierarchical ambiguities in late capitalism. *Organization* 21(2): 141–58.

Empson, L. 2000. Mergers between professional service firms: Exploring an undirected process of integration. *Advances in Mergers and Acquisitions (JAI Series)* 1: 205–37.

Empson, L. 2001. Fear of exploitation and fear of contamination: Impediments to knowledge transfer in mergers between professional services firms. *Human Relations* 54(7): 839–62.

Empson, L. 2001. Introduction: Knowledge management in professional service firms. *Human Relations* 54(7): 811–17.

Empson, L. 2004. Organizational identity change: Managerial regulation and member identification in an accounting firm acquisition. *Accounting, Organizations and Society* 29(9): 759–81.

Empson, L. 2007. Surviving and thriving in a changing world: The special nature of partnership. In *Managing the modern law firm: New challenges, new perspectives*, ed. L. Empson. Oxford: Oxford University Press, 10–36.

Empson, L. 2012. Beyond dichotomies: A multi-stage model of governance in professional organizations, in *Handbook of research on entrepreneurship*, ed. M. Reihlen and A. Werr. Cheltenham: Edward Elgar, 274–95.

Empson, L. 2015. Leadership, power, and politics in law firms. In *Leadership for lawyers*, ed. R. Normand-Hochman. London: Globe Law and Business, 89–102.

Empson, L. and Chapman, C. 2006. Partnership versus corporation: Implications of alternative forms of governance in professional service firms. *Research in the Sociology of Organizations* 24: 139–70.

Empson, L., Cleaver, I., and Allen, J. 2013. Managing partners and management professionals: Institutional work dyads in professional partnerships. *Journal of Management Studies* 50(5): 808–44.

Empson, L. and Langley, A. 2015. Leadership and professionals. In *The Oxford handbook of professional service firms*, ed. L. Empson, D. Muzio, J. Broschak, and B. Hinings. Oxford: Oxford University Press, 163–88.

Empson, L., Muzio, D., Broschak, J., and Hinings, B. eds. 2015. *The Oxford handbook of professional service firms*. Oxford: Oxford University Press.

Empson, L., Muzio, D., Broschak, J., and Hinings, B. 2015. Researching professional service firms: An introduction and overview. In *The Oxford handbook of professional service firms*, ed. L. Empson, D. Muzio, J. Broschak, and B. Hinings. Oxford: Oxford University Press, 1–24.

Equal Employment Opportunities Commission v. Sidley Austin Brown & Wood, 315 F.3d 696 (7th Cir. 2002).

Fairhurst, G. T. and Uhl-Bien, M. 2012. Organizational discourse analysis (ODA): Examining leadership as a relational process. *The Leadership Quarterly* 23: 1043–62.

Fama, E. and Jensen, M. 1983. Separation of ownership and control. *Journal of Law and Economics* 26: 301–25.

Faulconbridge, J. 2015. Knowledge and learning in professional service firms. In *The Oxford handbook of professional service firms*, ed. L. Empson, D. Muzio, J. Broschak, and B. Hinings. Oxford: Oxford University Press, 425–51.

Faulconbridge, J. R., Beaverstock, J. V., Muzio, D., and Taylor, P. J. 2008. Global law firms: Globalization and organizational spaces of cross-border legal work. *Northwestern Journal of International Law and Business* 28(3): 455–88.

Fayol, H. 1949. *General and industrial management*. London: Pitman.

Ferris, G. R., Treadway, D. C., Perrewe, P. L., Brouer, R. L., Douglas, C., and Lux, S. 2007. Political skill in organizations. *Journal of Management* 33: 290–320.

Financial Reporting Council. 2016. The UK corporate governance code. London: Financial Reporting Council. <https://www.frc.org.uk/Our-Work/Publications/Corporate-Governance/UK-Corporate-Governance-Code-April-2016.pdf>, accessed 14 October 2016.

Fleming, P. and Spicer, A. 2014. Power in management and organization science. *Academy of Management Annals* 8(1): 237–98.

Foucault, M. 1991. *Discipline and punish: The birth of a prison*. London: Penguin.

Freidson, E. 1984. The changing nature of professional control. *Annual Review of Sociology* 10: 1–20.

Gabbioneta, C., Prakash, R., and Greenwood, R. 2014. Sustained corporate corruption and processes of institutional ascription within professional networks. *Journal of Professions and Organization* 1(1): 16–32.

Galanter, M. and Henderson, W. 2008. The elastic tournament: The second transformation of the Big Law firm. *Stanford Law Review* 60: 102–64.

Galanter, M. and Palay, T. 1991. *Tournament of lawyers: The transformation of the Big Law firm*. Chicago: University of Chicago Press.

Garud, R., Hardy, C., and Maguire, S. 2007. Institutional entrepreneurship as embedded agency: An introduction to the special issue. *Organization Studies* 28: 957–69.

Gerson, B. 2005. The limits of professional behaviour. *Harvard Business Review* 83 (April): 14–16.

Gibeau, E., Reid, W., and Langley, A. 2015. Co-leadership: Contexts, configurations and conditions'. In *The Routledge companion to leadership*, ed. J. Storey, J. Hartley, J.-L. Denis, P. 't Hart, and D. Ulrich. London: Routledge, 225–40.

Granovetter, M. 1985. Economic action and social structure: The problem of embeddedness. *The American Journal of Sociology* 91(3): 487.

Grant, R. M. and Spender, J. C. 1996. Knowledge and the firm. *Strategic Management Journal* 17 (Winter): 5–11.

Greenberg, D. and Guinan, P. J. 2004. Mergers and acquisitions in technology-intensive industries: The emergent process of knowledge transfer. In *Mergers and acquisitions: Creating integrative knowledge*, ed. A. L. Pablo and M. Javidan. Oxford: Blackwell, 135–55.

Greenwood, R. and Empson, L. 2003. The professional partnership: Relic or exemplary form of governance? *Organization Studies* 24: 909–33.

Greenwood, R. and Hinings, C. R. 1988. Organizational design types, tracks and the dynamics of strategic change. *Organization Studies* 9(3): 293–316.

Greenwood, R., Hinings, C. R., and Brown, J. 1990. 'P²-form' strategic management: Corporate practices in professional partnerships. *Academy of Management Journal* 33: 725–55.

Greenwood, R. and Suddaby, R. 2006. Institutional entrepreneurship in mature fields: The Big Five accounting firms. *Academy of Management Journal* 49: 27–48.

Greiner, L. E. 1972. Evolution and revolution as organizations grow. *Harvard Business Review* 50(4): 37–46.

Greiner, L. E. 1998. Evolution and revolution as organizations grow. *Harvard Business Review* 76(3): 55–68.

Greiner, L. E. and Malernee, J. K. 2005. 'Managing growth stages in consulting firms'. In *The contemporary consultant*, ed. L. E. Greiner and F. Poulfelt. Mason, OH: Thomson South-Western, 3–22.

Grey, C. 1994. Organizational Calvinism: Insecurity and labour power in a professional labour process. Paper presented at the 13th International Labour Process Conference.

Gronn, P. 2002. Distributed leadership as a unit of analysis. *The Leadership Quarterly* 13: 423–52.

Gronn, P. and Hamilton, A. 2004. 'A bit more life in the leadership': Co-principalship as distributed leadership practice. *Leadership and Policy in Schools* 3(1): 3–35.

Haight, A. 2001. Burnout, chronic fatigue, and Prozac in the professions: The iron law of salaries. *Review of Radical Political Economics* 33: 189–202.

Hanks, S. H., Watson, C. J., Jansen, E., and Chandler, G. N. 1993. Tightening the life-cycle construct: A taxonomic study of growth stage configurations in high-technology organizations. *Entrepreneurship: Theory and Practice* 18: 5–29.

Hart, O. and Moore, J. 1990. Property rights and the nature of the firm. *Journal of Political Economy* 98(6): 1119–58.

Harvey, W. and Mitchell, V. 2015. Marketing and reputation within professional service firms. In *The Oxford handbook of professional service firms*, ed. L. Empson, D. Muzio, J. Broschak, and B. Hinings. Oxford: Oxford University Press, 279–303.

Haspeslagh, P. and Jemison, D. 1991. *Managing acquisitions: Creating value through corporate renewal.* New York: The Free Press.

Hatch, M. J. and Schultz, M. 2002. The dynamics of organizational identity. *Human Relations* 55(8): 989–1018.

Heydebrand, W. 1973. Autonomy, complexity, and non-bureaucratic coordination in professional organizations. In *Comparative organizations: The results of empirical research*, ed. W. Heydebrand. Englewood Cliffs, NJ: Prentice Hall, 158–89.

Hill, M. 2011. Inside McKinsey. *Financial Times*, 25 November. <http://www.ft.com/cms/s/2/0d506e0e-1583-11e1-b9b8-00144feabdc0.html>, accessed 25 April 2015.

Hinings, C. R., Brown, J., and Greenwood, R. 1991. Change in an autonomous professional organization. *Journal of Management Studies* 28: 376–93.

Hodgson, R., Levinson, D., and Zaleznik, A. 1965. *The executive role constellation.* Boston, MA: Harvard University Press.

IBISWorld. Global accounting services: Market research report. <http://www.ibisworld.com/industry/global/global-accounting-services.html>, accessed 14 October 2016.

IBISWorld. Global advertising agencies: Market research report. <http://www.ibisworld.com/industry/global/global-advertising-agencies.html>, accessed 14 October 2016.

IBISWorld. Global architectural services: Market research report. <http://www.ibisworld.com/industry/global/global-architectural-services.html>, accessed 14 October 2016.

IBISWorld. Global commercial banks: Market research report. <http://www.ibisworld.com/industry/global/global-commercial-banks.html>, accessed 14 October 2016.

IBISWorld. Global engineering services: Market research report. <http://www.ibisworld.com/industry/global/global-engineering-services.html>, accessed 14 October 2016.

IBISWorld. Global investment banking & brokerage: Market research report. <http://www.ibisworld.com/industry/global/global-investment-banking-brokerage.html>, accessed 14 October 2016.

IBISWorld. Global management consultants: Market research report. <http://www.ibisworld.com/industry/global/global-management-consultants.html>, accessed 14 October 2016.

IBISWorld. Global pharmaceuticals & medicine manufacturing: Market research report. <http://www.ibisworld.com/industry/global/global-pharmaceuticals-medicine-manufacturing.html>, accessed 14 October 2016.

IBISWorld. Global reinsurance carriers: Market research report. <http://www.ibisworld.com/industry/global/global-reinsurance-carriers.html>, accessed 14 October 2016.

Jarzabkowski, P., Sillince, J., and Shaw, D. 2010. Strategic ambiguity as a rhetorical resource for enabling multiple interests. *Human Relations* 63(2): 219–48.

Jensen, M. C. and Meckling, W. H. 1976. Theory of the firm: Managerial behaviour, agency costs, and ownership structure. *Journal of Financial Economics* 3(4): 305–60.

Kerr, M. E. 2000. One family's story: A primer on Bowen theory. The Bowen Center for the Study of the Family. <http://www.thebowencenter.org>, accessed 6 October 2016.

Kerr, M. E. and Bowen, M. 1988. *Family evaluation*. New York: W. W. Norton & Company.

Kets de Vries, M. 2005. The dangers of feeling like a fake. *Harvard Business Review* 83(9) September: 108–16.

Kets de Vries, M. 2012. Star performers: Paradoxes wrapped up in enigmas. *Organizational Dynamics* 41(3): 173–82.

Kets de Vries, M. and Balazs, K. 2011. The shadow side of leadership. In *The SAGE handbook of leadership*, ed. A. Bryman, D. L. Collinson, K. Grint, B. Jackson, and M. Uhl-Bien. London: SAGE Publications, 380–92.

King, D. R. et al. 2004. Meta-analyses of post-acquisition performance: Indications of unidentified moderators. *Strategic Management Journal* 25(2): 187–200.

Knights, D. and Clarke, C. 2014. It's a bittersweet symphony, this life: Fragile academic selves and insecure identities at work. *Organization Studies* 35(3): 335–57.

Krause, R., Semandi, M., and Cannella, A. 2014. CEO duality: A review and research agenda. *Academy of Management Annals* 40(1): 256–86.

Kunda, G. 1992. *Engineering culture: Control and commitment in a high-tech corporation.* Philadelphia: Temple University Press.

Law Society Gazette. 1996. 'Bringing in the administrators'. 17 April: 14.

Lawrence, T., Malhotra, N., and Morris, T. 2012. Episodic and systemic power in the transformation of professional service firms. *Journal of Management Studies* 49(1): 102–43.

Lawrence, T. and Suddaby, R. 2006. Institutions and institutional work. In *The SAGE handbook of organization studies*, ed. S. Clegg, C. Hardy, T. Lawrence, and W. Nord. London: SAGE Publications, 215–54.

Legal Business. 1994. 'Managing the managing partners'. January/February: 10–15.

Legal Business. 2003. 'Linklaters' bear market'. May: 49–55.

Legal Business. 2010. 'Burning platforms'. March: 49–53.

Legal Week. 2002. 'The end of the amateur'. 28 March: 19.

Leibowitz, A. and Tollison, R. 1980. Free-riding, shirking, and team production in legal partnerships. *Economic Inquiry* 18(3): 380–94.

Leicht, K. and Fennel, M. 2001. *Professional work: A sociological approach*. Oxford: Blackwell.

Lupu, I. and Empson, L. 2015. *Illusio* and overwork: Playing the game in the accounting field. *Accounting, Auditing, and Accountability Journal* 28(8): 1310–40.

Mandis, S. 2013. *What happened to Goldman Sachs: An insider's story of organizational drift and its unintended consequences*. Boston: Harvard Business Review Press.

MarketLine. 2016. MarketLine Industry Profile: Global Legal Services. June 2016.

Mazmanian, M., Orlikowski, W. J., and Yates, J. 2013. The autonomy paradox: The implications of mobile email devices for knowledge professionals. *Organization Science* 27(5): 1337–57.

Meiksins, P. and Watson, J. 1989. Professional autonomy and organizational constraint: The case of engineers. *The Sociological Quarterly* 30(4): 561–85.

Michel, A. 2007. A distributed cognition perspective on newcomers' change processes: The management of cognitive uncertainty in two investment banks. *Administrative Science Quarterly* 52: 507–57.

Michel, A. 2011. Transcending socialization: A nine-year ethnography of the body's role in organizational control and knowledge workers' transformation. *Administrative Science Quarterly* 56(3): 325–68.

Miller, D. and Friesen, P. 1980. Archetypes of organizational transition. *Administrative Science Quarterly* 25(2): 268–99.

Mintzberg, H. 1989. *Mintzberg on management: Inside our strange world of organizations*. New York: Free Press.

Mintzberg, H. 1993. *Structure in fives: Designing effective organizations*. Englewood Cliffs, NJ: Prentice-Hall.

Moloney, R. 2016. The long read: The numbers game at Slaughter and May. <https://www.thelawyer.com/issues/6-june-2016/the-numbers-game-at-slaughter-may/>, accessed 19 October 2016.

Moore, J., Higham, L., Mountford-Zimdars, A., Ashley, L., Birkett, V., Duberley, J., and Kenny, E. 2016. Socio-economic diversity in life sciences and investment banking. London: Social Mobility Commission. <https://www.gov.uk/government/uploads/system/uploads/attachment_data/file/549994/Socio-economic_diversity_in_life_sciences_and_investment_banking.pdf>, accessed 14 October 2016.

Morris, T. and Empson, L. 1998. Organization and expertise: An exploration of knowledge bases and the management of accounting and consulting firms. *Accounting, Organizations and Society* 23(5–6): 609–24.

Morris, T., Greenwood, R., and Fairclough, S. 2010. Decision making in professional service firms. In *Handbook of decision making*, ed. P. Nutt and D. Wilson. Chichester: John Wiley & Sons, 275–306.

Muhr, S. L. 2010. The leader as cyborg: Norm-setting, intimidation and mechanistic superiority. In *Metaphors we lead by: Understanding leadership in the real world*, ed. M. Alvesson and A. Spicer. London: Routledge, 138–61.

Muhr, S. L., Pedersen, M., and Alvesson, M. 2012. Workload, aspiration, and fun: Problems of balancing self-exploitation and self-exploration in work life. In *Managing human resources by exploiting and exploring people's potentials*, ed. M. Holmqvist and A. Spicer. Research in the Sociology of Organizations 37. Bingley: Emerald Group Publishing Limited, 193–220.

Muzio, D., Faulconbridge, J., Gabbioneta, C., and Greenwood, R. 2016. Bad apples, bad barrels and bad cellars: A 'boundaries' perspective on professional misconduct. In *Organizational wrongdoing*, ed. D. Palmer, R. Greenwood, and K. Smith-Crowe. Cambridge: Cambridge University Press: 141–75.

Nahavandi, A. and Malekzadeh, A. R. 1988. Acculturation in mergers and acquisitions. *Academy of Management Review* 13(1): 79–90.

von Nordenflycht, A. 2007. Is public ownership bad for professional service firms? Ad agency ownership, performance, and creativity. *Academy of Management Journal* 50(2): 429–45.

O'Reilly, C. and Chatman, J. 1996. Culture as social control: Corporations, cults, and commitment. *Research in Organizational Behaviour* 18: 157–200.

Panel on Fair Access to the Professions. 2009. *Unleashing aspiration: The final report of the Panel on Fair Access to the Professions*. London: Cabinet Office. <http://webarchive.nationalarchives.gov.uk/+/http:/www.cabinetoffice.gov.uk/media/227102/fair-access.pdf>, accessed 14 October 2016.

Parker, C., Dipboye, R., and Jackson, S. 1995. Perceptions of organizational politics: An investigation of antecedents and consequences. *Journal of Management* 21: 891–912.

Pentland, B. T. 1993. Getting comfortable with the numbers: Auditing and the micro-production of macro-order. *Accounting, Organizations and Society* 18(7): 605–20.

Pfeffer, J. and Salancik, G. R. 1978. *The external control of organizations: A resource dependence perspective*. New York: Harper and Row.

Phelps, R., Adams, R., and Bessant, J. 2007. Life cycles of growing organizations: A review with implications for knowledge and learning. *International Journal of Management Reviews* 9(1): 1–30.

Pickering, M. E. 2017. Post-acquisition integration processes in publicly owned professional service companies: Senior professional behaviour and company performance. *Journal of Organizational Behavior*.

Podolny, J. M. 1993. A status-based model of market competition. *American Journal of Sociology* 98(4): 829–72.

Raelin, J. 1985. *Clash of cultures: Managers managing professionals*. Boston, MA: Harvard Business School Press.

Ranft, A. L. and Lord, M. D. 2002. Acquiring new technologies and capabilities: A grounded model of acquisition implementation. *Organization Science* 13(4): 420–42.

Raven, B. H. 1965. Social influence and power. In *Current studies in social psychology*, ed. I. D. Steiner and M. Fishbein. New York: Holt, Rinehart, Winston, 371–82.

Reid, W. and Karambayya, R. 2009. Impact of dual executive leadership dynamics in creative organizations. *Human Relations* 62(7): 1073–112.

Reid, W. and Karambayya, R. 2015. The shadow of history: Situated dynamics of trust in dual executive leadership. *Leadership* 12(5): 609–31.

Robertson, M. and Swan, J. 2003. 'Control—what control?' Culture and ambiguity within a knowledge intensive firm. *Journal of Management Studies* 40(4): 831–58.

Schad, J., Lewis, M. W., Raisch, S., and Smith, W. K. 2016. Paradox research in management science: Looking back to move forward. *The Academy of Management Annals* 10(1): 5–64.

Schoenberg, R. 2001. Knowledge transfer and resource sharing as value creation mechanisms in inbound continental European acquisitions. *Journal of Euromarketing* 10(1): 99–114.

Schweiger, D. M. and Denisi, A. S. 1991. Communication with employees following a merger: A longitudinal field experiment. *Academy of Management Journal* 34(1): 110–35.

Shafer, W., Lowe, D., and Fogarty, T. 2002. The effects of corporate ownership on public accountants' professionalism and ethics. *Accounting Horizons* 16: 109–25.

Sharma, A. 1997. Professional as agent: Knowledge asymmetry in agency exchange. *Academy of Management Review* 22(3): 758–98.

Sherer, P. and Lee, K. 2002. Institutional change in large law firms: A resource dependency and institutional perspective. *Academy of Management Journal* 45: 102–19.

Sillince, J., Jarzabkowski, P., and Shaw, D. 2012. Shaping strategic action through the rhetorical construction and exploitation of ambiguity. *Organization Science* 23(3): 630–50.

Silvester, J. 2008. The good, the bad, and the ugly: Politics and politicians at work. *International Review of Industrial and Organizational Psychology* 23: 107–48.

Sirower, M. 1997. *The synergy trap: How companies lose the acquisition game*. New York: The Free Press.

Smets, M., von Nordenflycht, A., Morris, T., and Brock, D. Forthcoming. *25 years since 'P2': Taking stock and charting the future of the professional organization*. Special issue of *Journal of Professionals and Organizations*.

Smircich, L. and Morgan, G. 1982. Leadership: The management of meaning. *Journal of Applied Behavioral Science* 18(3): 257–73.

Smith, W. K. and Lewis, M. W. 2011. Toward a theory of paradox: A dynamic equilibrium model of organizing. *Academy of Management Review* 36(2): 381–403.

Smith, W. K., Lewis, M. W., and Tushman, M. 2016. 'Both/and' leadership: Don't worry so much about being consistent. *Harvard Business Review* 94 (May): 63–70.

Sorenson, J. and Sorenson, T. 1974. The conflict of professionals in bureaucratic organizations. *Administrative Science Quarterly* 19(1): 98–106.

Stevens, A. 2006. The archetypes. In *The handbook of Jungian psychology: Theory, practice and applications*, ed. R. Papadopoulos. Hove: Routledge, 74–93.

Tolbert, P. 1988. Institutional sources of organizational culture in major law firms. In *Institutional patterns and organizations: Culture and environment*, ed. L. Zucker. Cambridge, MA: Ballinger Press, 101–13.

Tolbert, P. and Stern, R. 1991. Organizations of professionals: Governance structures in large law firms. In *Research in the sociology of organizations, Vol. 8: Organizations and professions*, ed. P. Tolbert and S. Barley. London: JAI Press, 97–118.

Tourish, D. 2011. Leadership and cults. In *The SAGE handbook of leadership*, ed. A. Bryman, D. L. Collinson, K. Grint, B. Jackson, and M. Uhl-Bien. London: SAGE Publications, 215–29.

Treadway, D. C., Hochwarter, W. A., Kacmar, C. J., and Ferris, G. R. 2005. Political will, political skill, and political behavior. *Journal of Organizational Behavior* 26: 229–45.

Tsoukas, H. 1991. The missing link: A transformational view of metaphors in organizational science. *Academy of Management Review* 16(3): 566–85.

Tuch, C. and O'Sullivan, N. 2007. The impact of acquisitions on firm performance: A review of the evidence. *International Journal of Management Reviews* 9(2): 141–70.

Uhl-Bien, M., Marion, R., and McKelvey, B. 2007. Complexity leadership theory: Shifting leadership from the industrial age to the knowledge era. *The Leadership Quarterly* 18: 298–318.

Uhl-Bien, M., Riggio, R. E., Lowe, K. B., and Carsten, M. K. 2014. Followership theory: A review and research agenda. *The Leadership Quarterly* 25: 83–104.

Wikipedia. 'Borg (*Star Trek*)'. <https://en.wikipedia.org/wiki/Borg_(Star_Trek)>, accessed 26 August 2016.

Willmott, H. 1993. Strength is ignorance; slavery is freedom: Managing culture in modern organizations. *Journal of Management Studies* 30(4): 515–52.

Yukl, G. 1989. Managerial leadership: A review of theory and research. *Journal of Management* 15(2): 251–89.

Index